THE AZUSA STREET MISSION AND REVIVAL

∞

The Birth of the
Global Pentecostal Movement

CECIL M. ROBECK JR.

NELSON REFERENCE & ELECTRONIC
A Division of Thomas Nelson Publishers
Since 1798
www.thomasnelson.com

Portions of the Afterword were originally published as Cecil M. Robeck, Jr, "Reflections on the Role of Revival." *The Church of God Evangel* 91:11 (November 2001), 28–30. The author wishes to thank *The Church of God Evangel* for permission to reprint them here.

Illustrations on the following pages are from the personal collection of Cecil M. Robeck, Jr., 28, 32, 37, 45, 47, 51, 54, 55, 58, 61, 64, 79, 90, 97, 113, 120, 122, 134, 170, 172, 191, 193, 194, 199, 201, 202, 211, 205, 228, 251, 257, 263, 265, 308. Illustrations reproduced by the kind permission of the following institutions and persons: Apostolic Faith Mission, Portland, Oregon, 215; Apostolic Faith Mission of South Africa, 274; Esther Brinkley, 273; Flower Pentecostal Heritage Center, 36, 42, 44, 68, 71, 100, 110, 130, 192, 203, 206, 220, 226, 232, 233; International Pentecostal Holiness Church Archives and Research Center, 217; Maxine Van Dyke, 264; and The Miriam Matthews Collection, 70.

Library of Congress Cataloging-in-Publication Data available upon request
Robeck, Cecil M.
The Azusa Street Mission and revival : the birth of the global
Pentecostal movement / Cecil M. Robeck, Jr.
p. cm.
ISBN 1-4185-0624-9
1. Pentecostalism. 2. Pentecostal churches—Missions. 3. Azusa
Street Mission (Los Angeles, Calif.) I. Title.
BR1644.R59 2006   277.3'082—dc22   2005033675

Book design and composition by Mark McGarry, Texas Type & Book Works
Set in Monotype Dante

Printed in the United States of America
1 2 3 4 5 6 7 — 10 09 08 07 06

CONTENTS

ACKNOWLEDGMENTS

❧

I don't remember where and when this project first began. I suppose it was in the testimonies of the old-timers that I heard as a boy. Their stories kindled a fire in me that I have never been able to quench. When I moved to Pasadena, California in 1970, I was fortunate to get to know four "Azusa Street" participants quite well: Clyde Rogers, Fred Griesinger, Harold Fisher, and John Bartleman. I was also able to interview several others.

Some of the impetus for this project belongs with the late Dr. Art Glass. He hoped that I would publish the story of "Azusa Street" in a popular format that would instill a sense of pride in the young people of the Church of God in Christ. I wish he were here to tell me whether this is the book he had in mind. For help and insight into parts of the African American story, I am deeply indebted to Drs. Anthea Butler, Leslie Callahan, David Daniels, Sherry Sherrod Dupree, Leonard Lovett, A. G. Miller, the late James Tinney, Mr. Alexander C. Stewart, and the late Bishop Ithiel Clemmons.

I owe a debt of gratitude to my friend Dr. George O. Wood, General Secretary of the Assemblies of God, who a decade ago invited me to take him, his wife, and a few of their friends on a tour of the Los Angeles sites related to the Azusa Street Mission and revival. I want to thank George and the seventy-five hundred other people who have since taken this day-long pilgrimage with me. Your challenges, questions, and suggestions have made this project all the more worthwhile.

And then there are my students. I wish to extend a deep and heartfelt "Thanks" to each of the many students at Fuller who have taken my course on the history of the Pentecostal and charismatic movements. Your willingness to undertake a number of creative research assignments related to this study places me very much in your debt!

Along the way, I have been encouraged repeatedly to continue my research as part of Fuller Theological Seminary's generous sabbatical program. Its president, Dr. Richard J. Mouw, has provided me with occasional, good-natured goads: "Robeck, when are you going to write something ordinary people will read?" I sure hope this works! My dear friend and former colleague Dr. Russell P. Spittler has been a consistent source of encouragement and a primary sounding board on many aspects of this study, especially on issues related to Pentecostal/charismatic spirituality.

The John Randolph Haynes and Dora Haynes Foundation gave me a substantial grant that first enabled me to travel to several key cities and undertake a year of mind-numbing detail-chasing that lies behind this volume and several others that I expect will follow. The Huntington Library granted me a quiet space during one of my year-long sabbaticals. The Assemblies of God has given a great gift to me in the Flower Pentecostal Heritage Center and its incredibly helpful staff—especially Mr. Wayne Warner, Mrs. Joyce Lee, and Mr. Glenn Gohr. The Morgan City Historical Society staff helped me understand the southern Louisiana coastal parishes. Mr. Darrol Pierson of the Indiana State Library pointed me in several fruitful directions. Wilma L. Gibbs, director of the Indiana Historical Society, was always ready to respond to my questions. Ms. Carolyn Garner-Reagan, a former research librarian at the Pasadena Public Library, guided me to valuable resources on the history of Southern California and helped me to find the passenger list of the SS Campania.

A word of thanks also goes to Mrs. Karen Barrett and to the Rev. Dwight Baltzell, former General Superintendent of the Apostolic Faith Mission (Portland, OR), for access to the archive there; to Dr. Harold D. Hunter, director of the International Pentecostal Holiness Archive and Research Center, and his assistant Ms Erica Rutland for their repeated help; and to Mr. Peter DeWitt and Dr.

François Möller for making it possible for me to explore the archival holdings of the Apostolic Faith Mission in South Africa.

Many are the friends and associates who have contributed to this study as well. Drs. Allan Anderson, Edith Blumhofer, David Bundy, Augustus Cerillo, Joseph Coletti, Donald Dayton, Gastón Espinosa, William Faupel, Harold Helms, Philip Hilliard, Walter Hollenweger, Gary McGee, Wonsuk Ma, Robert Meye, Douglas Nelson, Jean Daniel Plüss, Jim Phillips, and Grant Wacker have all been wonderful dialogue partners providing helpful insights and gentle provocations through the years. Mr. G. Wayne Pendleton provided information and photographs on the Pendleton family. Maxine Van Dyke gave me materials on Antoinette Moomau. The late Mrs. Grace (Smale) Westberg shared information and materials on Joseph Smale. Esther Brinkley furnished materials on Daniel Awrey. And Robert Fisher supplied me with information and photographs on his grandfather, Elmer K. Fisher. Mr. Jan-Endy Johanneson took me to used book stores in Stockholm and gave me complete access to a number of early Swedish sources. Mr. Helge Christenson turned my crude attempts at translation from these documents into understandable English. And Mr. Glen Blossom provided me with copies of the *Full Gospel Tabernacle News*, which supplied valuable information on the layout of the Azusa Street Mission.

I want to thank Dr. Michael S. Stephens, a senior editor at Thomas Nelson, who caught the vision for this book and championed it through the long process of publication. Thomas Nelson Publishers deserves a note of appreciation as well. Such history books are not their normal fare, but they took a risk that I hope will be an encouragement to them.

When I began working on "Azusa Street" in earnest, I was an associate dean and Ms. Jennifer Stock was my administrative assistant. Like me, she was captivated by the project and the people we met along the way. Through the years Jennifer has contributed more than anyone else (other than me) to the actual work on this project. Her tenacity at following up leads has been nothing short of amazing! I am also in debt to her husband, John Barrios, for encouraging her to continue to help me locate valuable resources and information and to scan microfilm for many long hours on her days off—solely for the price of lunch.

This project could never have seen the light of day without the complete support and complicity of my wife, Patsy, and our sons, Jason, John Mark, Peter, and Nathan. They have felt my passion. They have heard the stories. They have been introduced to the people. They have scoured used-book stores on our "vacations" up the coast of California, from Los Angeles to San Francisco, and back down the central valley. They have endured long and sometimes lonely hours as I hid myself away to write and rewrite. They have prayed for me and loved me with all my imperfections as I have sought to find answers to the many, many questions this story has raised for me. Patsy even joined me for a couple of tedious weeks of microfilm work and has read many of the pages I have written.

Finally, I hope and pray that this volume will encourage my readers to "draw nigh to God," for with that imperative comes the assurance that the age-old promise of James 4:8 is still true—"and he will draw nigh to you." That verse of Scripture hung on the wall of my bedroom when I was a boy, and it brought me great comfort at night. As I have explored the Azusa Street revival, however, that verse has come back to me in a different but equally powerful way. The whole purpose of telling this story is to bring glory to God. The best way I can do that is to point my readers back to the God who stands ready to meet them, even as he encountered the people who found their way through the dusty streets of Los Angeles a hundred years ago. There they knelt before him in a humble building with a dirt floor and a plague of flies. There he found them and filled them to overflowing in a revival that has changed the face of Christianity forever. I am quite sure that one hundred years later, they would find the answers to their prayers as nothing less than astonishing! So it is that I offer this work to the glory of the Lord who first lit the fire within me. And I close with a shout that is often on the lips of my Latin American Pentecostal sisters and brothers. *Gloria a Dios! Gloria a Dios! Gloria a Dios!*

INTRODUCTION:
THE SIGNIFICANCE OF AZUSA STREET

ℰᑯ

All classes of people gathered in the temple last night. There were big Negroes looking for a fight, there were little fairies dressed in dainty chiffon who stood on the benches and looked on with questioning wonder in their baby-blue eyes. There were cappers from North Alameda Street, and sedate dames from West Adams Street. There were all ages, sexes, colors, nationalities and previous conditions of servitude. The rambling old barn was filled and the rafters were so low that it was necessary to stick one's nose under the benches to get a breath of air.

It was evident that nine out of every ten persons present were there for the purpose of new thrills. This was a new kind of show in which the admission was free—they don't even pass the hat at the Holy Rollers' meeting—and they wanted to see every act to the drop of the curtain. They stood on benches to do it. When a bench wasn't handy they stood on each other's feet.

Los Angeles Herald

IT IS IMPOSSIBLE to find such colorful descriptions in today's newspapers. Complaints would be filed before the ink was dry, with claims of offenses committed against any number of folk. In the politically correct world in which we now live we have lost some things to other sensibilities. We have given up much of the texture and color made possible by such descriptive language. But here we have it in a nutshell—the stereotypical portrait of those who attended the Azusa Street Mission[1]—the rich and the poor, the young and the old, the black and the white, male and female.

Whatever their reasons or their expectations, they all gathered in this one place. If you close your eyes and let your imagination run with the pictures painted by these sentences, the sights, the sounds, the smells, and the sensations, you can experience a bit of the energy that was unleashed when the revival was at its height at the Azusa Street Mission.

Throughout this book I will quote directly from a number of such articles that ran in local newspapers during the Azusa Street revival. At times the language in these articles may be offensive to the twenty-first-century ear. I have chosen to leave these accounts unchanged because they demonstrate exactly how African Americans and others were viewed or valued at the time. In some cases, the lavishly picturesque language reflects the intent of the various reporters to convey an emotional sense of what it was like to be in the mission itself. In others, it betrays the prejudicial and arrogant positions that many held.

While the mission would become the spiritual home for hundreds, it was also a tempting, if not a satisfying watering hole for thousands more. Some people came to drink deeply from its artesian abundance out of their thirst of desperation. They went away refreshed and renewed. Others came merely to be titillated, to be splashed with its overflow. More often than not, their reward was simply the entertainment they received as they watched those who were serious about meeting God enter into states of religious ecstasy. Still others came to cast stones at the "misguided," even the "dangerous" direction that they believed the revival was taking. Their criticisms may have seemed to be justified to sectarians who joined them in spirit, but more often than not, those who knew better pitied them. Whatever people expected as they entered the mission, they seem to have found. It was impossible to be neutral. It was impossible to remain untouched by what went on there.

Since 1906 when the mission first came onto the world's stage, two types of people have frequented the multiplied thousands of Pentecostal and Charismatic churches around the world. There are those who were part of the Azusa Street Mission and revival, and there are those who wish they had been. It is difficult to be anything else.

For decades, the story of what went on in that bygone era typically came in vibrant and compelling testimonies. "This is what God did among us," they proclaimed. On other occasions, those who had been privileged to attend the mission's meetings gave them further expression in the romantic yearnings for the "good old days." While their eyes twinkled with delight, or explored the visions found only in their memories, old-timers often told their stories with wit, but always with enthusiasm. Their memories of how God had met them in that place held them captive with a vitality unmatched by anything else they had ever experienced. Nothing would ever be the same. God had touched them!

Some spoke of their spiritual encounters with hushed, awe-filled tones as they were once again caught up in the memory of those precious moments. Others shouted with all the urgency they could summon as they exhorted a new generation to seek God like they had done. Always they tempted and teased and tantalized newer converts in a kind of romanticized wonder. "God can do it again," they promised. "Expect it to happen to you," they urged. "All you have to do is tarry and mean business," they instructed.

These promised encounters might not come with the same visceral passion, the same arduous abandonment, or the same fervent liberty that they had enjoyed in the beginning. But they would come! And those who challenged their audiences to wrestle with God knew beyond a shadow of a doubt that God stands ready to pour out His Spirit in fresh ways once again, if only our souls, like the deer that pants after streams of water, would pant with the same level of passion after God (Ps. 42:1). Something new, something wonderful had happened before their eyes. They had encountered God in all God's fullness! And while these saints instructed their children and grandchildren and anyone else who would listen to them, to pursue God until God encountered them in power, they also bore compelling testimony to what had already happened to them at "Azusa Street."

Today it is no longer possible to hear "those who were there" tell their stories with such awe or enthusiasm. Their voices have been silenced by death. But their stories live on as though they happened only yesterday. They live on in the articles, diaries, letters, recorded testimonies, and written reports that they have left, and in the memories of those who heard them speak. The story of the Azusa Street Mission is really the account of God fulfilling a longtime promise that He would pour out His Spirit upon all flesh (Joel 2:28–29; Acts 2:17–18). It is a series of human testimonies of a Divine encounter between some quite ordinary people and their God. It is the story of a simple, humble people who reached out to God and were rewarded in their quest for spiritual power so that they might become more effective in their calling to share the gospel story (Acts 1:8). It is this story of their encounter with God and the actions to which it led, that I hope to tell in a fresh way.

The Azusa Street Revival in a Nutshell

William Joseph Seymour, the African American pastor of the Azusa Street Mission, was the son of former slaves. Born in 1870, he was reared in a Catholic home just a few miles from the Gulf Coast in southern Louisiana. Between 1895 and 1905, William Seymour traveled to Indianapolis, Cincinnati, and Houston where he became a participant in the Wesleyan holiness movement. It was in 1905, in Houston, Texas, where Seymour came into contact with Charles F. Parham, the founder of the Apostolic Faith movement.

In January 1906, William J. Seymour enrolled in Parham's short term Bible school where he studied for about six weeks. While Seymour was not allowed to take a seat inside the classroom because of segregation laws, Parham made space available for him in the hallway. It was here that Parham taught his theory about "baptism in the Holy Spirit" to his students, and during this period, Parham accompanied Seymour into the African American community where Seymour preached and Parham critiqued him. Shortly after he began his studies under Parham, William J. Seymour was invited to Los Angeles, to serve as the pastor of a small storefront mission at Ninth and Santa Fe Street. The founding pastor of that congregation, an African American woman named Mrs. Julia Hutchins, was hoping to go to Africa as a missionary and intended for William Seymour to be her replacement. She had heard great things about Pastor Seymour and looked forward to his arrival.

Parham counseled Seymour not to go, but because of Seymour's firm conviction that this call was from God and he must go, Parham relented. Seymour arrived in Los Angeles on February 22,

1906. Two days later he began to preach. By Sunday, March 4, Mrs. Hutchins had decided that Seymour was not the man for the job. She rejected his ministry in a doctrinal dispute over the nature of the "baptism in the Spirit" and refused to allow him to continue. Turned away from his congregation and with no resources to leave the city, Seymour needed help. Fortunately, Edward and Mattie Lee invited him to stay at their tiny home until he could decide what to do. Each evening they gathered in their parlor for prayer together, and Seymour spoke to them. Before long, they had established a prayer meeting that others visited as well.

By mid-March the growth of that prayer meeting forced them to move two blocks to the larger home of Richard and Ruth Asberry at 214 (now 216) North Bonnie Brae Street. On April 9, 1906, this Bible study was visited by a move of the Holy Spirit in which people began to speak and sing in tongues. Within days this small group had grown so large that it was forced to find a more suitable facility for their meeting. They located such a building at 312 Azusa Street. It had been built in 1888 by Stevens African Methodist Episcopal Church (AME), a congregation founded by the celebrated African American woman, Biddy Mason, who after walking as a slave behind a wagon train from Mississippi to Salt Lake City, Utah, and then down to Southern California, took advantage of California's "free" position, and won her freedom from her owner in the California courts.

In 1904 Stevens AME Church moved to a new facility at Eighth and Towne and changed its name to First African Methodist Episcopal Church. This move left the Azusa Street property vacant. The people of First AME Church did some remodeling of the old church on Azusa Street and offered it for lease. Seymour and his friends investigated, negotiated a short-term lease and cleaned it up. It became known officially as the Apostolic Faith Mission, but popularly it was known as the Azusa Street Mission.

From 1906 through 1909 the Azusa Street Mission became the focus of attention not only of Los Angeles, but of thousands of people around the world as news spread about the mission that stood at the heart of a revival. People were spellbound by the claims of what God was doing there! Revival had come to the mission in a profound way, and literally thousands of people flocked there from all over the world. They came to see it for themselves, to be challenged, to pray, to encounter God, and to be empowered. Many left in just days, newly energized by their encounter with God, to tell the world of their personal story as part of the larger gospel story.

As far as we know, the story of the Azusa Street Mission made its public debut on the pages of the *Los Angeles Daily Times*, April 18, 1906. It was the morning of the great San Francisco earthquake,[2] and many of the mission's participants saw both events as signs that God was intervening in everyday California life. It was this controversial beginning to the mission that initially attracted the attention of believers and cynics. The article carried in the *Times* was the first of scores of articles to appear in the Los Angeles press as well as the press in surrounding communities. Together, they helped document the progress of the revival, the antics of the faithful, and the status of the mission over the next several years. News reports on the revival and its impact would eventually number in the hundreds.

There are several reasons this African American mission received so much coverage and why the story bears retelling today.

First, it grew with unparalleled speed. The Azusa Street Mission was aggressively evangelistic. In a day of "church growth" schemes, burgeoning "megachurches" and "emergent" churches on the one hand, and declining church membership in many historic congregations on the other, it is important for us to hear once again how a small prayer meeting of some fifteen people, including children, grew into an internationally acclaimed congregation of hundreds in just three months. In a day when the growing challenge of secularism questions the legitimacy of evangelistic and missionary activities by the church, when governments around the world are increasingly enacting "anti-proselytism" laws or are challenging the church's freedom to proclaim the gospel in the public square without censorship, the successes and failures of the Azusa Street Mission's policies need to be studied anew.

Within days of its beginning, meetings at the mission exploded as crowds swarmed the place, filling the building and spilling outside. There they listened for hours even through the open windows of the mission, where they hoped to catch a glimpse or hear a snippet of what was happening inside. Estimates from the period suggest that crowds grew to as many as fifteen hundred people on any given Sunday during 1906. From time to time, literally hundreds of hymn-singing celebrants, candidates, and members of the mission made trips to nearby San Pedro and Terminal Island, commandeering trains and streetcars that took them to all day baptismal services at the beach. It was common to find as many as 150 to 250 new converts being baptized at each of these events.

By late-summer 1906, less than six months after it was founded, members and sympathizers had established several related congregations in Los Angeles and surrounding communities. Leaders participating in the Azusa Street revival used the public transportation system to spread the revival. The streetcar lines provided easy access for the Azusa Street faithful to take their message to the surrounding suburbs. As a result, many Azusa Street participants moved out of the mission to hold meetings on heavily trafficked street corners in the nearby towns of Pasadena, Monrovia, Whittier, Anaheim, Long Beach, and San Pedro. They distributed tracts, set up tents, or rented storefronts, plotting out where they would be most effective as they established other permanent places for Pentecostal worship.

By September 1906, the mission had sent a score of evangelists up and down the west coast of the United States to places such as San Jose, San Francisco, and San Diego, California, to Salem and Portland, Oregon, and to Spokane and Seattle, Washington. By December 1906 they were in Denver and Colorado Springs, in Indianapolis and Minneapolis, in Akron, Alliance, and Cleveland, Ohio, in Chattanooga, Tennessee, in Norfolk, Virginia, and even in New York City. By December 1906 the mission had commissioned and sent at least thirteen missionaries to Africa. Four of them were white; they all went to Angola. Nine of them were African Americans who, in their travels across the United States, recruited three more people to join them for ministry in Liberia. By January 1907 they had begun ministering in Monrovia, Liberia and surrounding outstations and by 1909 an Apostolic Faith Mission, which boasted 154 baptized converts, had been firmly established there. By early 1907, missionaries from the Azusa Street Mission had entered Mexico, Canada, Western Europe, the Middle East, West Africa, and several countries in Asia. By 1908, the movement had spread to South Africa, Central and Eastern Europe, and even Northern Russia. It is because of the singular success of Azusa Street's missionary program, before any others were in place, that I have chosen to claim that its story is unique to the birth of global Pentecostalism.

Successes like these did not come easily. They often took their toll. Most of the earliest missionaries to Liberia died of malaria and related diseases within weeks of their arrival. Evangelists and missionaries with an uncommon experience of God, and a headstrong zeal for telling others of what had happened to them, were often ridiculed or arrested for their troubles. Sometimes they were so noisy that they could be heard blocks away. And their antics were often unseemly. Sometimes they violated the public peace and even disrupted common standards of public decency. They were harassed by neighbors seeking peace so that they could sleep. The unwillingness of many of these people to seek medical attention and their dogged reliance upon healing through the prayer of faith, led to scrapes with the law over the nature and limits of acceptable medical practice. Their initial reliance on prayer instead of doctors, and complaints lodged by neighbors who were concerned with the exposure of children to what they perceived to be nothing more than psychological manipulation, led child welfare agencies to investigate charges of child abuse. Their noise, their antics, and their belief in divine healing even fueled the fires of public debate on the legitimate limits of the free exercise of religion in the United States.

The second reason to explore the story of Azusa Street is that it had a profound effect on other congregations. In a day marked by the postmodern rejection of most overarching or shared forms of authority, when arguments are made for greater expressions of individual freedom and individual spirituality, when institutional cooperation between churches is on the decline and the emergence of new, independent and emerging churches is at an all time high, Pastor Seymour's vision of shared experience and communal cooperation between various Christian groups needs to be rediscovered. Repeatedly, Seymour published the mission's position: "The Apostolic Faith movement stands for the restoration of the faith once delivered unto the saints—the old-time religion, camp meetings, revivals, missions, street and prison work, and Christian unity everywhere." "We are not fighting men or churches, but seeking to displace dead forms and creeds and wild fanaticisms with living, practical Christianity. 'Love, Faith, Unity' is our watchword." But Seymour's persistent calls for "unity" seemingly fell and continue to fall on deaf ears.

The mission's evangelistic success so deeply affected other congregations that preachers became defensive. Some used their pulpits to attack the mission. One Los Angeles pastor ridiculed the mission before his Sunday morning congregation, with the following descriptive prediction.

> They come with the blare of trumpets out of tune and harmony, but lustily blown with all the power of human or inhuman lungs; they shine with phosphorescent gleam, strangely like that of brimstone, and with odor more or less tainted; they distract the affrighted atmosphere with a bewildering jargon of babbling tongues of all grades—dried, boiled, and smoked; they rant and dance and roll in a disgusting amalgamation of African voudou superstition and Caucasian insanity, and will pass away like the hysterical nightmares that they are.

At least two Los Angeles newspapers carried his words. They represented the thoughts of many of the mission's critics—African Voodoo mixed with Caucasian insanity!

Meanwhile, the Los Angeles Church Federation, which represented many of the city's historic Protestant churches, held meetings they hoped would compete favorably with those offered at the Azusa Street Mission. In fact, just three months after the Azusa Street Mission held its first services, the churches of the federation counseled together to develop a plan that would counter the mission's impact on the city.

Results were not always predictable. The actions taken by the federation not only led the members of many federation related congregations to expect revival in their own churches, but the newspaper coverage that the federation's actions elicited, essentially provided free advertisement for the activities of the Azusa Street Mission. This led several other congregations to join this emerging "Pentecostal" movement. It also led to the establishment of other new Pentecostal congregations in the greater Los Angeles area.

By 1908, the same situation had been replicated nationwide when several Wesleyan-holiness denominations embraced the message of the Azusa Street Mission and its revival. Among them were the Fire-Baptized Holiness Church, the Church of God in Christ, the Church of God (Cleveland, TN), and the Pentecostal Holiness Church. Others lost such large numbers of members to the revival that new denominations with similar names were formed. Alongside the Free-Will Baptist Churches, for instance, a new group, a group that took signs and wonders and speaking in tongues in its stride, the Pentecostal Free-Will Baptist Churches sprang into existence.

Third, "Azusa Street" rightfully continues to function as the primary icon expressing the power of the worldwide Pentecostal movement. A common "story" or "myth" (that is an animating narrative—not necessarily something fictional or untrue) motivates all successful movements. At a time when postmodern thinking attempts to cut the heart out of history and tradition, the recovery of the Azusa Street "story" can still provide a new impetus toward an encounter with God and spiritual growth. The mission taught its faithful that Jesus Christ had provided salvation for them, that He is "the same, yesterday, today, and forever" (Heb. 13:8). It instructed its people that if they wanted to become effective witnesses for Christ they needed to be baptized in the Holy Spirit (Acts 1:8). They were expected to pursue God, and then to be overwhelmed and transformed by God in the resulting encounter. The initial proof of this encounter, though by no means the only thing expected to bear witness to it, was speaking in "other tongues as the Spirit gave them utterance" (Acts 2:4). Many at the mission anticipated that these tongues pointed to the places where God had equipped them to minister. By lifting up such a distinctive teaching, the Azusa Street Mission continues to play a foundational role in the ongoing pursuit and understanding of Pentecostal and Charismatic spirituality.

Today, among the hundreds of congregations in the Los Angeles area that are part of the movement that emerged from this mission stand are West Angeles Church of God in Christ, the Cathedral of Faith, the City of Refuge, Faithful Central Bible Church, and the Church on the Way. While it may be interesting to note that none of these congregations carries a denominational name, though most are part of a Pentecostal denomination, all of these congregations have a membership closely approaching or easily surpassing twenty thousand.

Many of the televangelists and religious broadcasters such as Pat Robertson, Oral Roberts, Kenneth and Gloria Copeland, and T. D. Jakes have spoken of the role that Azusa Street has played and continues to play in their ministries. The Trinity Broadcasting Network has repeatedly demonstrated its link with the mission through its many Pentecostal and Charismatic broadcasts through the years.

Representative of many additional Pentecostal groups in the United States that acknowledge the revival as an important factor in their later origin are the Assemblies of God, the Pentecostal Assemblies of the World, the United Pentecostal Churches, the Vineyard Christian Fellowship, Victory Outreach, La Asamblea Apostólica de la Fe en Cristo Jesús, Inc. and its Mexican counterpart, La Iglesia Apostólica de la Fe in Cristo Jesús. Their impact on the world can be illustrated by looking at the number of members and adherents of just the Assemblies of God. It came into existence in 1914 when it emerged from a gathering of people, many of whom had been directly touched by the Azusa Street revival and those it sent out from the mission. Yet, today the Assemblies of God claims 2.5 million members and adherents in the United States and 53 million worldwide. These are only a few of the stories that could be told to illustrate the impact of the Azusa Street Mission on the spread of the Pentecostal/Charismatic movements throughout the world.

In Latin America, the poor and the marginalized have enthusiastically embraced this movement as their own, even when various forms of "liberation theology" in the region had been designed specifically with the poor and marginalized in mind. At the Azusa Street Mission, people spoke in tongues, prophesied, preached divine healing, went into trances, saw visions, and engaged in other phenomena such as jumping, rolling, laughing, shouting, barking, and falling under the power of the Holy Spirit, that were highly unusual within the established religious community of Los Angeles. As a result, the mission's members were subjected to regular and frequent ridicule, both public and private. Viewed as fanatics, many of its members were arrested, fined, and jailed on grounds that they were "insane." The Los Angeles Police Department assigned special officers to monitor the mission's ongoing services. Sometimes these officers interrupted the worshippers when the officers thought that the services got too loud or ran too late. At the same time, the public debated whether the mission should even be allowed to exist. Many of these same actions have been taken throughout Latin America. The Pentecostals in that region of the world have been ridiculed as "alleluias" and "tambourines," they have been labeled as "sects" and "ravenous wolves," and they have been persecuted. But the icon of the Azusa Street Mission has been a source of empowerment, encouraging members to receive their power directly from God and then exercise it on behalf of the community.

A similar story emerged at the height of the apartheid era in South Africa, "colored" and "black" Pentecostals turned their attention to the Azusa Street Mission as their symbol of hope for their own situation. Its pastor William J. Seymour after all was of African descent, the son of former slaves. In spite of these odds, God called him, and he rose to become the leader of a racially inclusive congregation with a massive revival in the midst of an otherwise segregated society. South African blacks and coloreds came to believe that the same thing could also be true in apartheid South Africa, and that Seymour's message of racial and ethnic equality could be affirmed as broadly as the nation itself.

Today, the largest competitor to the Roman Catholic majority in Latin America is the Pentecostal one, and the majority of African churches are Pentecostal/Charismatic in practice. Between 1985 and 2005, for instance, the Lutheran Church in

Ethiopia has grown from two hundred thousand members to over four million members, and almost all of them describe themselves as Charismatics. Many of Africa's independent or indigenous churches hark back to the Apostolic Faith Mission. The Anglican community in Singapore is highly charismatic. The Orthodox Church in Kenya is renowned for the healing and deliverance services it holds in which people also speak in tongues and prophesy. The fastest growing churches in Asia, especially in places like Singapore, the house churches on mainland China, among Roman Catholics in the Philippines, and among the people of Korea are Pentecostal/Charismatic congregations and/or movements. The largest church in the world, Yoido Full Gospel Church in Seoul, Korea with its more than eight hundred thousand members is one more example of the mission's global impact. As long as the number of Pentecostal/Charismatic Christians around the world continues to grow, the impact of the Azusa Street Mission grows with it.

The fourth important aspect of the Azusa Street Mission and revival is that it continues to serve as an example for its outreach to the marginalized—the poor, women, and people of color. In a day that is marred by endless racial strife and tension, strong anti-immigration sentiment, and ethnic mistrust and intolerance, it is important to hear how this one congregation attempted to live out a vision of racial and ethnic inclusion.

One of Pastor Seymour's favorite biblical texts was Luke 4:18–19.

> *The Spirit of the Lord is on me,*
> *Because he has anointed me*
> *To preach good news to the poor,*
> *He has sent me to proclaim freedom for the prisoners*
> *And recovery of sight for the blind,*
> *To release the oppressed,*
> *To proclaim the year of the Lord's favor.*

While many white Pentecostals are tempted to interpret this text solely in a spiritual sense, Seymour believed—and he is followed by most Pentecostals around the world—that it conveys an equally important literal message. The poor, those incarcerated in the city's jail, those without physical sight or with other physical needs, and the oppressed, whether through addictions or prejudice were all high on the mission's agenda. Seymour's commitment to the poor can be seen in his statement, "The Apostolic Faith movement stands for 'missions' and for 'street . . . work.'" His commitment to prisoners is present in his declaration that "The Apostolic Faith Movement stands for . . . 'prison work.'" His commitment to the blind and to all who needed physical healing came in his claim that "God is able to heal" and his desire to lay his hands upon the sick and pray the prayer of faith. But his commitment to the oppressed, whether they were former slaves, or women, or members of any other race or class, was always uppermost in his mind.

According to the *California Eagle*, Los Angeles' African American newspaper, Pastor Seymour came to Los Angeles *with the intention* of founding a congregation in which members of all races would be welcome. It would be a place where everyone could make a contribution, and where they could all be accepted as equals. While Los Angeles was not yet the hotbed of "Jim Crow" activity that many other parts of the nation were at the time, the racial sensitivities of many Angelinos were deeply challenged by the mingling of races, classes, and genders at the mission. From the perspective of the worshippers, the ease with which these groups mixed became a testimony to the power of the gospel to change individual hearts as well as the larger society. From the perspective of many Angelinos, it was a scandal that carried far reaching implications for the status quo of the larger social order in the United States.

From the outset, the leadership group that surrounded Seymour was racially mixed and included both women and men. For several years, under Pastor Seymour's unique ministry, the mission attracted and held the ongoing participation of African Americans, European Americans, Hispanic Americans, Asian Americans, Native Americans and others. As a result, the Azusa Street Mission provides a glimpse of what is possible if we allow space for the Holy Spirit to change hearts and minds. It may also provide a model for congregations in our own day to embrace this same kind of diversity, to demonstrate before the world the power of the gospel to break down the artificial racial and ethnic walls that otherwise divide us, as the apostle so eloquently noted in Ephesians 2:11–22.

Thus, the mission resulted in a movement which, in keeping with God's promise to pour out His Spirit upon all flesh, male or female, frequently recognizes the ministry of women as legitimate and as equal with that of men. This was an important witness over claims by fundamentalists, evangelicals, historic Protestants, Catholics, and Orthodox alike, that women are simply to be "silent in the church." And it came to Pentecostalism long before most historic Protestant denominations reached the conclusion that women should play a greater role in ministry. The differences in how Pentecostals and most Protestants reached this conclusion serve to underscore a key distinction between them. Pentecostals justified their position based largely on their understanding of Joel's promise (Joel 2:28–32). Protestants came to similar conclusions primarily after they had been subjected to the criticism of secular feminists.

Exploring the Azusa Street Revival

The most widely read account of the revival that emerged at Azusa Street is still Frank Bartleman's *How Pentecost Came to Los Angeles*, first published in 1925. In the eight decades since, this account has appeared under a number of titles and in countless editions. Bartleman is unquestionably unique as the primary witness to the revival. Still, subsequent investigation has unearthed hundreds of sources that enrich and broaden his brief account of the subject.

Most subsequent studies of Azusa Street have been limited to only one part of the conversation that took place in the original context, that is, of insiders who uncritically supported the revival. There were, however, many other people who gave their opinions on the subject. Their accounts also need to be taken seriously in order to recover the full story. Some of them were supportive of what was taking place, while others were vociferously opposed to what they saw. Thus, in this new study of the Azusa Street revival, I will draw from many of these sources, including the mission's periodical *The Apostolic Faith*, published intermittently between September 1906 and June 1908. In addition, I will draw from many of the articles published in local newspapers from the period, as well as public records such as property deeds, census reports, city directories, photographs, cartoons, maps, diaries and personal correspondence that I have unearthed along the way, and interviews that I have conducted with people who were there. I will also draw from my more than thirty years of living with the subject.

I hope to provide a new perspective on the life and ministry of William J. Seymour at the Azusa Street Mission by placing the revival within the larger social, cultural, racial, and religious contexts of their world, especially of 1906 Los Angeles. Revival and renewal always come within existing contexts and they are affected by these contexts. Along the way I will point out various factors that I believe the Azusa Street context contributed to the growth and decline of the Azusa Street revival. I will show how Los Angeles became the paramount center from which the Pentecostal movement spread prior to 1915. The identification of factors that attracted people from around the world to this multicultural and interracial religious experiment before scattering them like feathers or seeds blown by the winds of the Holy Spirit across the globe to tell what they had seen and experienced, should help us to understand the success of global Pentecostalism as it entered new locations and cultures.

In the century since the beginning of the Azusa Street Mission, some distortion in our popular understanding of those early events and their significance has taken place.[3] I hope that this new and expanded accounting of those events will give way to a rich appreciation for Pentecostal/Charismatic spirituality to which these early witnesses bore testimony. Even in a postmodern age, people remain hungry for a life-transforming encounter with the living God. My hope is that in retelling this story, this book will contribute to their hunger even as it leads them to seek the only One who is able to quench their spiritual thirst.

1

WILLIAM J. SEYMOUR
AND THE BEGINNINGS OF PENTECOSTALISM

ைை

> God raised up Ezekiel to prophesy to the dry bones and they
> lived. He was a blessed Holy Ghost man, though he did not have
> the baptism with the Holy Ghost. . . .
> He preached as he was commanded and the bones all came
> together, bless His holy name, and a great army was raised up.
> So we have this same privilege in these last days when God is
> pouring out His Spirit upon all flesh and our sons and daughters
> are prophesying in His mighty name.
>
> WILLIAM J. SEYMOUR

THE STORY OF THE Azusa Street Mission must begin with the
story of its pastor, William Joseph Seymour. Just as our own experiences affect the way we come to think and act later on, so too, the
circumstances under which William J. Seymour grew up played a
role in forming him into the person he became. Each of us has a
different starting point even when we are reared in the same family.
But to grow up in the American South, as an African American, the
child of former slaves, during the period of Reconstruction immediately following the Civil War (1861–1865), is an experience that
the majority of the world has never had. As a result, I want to
review some of the facts of life from that period that undoubtedly
affected the way Pastor Seymour later thought and acted.

Centerville and Verdunville, Louisiana

William Seymour was born to Simon and Phillis Seymour on Monday, May 2, 1870, in Centerville, Louisiana. Centerville lies in the

heart of bayou country, in St. Mary Parish, a dozen miles from the southern coast of Louisiana. In 1682 the explorer, Robert Cavalier de La Salle, claimed for France the entire Mississippi Valley including what would later become Louisiana. The region quickly became the realm of explorers, trappers, traders, and settlers. While most immigrants came directly from France, a sizable group of French settlers who had been driven by the British from the Maritime Province of Acadia off the coast of eastern Canada joined them after 1755. They would become known as Cajuns and they would settle in and around St. Mary Parish.

Most immigrants entered the region through the port of New Orleans. They fanned out across the region, moving as far west as Lake Charles and as far north as Alexandria. With them, they brought their languages and cultures as well as their hopes and dreams. And they brought their Roman Catholic faith. To help them tame this new land, many of them also brought slaves. The fact that control of this region moved back and forth between the Spanish and the French meant that ultimately a rich mix of French, Cajun, Spanish, Portuguese, and Afro-Caribbean cultures such as Creoles dominated in the region. This also resulted in a population of slaves who came in varying shades of color.

Slaves were typically graded according to color. Those of a lighter hue—often the offspring of forced interracial unions between female slaves and their white owners—generally drew higher prices. Slaves with light skin were often given the more highly prized designation of "mulatto" and frequently, though not always, they were assigned work in and around the homes of their owners. The rest, the darker skinned slaves who were designated as "blacks," typically bore the brunt of the field labor in the region's stiflingly hot and humid corn and sugar cane fields. Many of them made bricks and brick furnaces, and then built and worked in small plantation refineries where the sugar cane was crushed, then boiled down to produce molasses and sugar under sweltering summer conditions.

William Seymour's father, Simon, was born about 1837. He was known as Simon Simon until sometime between 1867 and 1870 when he changed his name to Simon Seymour. William Seymour's mother, Phillis Salaba, was born November 23, 1844. Both of William Seymour's parents were born into slavery. Their parents had been slaves before them. Simon would later be described in census reports as a "mulatto." In spite of this designation denoting a lighter skin color, he was assigned to work as a brickmaker and was undoubtedly employed in sugar production. Phillis, described as "black" in these same reports, worked the fields alongside her parents and her sisters and brother.

We do not yet know who owned William Seymour's father, but we do know who owned his mother. It was Mr. Adelard Carlin, among the wealthiest plantation owners in St. Mary Parish. It is difficult for most people who live today to imagine what slavery was like. Simon Simon and Phillis Salaba were not merely farm workers who worked the fields when the corn ripened or it came time to harvest the sugar cane. They were not treated with such respect. They were simply viewed as property.

It might help to put things into perspective if we look at a report that Mr. Carlin filed with the U.S. government in 1860, the year before the Civil War broke out. That year, Adelard Carlin reported that he owned 2,110 acres of land. A quarter of the land, some 560 acres, was in production, with two crops—corn and sugar cane. The rest was pasture land or simply undeveloped real estate. In addition, Mr. Carlin claimed that he owned 112 slaves, 80 horses, 40 mules, 30 milk cows, 16 oxen, 150 sheep, 150 pigs, and 150 "other" cattle. The placement of the slaves in a list that also reports the number of animals by species may seem crass by today's standards, but in reality, this is the way slaves were viewed at the time. They were nameless pieces of property that could be bought and sold without any consideration of their desires. Many reports merely gave them a number instead of a name.

In this report, William Seymour's mother, Phillis Salaba, her parents, Michel and Lucy Salaba, and all of her siblings were numbered among those 112 slaves. They provided the back breaking labor that produced Mr. Carlin's crops and made him rich. They cared for the animals that contributed to the farming, processing, and marketing of Mr. Carlin's products. They sowed, tended, and harvested the fields that yielded five thousand bushels of corn and 105 tons of cane sugar that year. And they refined 13,200 gallons of molasses for which Mr. Carlin was paid.[4] They worked hard, had few rights, and carried many responsibilities, while Mr. Carlin grew wealthy from their sweat.

On two occasions during the Civil War, there were skirmishes between Union and Confederate forces in and around Centerville, Louisiana. On the whole, however, the region was relatively stable. Union forces captured New Orleans early in the war and carefully occupied and patrolled the coastal sugar parishes of southern Louisiana to ensure stability in the region. On September 22, 1862, President Abraham Lincoln issued his famous "Emancipation Proclamation." With a couple of notable exceptions, Lincoln declared that as of January 1, 1863, all slaves would be free. The exception clauses included the sugar parishes of southern Louisiana, and St. Mary Parish where Seymour's parents were slaves, was one of them. While slaves throughout the South would be freed with Lincoln's "Proclamation," Simon Simon and Phillis Salaba would remain slaves.

The primary reason for Lincoln's exception was a pragmatic one. While slavery was an abominable institution and Lincoln was committed to ending it, as long as the people of this area continued as slaves, they had housing, clothing, food, "full employment," and their masters were forced to keep them healthy if they wanted their slaves to work. If the slaves in that strategic area were freed while the military was fighting a war, the Union army would immediately be confronted with caring for a huge, unemployed, homeless population and it would be unable to complete its military duties. Thus, the status of these slaves would change only with the end of the war and the passage of the 13th Amendment to the Constitution of the United States of America, December 18, 1865.

There was, however, another exception clause. Immediate freedom would be granted to those slaves who would willingly join the Union army and take up arms against the South. Simon was among some fifteen thousand African American volunteers who made the decision to join the Union army. On October 10, 1863, he became an infantryman in the famous *Corps d'Afrique*, later called the U.S. Colored Infantry. He served for three years in Louisiana and in Florida and was honorably discharged September 7, 1866.

Religious life in southern Louisiana was dominated by the Roman Catholic Church. The French who had settled in the region in the 18th century were indisputably Catholic. In 1724, the mayor of New Orleans, Jean Baptiste Le Moyne Bienville had issued *Le code noir*, "The Black Code." It required all slave owning settlers to instruct and baptize their slaves in the Roman Catholic faith shortly after their arrival in the region, or forfeit their slaves. While this law was never evenly enforced, most slave owners did what the law required. As a result, Louisiana still boasts the largest number of African American Catholics in the nation. The Seymours were among them.

At one level, when "The Black Code" became law in 1724, it could be understood as a measure intended to guarantee a single, consistent faith among the people of the region. It was viewed as an evangelistic tool. At another level, it was a means of mass control. It was intended to destabilize the slaves so that they would do the bidding of their masters. Slaves had been treated this way for centuries. Think for a moment of Daniel and his friends (Dan. 1:3–10). King Nebuchadnezzar took them from their native land and made them slaves. He did six things that most subsequent slaveholders have also found to be useful control mechanisms.

- He separated them from their families.
- He changed their names.
- He forced them to learn a new language.
- He attempted to change their cultural patterns.
- He attempted to change their diet in keeping with their new culture. And ultimately,
- He ordered them to change their religion by requiring that they bow down to an idol (Dan. 3:1–30).

The African slaves that came to Louisiana were subjected to all of these same forces. For most people in the United States, this experience is foreign. For African Americans, it holds profound implications. Most African Americans do not know from which African country they came. Many have a family tree that extends back no more than three or possibly four generations. As a result, these changes have contributed significantly to questions of identity and self-esteem among many African Americans.

One of the problems with forced conversions such as the French attempted to undertake is that they do not always produce the desired results. Most slaves embraced the faith of their masters under duress. They did not want to become Christians, and many of them found ways to maintain their traditional religions. They embraced the Christian faith by giving the correct answers and submitting to the forms or rites presented to them by the Catholic church. They participated in the liturgical life of the church, but they quickly filled that Christian form and ritual with double meanings. In a sense, they treated Christian forms and rituals in much the way they told the tales of Uncle Remus, with Brer Bear, Brer Fox, and Brer Rabbit. They told these colorful and entertaining tales even to their owners and the children of their owners. What the owners did not know was that Brer Rabbit represented the clever slave, while Brer Bear and Brer Fox represented what the slaves thought of their masters. They were dumb, bumbling, and incompetent. Thus, even in a story, they entertained the whites at one level and ridiculed them at another. At the same time, they entertained and empowered the blacks through their hidden ridicule of whites.

Many of the slaves that came to southern Louisiana in the late 18th and early 19th centuries came by way of various Caribbean islands. Sometimes they wove new religions using Catholic forms. Their syncretistic efforts gave rise to some kinds of "popular Catholicism," that is, expressions sometimes viewed by outsiders as "Catholic," although they may not be approved expressions, and in some cases they may even have been condemned by the church. One of the most dominant in Louisiana was one or another form of Voodoo. Voodoo took Catholic forms and rituals and wedded them to the religious realities that the slaves had brought with them from Africa. While Catholics might pray to or venerate specific saints, for instance, those involved in Voodoo gave their African gods new names, names that corresponded with those of the saints. Thus, when it appeared that they were venerating Christian saints, they were actually worshipping their African gods, all under the guise of being good Catholics.

Most slaves in southern Louisiana did not embrace classic Voodoo as such, but they did bring many of their beliefs, superstitions, and fears with them and they passed them on to the next generation of slaves. It was part of their attempt to remain African, to be faithful to the beliefs and practices that they remembered from their African past. What had developed by Seymour's time was a popular variation known as Hoodoo. Many of the slaves participated in a slave culture in which symbols, spells, incantations, sympathetic magic, and root work were a regular part of life. In spite of their differences, they held many things in common with the Christian worldview. They believed in a Divine spirit, in the supernatural including the empowerment of individuals, signs and wonders, miracles and healings, invisible spirits, trances and spirit possession, visions and dreams as a means of Divine communication, as well as other phenomena described in the Bible. They sang, clapped, trembled, shouted, danced, played drums, and developed a "call and response" preaching style. William J. Seymour was undoubtedly well aware of such things even as a child, for they formed an important part of African American slave culture and in many places in southern Louisiana they continue to exist into the present.

It was within this context that William Seymour's parents came of age. When Simon Simon and Phillis Salaba married July 27, 1867, neither of them was able to read or write. They signed their wedding license by placing an "X" on the license and having it witnessed. They soon had a daughter named Rosalie, and in 1870 Phillis gave birth to William. Over the next fifteen years, they would be joined by Simon, Amos, Julia, Jacob, Isaac, and finally in October 1885, by Emma. In each case, the children were taken to the Catholic Church in nearby Franklin, Louisiana, where they were baptized. William Seymour was baptized when he was four months old, on September 4, 1870. He would be reared a Roman Catholic. Seymour's formative years in the context where the supernatural was taken for granted, where spirits, both "good" and "evil" were commonly discussed, and where dreams and visions were understood to contain messages that sometimes foretold the future should be remembered as he moves through his spiritual pilgrimage.

During William Seymour's childhood, the road that ran through Centerville and connected it to Franklin was unpaved. The sidewalks that traversed the two-block length of Centerville were constructed of wood. Transportation was either by foot, on horseback, or by horse and buggy. Centerville is still a small, sleepy community, surrounded by verdant fields of corn, sugar cane, and open pastures where cattle are raised. While the majority of the homes there are small, wood-frame structures, a few old plantation mansions still stand guard along the nearby banks of Bayou Teche, which meanders slowly eastward toward nearby Morgan City before emptying into the Gulf. While the Catholic Church was in the county seat in Franklin, about six miles west of Centerville, the Presbyterians established a congregation in Centerville in 1860.

In 1883, when William Seymour was thirteen, his parents purchased a little over four acres of land in nearby Verdunville, about a mile and a half east of Centerville. The following year the family moved there. Adjacent to the Seymour home, the Baptists had started a church. It is very likely that because the Baptists were so close, the Seymours attended it from time to time while they maintained their membership in the Catholic Church in Franklin.

Before and during the Civil War, most slave owners prohibited their slaves from learning to read or write. They feared that such communication tools would enable the slaves to rebel against them. Thus, because Simon Seymour could neither read nor write, he had few options for employment after the war. He continued to make bricks for a living, but he also planted crops on the small family plot. Like most parents, however, Simon and Phillis Seymour wanted things to be better for their children. During the period of Reconstruction, when William Seymour was a child, things slowly began to change. The Methodists and Baptists sent evangelists and teachers throughout the South to establish schools for the children of former slaves. The Freedmen's Bureau, a grossly over-burdened and under-funded Federal agency bore primary responsibility for their ongoing welfare. The census for 1880, when William Seymour was ten years of age, reveals that William and his younger brother, Simon, were both enrolled in school where they were receiving basic literacy skills. When they were not in school, they worked as farm laborers.

Simon Seymour had become chronically ill with intestinal problems while serving in the Union army during the Civil War. It had required hospitalization. During the summer of 1891 these problems became acute, and he asked to be placed on permanent disability. He was about 54 years of age and clearly in declining health. The physician that examined him claimed that there was no reason to support Seymour's request and denied his application. Simon Seymour returned home and over the next several months his health deteriorated. He died November 14, 1891, and was buried the following day in the Providence Baptist Church Cemetery that lay adjacent to the Seymour property. Simon's death left the twenty-one-year-old William as the primary provider for the family. Ownership of the family plot passed to Phillis and the children. Phillis received a 50% interest, while a 10% interest went to each of the five surviving children.

The next few years were very difficult for the Seymour family. They managed to keep their property, but essentially the family existed at the poverty level. They continued to grow a little corn, a few potatoes, and some other vegetables, but they had very limited income from other sources. As a result, in 1895 William Seymour made his way to Indianapolis.

Indianapolis, Indiana

It was not yet common for former slaves or their children to leave the South. African American immigration to the urban centers of

the North and the West did not really take place until the 1920s. At
that time, the African American communities in New York and
especially in Chicago and Los Angeles grew by leaps and bounds.
In the 1890s most African Americans believed that it was just too
risky for them to travel to unknown areas of the country. It was the
case, of course, that following the Civil War, frustrated southern
whites were busy developing the equivalent of new "Black Codes"
in their attempts to keep African Americans disenfranchised. They
wanted to maintain a cheap labor force that they could control,
and they did so both through legislation and intimidation. In spite
of the prejudice and racism of so many whites and the rising number of "Jim Crow" laws throughout the South, most African Americans chose not to move. There were exceptions to this rule, such
as the planned migration that took as many as sixty thousand
African Americans to Kansas between 1874 and 1878, but they were
few.

The primary reason that African American men the age of
William Seymour left the South was almost inevitably related to
economic opportunity. They had job offers elsewhere or they
believed that they could get employment in such places. While we
do not yet have the full story that tells us why William J. Seymour
chose Indianapolis, it is likely that he knew someone in that city
who encouraged him to move north. There he could find work
that was not in the fields of some former plantation. Still, it was
rather risky for him to go to Indianapolis.

While Indiana had been aligned with the North during the Civil
War, and it was home to many Quakers and holiness people who
had worked to free the slaves, it was also on the way to becoming a
stronghold of white supremacy and in the 1920s, of the revitalized
Ku Klux Klan. After 1831, and for a generation to follow, all African
Americans in Indiana were required to register with county officials, much like the Jews were required to do in Hitler's Germany,
and they were required to post bond so that they would not
become a public liability. In 1851 Article XIII, Section I of the State
Constitution had spelled out that, "No Negro or mulatto shall
come into, or settle in the State, after the adoption of this Consti-

tution." Following the Civil War, the State Supreme Court ruled that this law was "null and void."[5]

In spite of the fact that Indiana had such a mixed history on racial affairs, William Seymour moved to Indianapolis and settled within the boundaries of the historic African American community at 127 1/2 Indiana Avenue (renumbered in 1898 to 427). His room was in a two-story apartment building with a central staircase. The area in which it stood was decidedly industrial in nature, with a railroad spur line running within 65 feet of his room. The stagnant Central Canal where neighbors emptied their garbage ran within a half block of Seymour's apartment. It was a noisy, stench-filled neighborhood, brimming with the sounds of sharp-toned whistles and hissing trains, and the clangs of pipes banging as they were moved. By 1898 he had found more suitable housing, this time on a narrow street at 309 Bird [alternatively known as Severin], essentially a fifteen foot wide alley in a residential neighborhood. He was surrounded by large yards, horse stables, a few small apartment buildings and a Methodist church. This place was also a bit closer to Indianapolis' downtown area where he worked.

Each edition of the *Indianapolis City Directory* published between 1896 and 1898 listed Seymour's occupation as a waiter. He was employed in three different upscale hotels in Indianapolis during the years that he lived in that city, the Bates House, the Denison House, and the Grand Hotel. President Abraham Lincoln had stayed at the Bates House. The Grand Hotel served as the unofficial headquarters of the state and national Democratic Party in the city. President Grant had stayed there. The Denison Hotel served as the state headquarters to the Republican Party for a number of years. The fact that Seymour, fresh from the fields of southern Louisiana found employment in the restaurants of such posh hotels strongly suggests that he had help in getting these jobs. It also says something about Seymour's willingness to adapt, to learn, and to serve.

It was during his years in Indianapolis that William Seymour claimed to have had a conversion experience. In 1914 Charles Shumway, a Methodist minister who was writing a baccalaureate thesis for the University of Southern California, interviewed

The Bates Hotel, where William J. Seymour worked as waiter in Indianapolis, later became the subject of a polka and a murder mystery, *The Bates House*. In 1861, Abraham Lincoln spoke to the public from its balcony when running for President.

William J. Seymour. He noted that while Seymour was in Indianapolis, he had been converted in a "colored Methodist Episcopal Church." While we do not know which congregation that was, there are several possibilities. Bethel African Methodist Episcopal Church is one such possibility because it was the strongest African American congregation in Indianapolis at the time and it was relatively near Seymour's apartment. A second possibility is the Meridian Street Methodist Episcopal Church, which stood across the street from Seymour's second address. A third possibility was the Simpson Chapel Methodist Episcopal Church in the city. It was led by an African American pastor.

While it was during this time that Seymour undoubtedly gained his appreciation for the teachings of John Wesley, the founder of Methodism, Shumway tells us that Seymour soon left the Methodist church over two important issues. First, the Methodist Episcopal Church, like most Protestant churches of that period,

did not subscribe to the doctrine of premillennialism. Premillenni-
alists believe in a literal return of the Lord before [pre] a literal
period of one thousand years [millennium] during which He will
rule over the earth. The Methodist church held to an "amillennial"
position, that is, a position in which the millennium is viewed as a
figurative or spiritual reality and not a literal reality to which the
return of the Lord might be tied. Most other Protestants were opti-
mistic postmillenialists, who embraced a form of Social Darwin-
ism, that is the progressive evolutionary theory by which society
would become better over a thousand years, after which [post] the
Lord returned to rule forever. Second, Seymour differed with the
Methodist church on the role of "special 'revelations'." The
Methodist church did not give them much value. Seymour did.

Mother Emma L. Cotton, an African American preacher, a
friend of Pastor Seymour's, and an early participant in the Azusa
Street Mission claimed that Seymour was converted and sanctified
among the Evening Light Saints. Today we know this group by the
name Church of God (Anderson, IN), and we have been touched
by its musicians from Sandy Patti to the Gaithers. It is probable,
therefore, that William J. Seymour worshipped with these people
during his time in Indianapolis, and that while he came to faith in a
Methodist Episcopal Church of some sort, he went on to be further converted and/or "sanctified" while attending services offered
by the Evening Light Saints.

Daniel S. Warner brought the Evening Light Saints, a radical
holiness group that prescribed plain clothing and banned the use
coffee and tobacco, into existence in 1880. Warner taught that a
new age of the Christian church, the Evening Light (named for
Zech. 14:7 "at evening time it shall be light"), was restoring the
church of the apostles. This belief in a new age of holiness
together with the fact that they addressed one another as "Saints"
led to their nickname, the "Evening Light Saints." They were very
active throughout Indiana at the time that Seymour was in Indianapolis. Their headquarters today lies in Anderson, Indiana, just
north of Indianapolis.

Seymour's time with the Evening Light Saints may help to

explain several key ideas that he adopted. Daniel S. Warner was committed to producing a new "Reformation" in the Church and as a result the Evening Light Saints were sometimes called the Church of God Reformation Movement. Warner committed the Saints to a position of non-sectarianism and non-creedalism. The group was committed to classical expressions of Christian doctrine, including the need for a salvation experience and a subsequent sanctification experience with a strong holiness code of ethics. Like many, though not all holiness groups, the Saints practiced three ordinances: the baptism of believers by immersion, the Lord's Supper, and the washing of one another's feet. Warner believed, however, that the notion of ministry and of church governance needed to be radically reformed. Warner's commitment to non-sectarianism meant that in most cases the group went so far as to oppose the keeping of a roll of members. His commitment to address all of his followers as "Saints" led him also to adopt a position of racial and gender inclusiveness. In the 1890s the Evening Light Saints was one of the few groups in which blacks and whites were treated equally and gifted women were encouraged to preach. Warner also placed considerable power in the hands of the local congregations.

In recent years, several historians of the Pentecostal movement have claimed that Seymour served as a minister with the Evening Light Saints at this time. While this claim has been made repeatedly, no historian has yet produced any evidence that documents this claim. While the Evening Light Saints generally kept no lists of members, they did attempt to keep lists of those who regularly served as evangelists and pastors. The reason for this was a pragmatic one. Ordained ministers were given special travel rates on the nation's railroads. Thus, the names of many ministers among the Evening Light Saints from the period, both black and white, were recorded. In the only attempt undertaken to document and list all known "Negro Leaders Reported Active within the Church of God Reformation Movement" between 1885 and 1903, however, Seymour's name does not appear.

When William J. Seymour ultimately arrived in Los Angeles, he was as committed to a policy of non-sectarianism, the equality of

the races, and the equality of women and men as Warner was. Seymour held to the same historic beliefs, the same high holiness standards, and he practiced the same three ordinances as Warner did,
baptism by immersion, the Lord's Supper, and the washing of feet.
While the impact of the Evening Light Saints is evident in Seymour's
subsequent ministry, he did not remain with the group for long. The
reasons were simple. Seymour did not share Warner's commitment
to the amillennial position on the Second Coming, and like the
Methodists, Warner was not a fan of special "revelation," in the
forms of dreams and visions. Seymour had obviously been influenced by another source, most likely from nearby Cincinnati.

During the summer of 1900 Seymour returned to his home in
Verdunville, Louisiana. He was working as a farm laborer at the
time the census was taken. His younger brother, Simon, would
continue to live on the family farm. His sister Julia, now twenty,
had become the primary on-site family caregiver for their mother
who was now 55 years of age, and her younger brother Jacob, who
was now physically handicapped. Throughout the years of his
absence, William J. Seymour had probably continued to contribute
to the family income.

Cincinnati, Ohio

Oral tradition originating in the African American "Apostolic" tradition in Indianapolis suggests that during his stay in Indianapolis,
William Seymour had been influenced by another holiness preacher
and teacher, Martin Wells Knapp. In many respects, Seymour's position was closer to the theology of Martin Wells Knapp than he was
to that of Daniel S. Warner. In 1900 Knapp had established "God's
Bible School and Missionary Training Home" in Cincinnati, Ohio. It
looks much the same today as it did at that time. The motto of the
school was "Back to the Bible." The advertisements for the school
that circulated in various publications described it as "Pentecostal"
and like Warner's work in Indiana, as "non-sectarian."

The term "Pentecostal" was commonly used across the holiness
movement at the time. It did not identify the school as having sym-

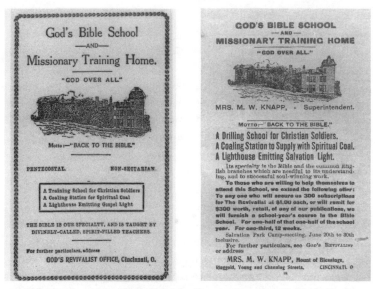

LEFT This advertisement for "God's Bible School" appeared in 1896. The Motto, "Back to the Bible" points to the founder's "primitive" convictions regarding how one should live as a Christian. The words such as "Pentecostal" and "Spirit-filled" were commonly used within the Wesleyan holiness movement and referred to the doctrine of sanctification. RIGHT This advertisement for Martin Wells Knapp's school appeared in 1901. Earlier claims that the faculty members were "Pentecostal" and "Spirit-filled," has been replaced by information regarding the course of study that was available at the school, the tuition rate, and an advertisement for the annual June camp meeting. The facility has changed little since 1901.

pathies with those who spoke in tongues, but rather, with those who held to two works of grace—salvation and sanctification. The ads that ran for the school claimed "The Bible is our specialty, and is taught by divinely-called, spirit-filled teachers." Like the term "Pentecostal," the phrase "Spirit-filled" was language commonly used to denote teachers who were part of the holiness movement. Later Pentecostals would appropriate the term "Pentecostal" for themselves, filling it with new meaning to identify those who believed that they had received the same baptism in the Spirit that the believers had received on the day of Pentecost that is described in Acts 2. Similarly, they would appropriate the term "Spirit-filled" to indicate those people who had received what they understood to be the baptism in the Holy Spirit with the biblical evidence of speaking in other tongues. Eventually, holiness people would release their grip on these terms in their desire to distance themselves from tongues-speaking, "Spirit-filled" Pentecostals. One powerful example of this eventually came when in frustration the Pentecostal Church of the Nazarene, which rejected the link between speaking in tongues and baptism in the Spirit, dropped the designation "Pentecostal" from its name in 1919 to become simply the Church of the Nazarene.

Three important factors must have attracted Seymour to study at "God's Bible School" that year. First, Knapp's school was racially inclusive; blacks and whites studied side by side. Second, Knapp was an avowed premillennialist. He taught that Jesus would return prior to a literal millennium. Third, Knapp took "special revelation" seriously. A decade earlier, Martin Wells Knapp had authored a book titled *Impressions*. It described how to discern whether a person had received "impressions" from God or "impressions" from Satan. Knapp was unique, for such subjects were rarely mentioned in traditional white, Christian circles and when they were discussed, they were typically set aside in favor of rational understandings of God's direction based largely on the interpretation and application of biblical texts.

Seymour's interest in "special revelation," however, may actually reflect another aspect of his years of formation. He had undoubtedly heard appeals to dreams and visions within southern Louisiana's African American community. There are many "slave narratives" going back to the 18th century, in which slaves talked about receiving guidance through visions and dreams, hearing voices, and experiencing different states of altered consciousness such as trances. All of these suggest that the role of what might be described as "special revelation" was widely accepted within the African American community.

Seymour was undoubtedly aware that similar things were frequently invoked in the "Hoodoo" tradition which was prevalent around Centerville and Verdunville. He was aware of the possibilities *and* the dangers that such phenomena provided. Dreams and visions had provided direction to many people in the Bible, especially in the Old Testament, where many African Americans identified with the slave past of the Israelites. Seymour must have found some resonance in the way Knapp wrote about the need to take visions, dreams, and internal voices seriously, while warning his readers to discern the spirits in order to recognize which manifestations came from God. Seymour's attention to this subject would pay dividends when people at the Azusa Street Mission, both black and white, began to claim visionary experiences, to interpret dreams, and to seek God for guidance. It would also be important when local spiritualists ultimately came looking for sympathy and acceptance at the Azusa Street Mission.

While Knapp superintended the Bible school, he also ran a publishing company known as the Revivalist Office. Among his publications were a number of books that circulated throughout the holiness community, often distributed by colporteurs, who carried them from door to door. He published a magazine called *God's Revivalist*. Students could matriculate at God's Bible School by selling subscriptions to the magazine. Tuition was $150 for a fifteen-week course.

There were over 70 students in the class that entered the school in 1900. Among those who studied there were several "Saints" from Warner's group as well as many others who found their way to the Bible school from a variety of independent congregations, holiness associations, and holiness camp meeting networks. While no known list of students from that period exists, it seems likely that William Seymour was among them. In their classes, students read the Bible as well as a number of Knapp's publications. In addition, students were offered courses in English grammar, rhetoric, orthography, penmanship, reading, and music. The curriculum was very basic, and students evidenced various levels of previous schooling.

William Seymour moved to Cincinnati that fall to pursue his studies, and once again he found work as a waiter. He rented his first room at 23 Longworth Street, and the next year moved several blocks down the street to an apartment at number 437. This section of the same street was known as Carlisle Avenue. In some ways, Seymour's

initial Cincinnati address was much like his initial address in Indianapolis. It was in the heart of "Little Buck," an area inhabited both
by African Americans and many newer immigrants. Seymour's apartment building was surrounded by the sounds and smells of light
industry, from a paste factory, to a typesetting and printing company,
to a variety of haberdasheries. His second address, four blocks west,
was quieter. A synagogue and several hotels stood nearby. Seymour
may well have been employed in one of these hotels.

During the few years Seymour lived in Cincinnati, the city was
swept by an invasion of smallpox. William Seymour contracted the
disease. In his bout with this deadly disease, Seymour incurred
some of the scarring that usually comes to survivors. As a result,
he lost one eye and it was replaced with an artificial one. As Seymour later reflected on this event, he saw the Lord's hand in it. He
came to believe that the Lord had called him into ministry and he
had been too slow to respond. The result was that God had sent
this plague upon him as a form of chastisement, a reminder of his
call to ministry. In 1903 Seymour left Cincinnati intent upon fulfilling that call.

Jackson, Mississippi

When Seymour left Cincinnati he traveled to Houston, some say in
search of relatives. Whatever the reason, from 1903 through 1905
Seymour made Houston his home base. During these years he
traveled to Chicago, where he ran into John G. Lake, a minister
then working with the holiness healing evangelist and utopian
community leader John Alexander Dowie of Zion, Illinois. While
staying at a Chicago Hotel, Lake and Seymour talked of spiritual
things. According to Lake, Seymour told him that for two and a
half years he had been praying for five hours a day because he had
such a hunger for God. During this same period of time, Seymour
reportedly held meetings in Lake Charles, Louisiana. Finally,
Shumway reported that in the winter of 1904–1905, Seymour was
directed "by special revelation" to Jackson, Miss[issippi], to receive
spiritual advice from a well-known colored clergyman." But who
was this clergyman?

Two possibilities quickly emerge. That clergyman was either Charles Price Jones or he was Charles Harrison Mason. Both men had originally been ministers in the Missionary Baptist Church Association, but following their acceptance of the holiness position regarding sanctification as a second work of grace, they were asked to leave the Association. Together they formed the Church of God in Christ.

Jones was the highly successful pastor of Christ's Tabernacle Church in Jackson, Mississippi at the time. He is best known in Pentecostal circles as the co-founder of the Church of God in Christ, and for a number of hymns that he wrote, including "Deeper, Deeper, in the Love of Jesus," and "Jesus Christ Is All I Need." He was a brilliant preacher and he had brought a number of congregations under his oversight. Charles Harrison Mason, who had come up with the name for their group, was serving as a pastor in nearby Tennessee. While it is impossible to know all that these men may have shared with one another, it is important to note that Seymour claimed that he was led to

Charles Price Jones

visit this clergyman by "special revelation." It may even be the case that Seymour wanted to learn something about how Jones and/or Mason understood the notion of "special revelation."

The African American church historian, Albert Raboteau, has argued that even if there is a *form* that connects the African past with the African American present, the *content* is new, and thus, the meaning has been utterly transformed.[6] Charles Mason, in particular, dealt with the subject of "special revelation" throughout his long career as Chief Apostle and Bishop of the Church of God in Christ. Many photographs show Mason surrounded by what are sometimes described as "oddities of nature."[7]

An outsider viewing such a photograph might view them as examples of slave religion's "conjuring culture." Mason would be seen as a shaman or a "conjure" man who divines these objects for

Bishop Charles H. Mason frequently posed with various "oddities of nature." From these items he claimed that by means of the Holy Spirit, he could discern the messages God had placed in them when they were created. This photograph must date from approximately 1950, though such photographs exist from the turn of the century.

some revelation. Mason appealed repeatedly to Psalm 19:1–4b to explain his actions.

> The heavens declare the glory of God;
> and the firmament sheweth His handiwork.
> Day unto day uttereth speech,
> and night unto night sheweth knowledge.
> There is no speech nor language,
> where their voice is not heard.
> Their line is gone out through all the earth,
> and their words to the end of the world.

He believed that through the help of the Holy Spirit, he could discern the message that God had placed in them yielding "words of knowledge" and "words of wisdom".

In the late 1960s, Elder C. G. Brown, First Secretary of the

Department of Home and Foreign Mission for the Church of God in Christ, remembered Mason's "demonstrations from earthly signs" in the following manner.

> Very frequently, the Spirit gives Elder Mason his messages for the people from earthly signs, or what are known as freaks of nature.... This is given to him through the Spirit, from any sign which may be brought to him ... Elder Mason will calmly pick up a stick, shaped in the exact likeness of a snake in its growth, or a potato shaped in the exact likeness of the head and ears of a pig in its growth, and demonstrate with such power that thousands of hearers are put on a wonder. It appears that he is reading one of the recesses of the object from which he is preaching. To look with skepticism at his consideration of these things is to disclose short sightedness and a lack of spiritual vision.[8]

Brown's language was revealing. He noted that the Holy Spirit gave messages to Mason through these "signs," that is, through God's own handiwork. He was able to hear that voice in "any sign," and he was able to "read ... the recesses of the object." This language transcended any idea that these things merely provided "object lessons" even as it became enmeshed in genuine "conjure" or "hoodoo" language.

What Mason believed he was doing was giving voice to the wordless speech of God's creation about which the psalmist so eloquently wrote. There is a sense in which Mason baptized into Pentecostal practice something he had seen in the surrounding African American conjure culture. He stood in the place of the medium or shaman, in the place of the "conjure" doctor or root worker, and using the same signs as they would use, he gave them completely new meaning. He filled them with "Christian" meaning. Charles Mason thereby preserved something from an historic African cultural basis, a non-Christian "conjuring culture" while transforming it into a Christian means of communication. At the same time, he critiqued the existing "African" culture when he explained that it was the Holy Spirit of the Bible who revealed such things to him. All of his African American friends would have understood him as he pronounced the gospel in terms that were familiar to them. The *form* was that of the culture around him, but the *message* transcended the culture.[9]

When the Assemblies of God was formed in Hot Springs, Arkansas, in April 1914, C. H. Mason preached at one of the inaugural services. During that service Mason drew attention to a sweet potato that he had carried into the pulpit, and in part, he proceeded to give what he believed to be God's message to those gathered before him based on what the Holy Spirit had revealed in that sweet potato.[10]

We have no evidence that William J. Seymour ever participated in similar activities at the Azusa Street Mission. Seymour's interest in the field of "special revelation," however, may have provided sufficient space for him to recognize the legitimacy of Mason's unique ministry. In any case, the two men became close lifelong friends. Seymour was always comfortable with worship in the African American religious tradition, a fact that became a stumbling block for some who visited the Azusa Street Mission. Unlike Mason, however, Seymour had been exposed to a world that may ultimately have proven to be broader than Mason's—the breadth of the Wesleyan holiness world that embraced whites as well as African Americans. His quest was to find a way in which the two cultures could best be brought together so that everyone benefited from the exchange.

Houston, Texas

Following his visit to Jackson, Mississippi, William J. Seymour returned to Houston. There he attended a small holiness congregation led by an African American widow nearly twenty years his senior. Mrs. Lucy F. Farrow had been born into a slave family in 1851 and sold on the slave block in Norfolk, Virginia. She was also said to be a niece of the famous Abolitionist, Frederick Douglass. She had married at least twice, and had given birth to a total of seven children, of which only two survived. In 1905 she rented a house adjacent to the railroad tracks on the edge of Houston's downtown, where she lived with her son and his wife, James and

Florence Pointer. There is no question but that Lucy Farrow had lived a hard life. Even now, while serving as the pastor of this small holiness congregation, she had to work to make ends meet. Her jobs varied from cook to nanny. She must have been encouraged with the arrival of William Seymour.

In July 1905, shortly after Seymour's return, the Houston press announced the imminent arrival of the Rev. Charles F. Parham. Described as a "divine healer," the announcement stated that he would soon begin to hold public meetings. While the *Houston Daily Post* noted that Parham was not the founder of any church or any creed, in a sense he was advertised as another non-sectarian. The *Post* went on to announce that Parham's intention was to turn the people to "the apostolic faith."

Charles Fox Parham had first gained notoriety in January 1901, when students in his short-term Bible school in Topeka, Kansas, began to speak in other tongues. Born in 1873, he had been healed of a life-threatening illness as a boy. As a result, he believed that he had a call to preach, and in 1890 he attended Southwest Kansas College. Before long, he decided that education was not a priority for him as a minister and he dropped out. His obvious gifts and desire to preach allowed him to be appointed to supply positions in several small Methodist congregations in eastern Kansas. He began to participate regularly in various camp meetings in which personal holiness and entire sanctification were dominant themes. During this time he became disillusioned with what he believed to be the coldness and formality of the Methodist church.

As Parham spent time in these Wesleyan holiness meetings, he adopted their independent line of thinking. He began preaching a series of beliefs that were incompatible with Methodism. He preached premillennialism. He took the position that the righteous were immortal but that the wicked would be annihilated. He preached more pointedly on the subject of divine healing. But most importantly, he adopted a racist theology known as the Anglo or British-Israelite theory. According to this theory, the Twelve Tribes of Israel had gone into the Babylonian Captivity, but only two had returned to the land of Israel. Ten tribes had essentially disappeared, but they could now be identified with the

Anglo-Saxon people. The white, Anglo-Saxon Protestants were their heirs in the United States. This led him to become an ardent supporter of modern Zionism and the return of the Jews to Israel, which gave way to prophetic speculation about events that needed to be fulfilled prior to the Second Coming. For obvious reasons, he was soon at odds with his bishop, and by 1895 he had left the Methodist church to form an independent ministry.

Over the next several years, Parham focused on the doctrine and practice of divine healing. In 1898 he opened a successful crusade in Ottawa, Kansas and he established the Beth-el Healing Home in Topeka. He published a periodical called *The Apostolic Faith* [Topeka, KS] that allowed him to circulate his ideas more broadly. When readers began to write, asking for further instruction, he founded a Bible school where he could share his ideas with his students.

In June 1900 an evangelist from Maine, Frank Sandford, held a series of tent meetings in Topeka. Parham was captivated by what he heard. As a result, he decided to take a trip to Maine to see Sandford's work firsthand. Along the way Parham visited several holiness and healing centers, including a stop to observe the work of John Alexander Dowie in Zion, Illinois, as well as that of Albert Benjamin Simpson and the Christian Alliance in New York. His visit to Zion, Illinois, would prove to be important to Parham later, but for now his mind was on Sandford. Parham spent six weeks at the "Holy Ghost and Us Bible School" in Shiloh, Maine, watching Sandford work.

Like Parham, Sandford had embraced the holiness position, taught the Anglo-Israelite theory, was an advocate of divine healing, and as a result of Dwight L. Moody's summer conferences in Northfield, Massachusetts, he was committed to world evangelization. In 1892, following a trip around the world, Sandford came to believe that all current missionary and evangelistic methods were inadequate and ineffective. He decided that God wanted him to work along "apostolic lines," in which "signs, wonders and mighty deeds" would empower those working toward world evangelization. This shift would require the restoration of New Testament power, and would include such things as the restoration of the gift of tongues, that is, the recovery of an ability to speak languages of

Frank Sandford's Shiloh Community in Maine

the world without prior study, under the direct inspiration of the Holy Spirit and for the ultimate evangelization of the world.

Parham's visit to Shiloh had a profound effect on him. He concluded that the baptism in the Holy Spirit was available to all believers who lived a holy life and sought to attain it. He believed in the restoration of the gifts of the Holy Spirit listed in 1 Corinthians 12—14. He came to believe, like Sandford, that the gift of tongues meant the ability to speak different foreign languages of the world without prior knowledge or study. This would become the ultimate evangelistic tool, for the person with this gift would be able to proclaim the gospel in a foreign setting in complete reliance upon and under the direct inspiration of the Holy Spirit.

Parham returned to Topeka and beginning in October 1900, he began to offer classes. In December, he assigned his students the task of reflecting upon the question, "What is the Bible evidence of the Baptism with the Holy Ghost?" He obviously thought that he knew the answer after spending time with Sandford, but he wanted his students to study the Bible and arrive at their own conclusions. On December 31, 1900, he received their answer. They had searched the book of Acts and concluded that the "indisputable proof" on each occasion, was the fact that they had spoken in other tongues. A young woman named Agnes Ozman asked that

Parham place his hands upon her so that she might receive this baptism in the Spirit with the "Bible evidence." Parham and the others did as she asked, and soon she was speaking in other tongues. Over the next several days others in the class also began to speak in tongues and the Topeka, Kansas, newspapers began to publish the story. For a while, Parham was popular with many Kansans, but before long they lost interest. Parham then began to travel throughout Kansas, Missouri, and Texas, preaching this theory as part of what he called the "Apostolic Faith."

Following a highly publicized healing incident in one of his meetings in Old Orchard, Texas, Parham once again became a prominent figure. In June 1905 he made Melrose, Kansas his new headquarters and continued to publish *The Apostolic Faith* [Melrose, KS]. He gathered a number of workers around him, most of them students, and he sponsored a short-term, hands-on, Bible school. Together Parham and his students held street meetings, witnessed door-to-door, and conducted public rallies in rented halls. Parham's announced visit to Houston in July 1905 was one more of these events. He rented Bryan Hall. To drum up public interest, his students paraded through the streets of Houston carrying banners of the Apostolic Faith movement, arrayed in clothing of the Middle East from a collection that Parham had purchased. He announced that his topic would be "The Restoration of Religion's Birthplace to Its Rightful Heirs."

Parham's message could not have hit Houston at a better time. The papers were carrying news of a Congress of the Zionist Movement then meeting in Basel, Switzerland. Among their topics was where to found a homeland for the Jews. The crowd at Bryan Hall was so large that people had to be turned away. As a result, Parham was asked to give a summary of his speech to the local press for publication.

Parham continued to hold meetings in Houston, met with students, preached on divine healing, on baptism in the Spirit with the "Bible evidence" of speaking in tongues, and on evangelism. He also raised money intended to help restore the Jews to their historic homeland. Parham extended his stay in Houston through mid-August, preaching that the gift of tongues had been given for purposes of world evangelization. Late at night he took his students to

This photograph dates from 1905 when Charles F. Parham held meetings in Byran Hall in Houston Texas. He sits in the center of the front row, surrounded by his Apostolic Faith workers.

the various bordellos of the city where they engaged the prostitutes who came to the windows, in conversation about their souls. They even entered these houses of ill repute to make further appeals.

While Parham and his students ministered in Houston, Parham recruited Lucy Farrow, whom he described as a "very light colored woman," to serve as the organization's cook. While she worked, Lucy Farrow listened to Parham and his students interact with one another. She was challenged by what she heard. Parham was so pleased with Farrow's work, that as Parham's crusade in Houston drew to a close, he offered her a position as the nanny of his children while he held meetings in Kansas. Farrow agreed. Having accepted this temporary position with Charles Parham, Lucy Farrow turned her congregation over to William J. Seymour who would serve as pastor in her absence.

Charles Parham and his company of workers, now accompanied by Farrow, traveled to Melrose, Kansas. Parham began meetings in southeastern Kansas. During this time, three important events took place. A young woman from Los Angeles named Neely Terry was on a trip to visit relatives in Houston. She attended the church where Seymour preached. She was impressed with him and his preaching and when she returned to Los Angeles, she told her local congregation about Seymour. Her congregation had been founded by Mrs. Julia Hutchins, and Neely Terry's recommendation of Seymour would ultimately lead to his invitation to come to Los Angeles. Meanwhile, in Kansas, Farrow had concluded that Parham's teaching about baptism in the Spirit with the Bible evidence of speaking in tongues was correct. As a result, she sought and received this baptism and began to speak in tongues. Finally, in Brunner, Texas, a group of Parham's workers had convinced Warren Faye Carothers, pastor of the Christian Witness Tabernacle as well as an attorney, to join forces with them. After receiving his baptism in the Spirit, Carothers went to work for the Apostolic Faith movement. Carothers' conversion was a real coup. He was an articulate spokesperson with ready access to the press. He would quickly become Parham's primary advocate in Houston, as well as his chief lieutenant in Texas.

On October 20, Parham took his evangelistic team by overnight train to the Houston area once again. On Sunday, October 22 they engaged Bryan Hall once again, and the next day Parham and Carothers met and announced that together they would spread the message of the Apostolic Faith in Texas. By December, Parham had moved his family to Houston and set up his home and his Apostolic Faith headquarters at the corner of Rusk Avenue and Brazos Street. At this point Parham began to call himself the "Projector of the Apostolic Faith Movement." He announced that he would open an Apostolic Bible Training School beginning in January 1906. Taking a page from the work of Frank Sandford who likened his work to that of an army with Sandford as the general, Parham announced that the school would be conducted according to "military rule" with set hours for rising, eating, study-

Warren Faye Carothers

ing, and working. Students would be expected to submit to whatever orders they received. In return, by faith, they would receive room, board, and a tuition free Bible school education.

Parham advertised a "thorough finishing course for successful evangelistic work." Students would be privileged to undertake "any study in English," and those who wished would be able to study music. He anticipated that both vocal and instrumental instruction would be made available to them. Students would be given instruction in the Bible, and they would be expected to live up to what the Bible taught. In addition, for two hours each day Charles F. Parham would be available to pray for the sick.

Mrs. Farrow returned to Houston with the Parhams. She hurriedly contacted William Seymour. Her new experience of baptism in the Holy Spirit quickly became the topic of their conversation. She suggested that her congregation become part of Parham's Apostolic Faith movement. She and Seymour now became regular attendants at Parham's meetings. Seymour was anxious to hear more about Lucy Farrow's experience and he wanted to hear Parham for himself.

At first Seymour had his doubts about Parham's message. Like many holiness people, Seymour believed that he had been baptized in the Spirit when he had been sanctified. But Lucy Farrow convinced him that if he simply sought God, he would also receive what she had received. It would prove his earlier holiness understanding of baptism in the Spirit was wrong. Upon hearing Mrs. Farrow's testimony and after hearing Parham preach, Seymour began to pray that God would empty him of any false notions he might hold. He searched the Scriptures, looking up texts that dealt with sanctification as well as texts dealing with baptism in the Spirit. He finally concluded that Parham's position on baptism in the Holy Spirit with the Bible evidence of speaking in other tongues made sense as the best interpretation of the biblical facts.

Seymour and Farrow were both aware of the limitations that their skin color afforded them in Texas. The meetings that Parham held in Houston were segregated meetings, in keeping with local cultural expectations and local legislation. Whites were given the primary seats in the auditorium or sanctuary, while African Americans were required to sit or stand in the rear. Seymour had been excluded from seeking baptism in the Holy Spirit at the altar of one of Parham's meetings because Parham did not allow for a racially integrated altar. With the announcement of Parham's intention to open a Bible Training School, Seymour wondered whether it would ever be possible for him to study there. Unlike Cincinnati, Ohio, where schools could be racially integrated, the "Jim Crow" laws of Texas prohibited the free mixing of the races in schools.

Lucy Farrow apparently interceded on Seymour's behalf, and Parham conceded that Seymour could have a space in the class, though not in the classroom. He would have to take his seat in the hall outside the classroom door. Parham would not violate the letter of the local Jim Crow laws, but he would not allow them to keep him from educating a genuine seeker, regardless of his color. Although the curriculum called for students to engage in hands-on, practical ministry, Seymour would not be able to minister to whites. He would have to find a way to do his work among blacks. With these understandings, Seymour became a student in Parham's Apostolic Bible Training School.

During this period, the relationship between Parham and Carothers

Parham's Bible School in Houston, where William J. Seymour was a student in early 1906. This building was located at 503 Rusk Avenue, on the northeast corner of Rusk Avenue and Brazos Street.

grew more solid. Parham relied increasingly upon Carothers for input and advice. He trusted Carothers, who knew the community of Houston. As the Bible School opened in early January, the two evaluated the potential that various students had. Their conversation inevitably turned to William Seymour. They saw obvious gifts for ministry in him, and they concluded that he might ultimately be the primary person they would encourage to take the Apostolic Faith ministry to the African American people of Texas.

Without wishing to justify either the actions or the beliefs of Charles F. Parham and Warren Faye Carothers, it must be noted that they were both men of their time, and they were both white men ministering in the South. Carothers, a future Executive Presbyter of the Assemblies of God was, by his own admission, an ardent segregationist. He justified racial segregation in the South by arguing that although all humanity shared one blood (Acts 17:24–26), God had created a multiplicity of nations that God subsequently divided along color lines. He believed that the United States had been intended by God to become a nation for whites, just as Africa was intended to be a continent set apart by God for those with black skin. Sadly, he seems to have ignored the place of Native Americans altogether! The institution of slavery had confused this simple scenario because an entire "nation" of Africans had been "imported" into the South. That importation had broken down the natural "geographical barriers" that God had put into place. Racial friction was the inevitable result. The Holy Spirit would use this friction to preserve racial integrity, he contended, and he maintained that Pentecostal people in the South understood that, even if outsiders did not. As a result, strict lines of separation between the races would typify all meetings of the Apostolic Faith movement. While Parham may have differed with Carothers on his understanding of race at some levels in 1906, Parham's own commitment to the Anglo-Israel theory left him no room to criticize Carothers. Both men viewed white, Anglo-Saxon Protestants as in some way especially blessed by God, a superior people, and this inevitably placed African Americans and other people of color at a distinct disadvantage.

Parham's Bible School opened right after the New Year in 1906.

Bible instruction began daily at 9:00 A.M. The Bible was the primary textbook, and students were expected to work their way through it by looking at assigned topics. They were given topics such as conviction, repentance, conversion, consecration, sanctification, healing, the Holy Spirit in His different operations, and prophecies. In each case, the topics were consistent with popular holiness teaching and evangelistic concerns. Students traced these topics through the Bible, pulling out proof texts that would provide the mainstay of their understanding. The one book of the Bible mentioned as a source of study was the Book of Revelation. Parham undoubtedly used it to proclaim his Zionist position formed against the backdrop of his prophetic and restorationist presuppositions.

The style of instruction consisted of lectures by Parham, discussions involving the students, practical experience such as street preaching, and extended times of prayer. The students were expected to write out and share their findings on the assigned topical studies with the class each day. During the afternoons and many evenings, students participated in street meetings, visited the sick, taught Sunday school classes, filled pulpits in the absence of local pastors, and engaged in other practical aspects of the work.

Recognizing that William Seymour was already a seasoned worker, Parham seems to have allowed Seymour more latitude than some others. He accompanied Seymour as together they would preach to the "colored people" of Houston. Seymour even preached at least once at the Brunner Tabernacle, under the watchful eyes of its pastor, Warren Faye Carothers and his teacher, Charles Parham. During the time he was a student in Parham's school, Seymour remained silent on the issues with which he disagreed. He studied hard and he prayed many hours for his baptism in the Spirit. He was not successful in receiving it during his time with Parham, but at that time he was firmly committed to Parham's basic theological theory on the subject.

It is evident that even as a student, William Seymour did not accept all of Parham's theology. He was sufficiently discriminating to make his own theological decisions. He shared Parham's concern for evangelization, his emphasis upon sanctification and the pursuit of holiness, his teaching on the baptism in the Spirit with the Bible evidence of speaking in other tongues, his emphasis upon divine healing, and his premillennial position on the Second Coming. He was not fully convinced of Parham's claims that the language one received when he or she was baptized in the Spirit was a human language intended to be used for evangelistic purposes, though he was fully committed to speaking in tongues playing the evidential role in baptism in the Spirit. But he rejected completely Parham's notion of the annihilation of the wicked. And he totally rejected Parham's Anglo-Israelite theory.

Within a month after school began, Seymour received an invitation asking him to accept the position as pastor of a relatively new holiness mission in Los Angeles. Mrs. Julia Hutchins had founded this mission at 9th and Santa Fe. She had led the congregation for several months and now desired for the congregation to have a permanent pastor. Miss Neely Terry had given a very good review of William J. Seymour, describing him as a "very godly man." Mrs. Hutchins was anxious to go to Liberia as a missionary, and after consulting with her congregation, she issued the invitation to Seymour.

Charles Parham had been telling his students that they should pray that the Lord would send openings for them to serve in ministry, and they were instructed to follow God's leading in this matter. When Seymour received the invitation from Julia Hutchins, he was inclined to accept it. His acceptance of the invitation, however, would necessitate his dropping out of school. He decided to ask Charles Parham whether or not he should accept the call. If Parham agreed, it would be an offer that would allow Parham's influence to spread to the West Coast.

When Seymour shared the invitation with Parham, Parham was very resistant. Carothers would later write that he and Charles Parham had been "arranging to send [Seymour] out with the message among the African population of Texas." For Seymour to go to California was a big step that neither Parham nor Carothers had envisioned. They were not ready to expand that far, and Seymour's interest in going to Los Angeles apparently caught Parham and Carothers by surprise. They were further opposed to his going until he had been baptized in the Holy Spirit. In the meantime, Mrs. Hutchins forwarded money to Seymour intended to cover his railroad fare.

In spite of the lack of support he felt from Parham and Carothers, William J. Seymour decided to accept the invitation. He informed Parham of his decision and Parham made it clear to Seymour just how "disappointed" he was in his decision. Carothers conducted the service in which they all "bade him God speed." Parham had the students of the Bible Training School lay hands upon Seymour and pray for him. And Parham later claimed that he contributed further funds toward Seymour's travel expenses. When Seymour left Houston, Parham promised him that as soon as they were ready, he would send lapel buttons to Seymour that Seymour could distribute to his own workers. They would identify those who wore them as workers in the Apostolic Faith movement.

Seymour departed Houston by train about February 18, bound for Los Angeles by way of Denver, Colorado. In Denver he stopped to visit the "Pillar of Fire Training School" that a woman named Alma White had founded in 1898. Why Seymour visited Alma White's school is something of a mystery. He may have had a friend there, or he may have simply taken the opportunity to visit the site

Kent and Alma White were originally Methodist ministers. Both of them frequented the camp meeting circuit of the Wesleyan holiness movement. Alma White proved to be the superior preacher of the two, and ultimately founded the Pillar of Fire, a Wesleyan holiness denomination. When Kent White was baptized in the Spirit and spoke in tongues, Alma White did everything in her power to bring it to an end. Since neither of them believed that they should divorce, they endured a very long separation. Kent White moved to Britain, where he joined the Apostolic Church, the earliest Pentecostal denomination to form in Great Britain. In his final year, he returned home and was nursed by Alma White. After his death, she claimed that he had given a deathbed recantation of his Pentecostal commitments.

of a thriving ministry that was both well known and controversial in holiness circles. In either case, while he was there, Seymour was invited to share a meal with Alma White and some others at the school and he was also asked to pray over the food.

Several years later Alma White wrote a brief, but highly critical description of Seymour as she remembered him from this visit. "He was very untidy in his appearance," she began, "wearing no collar, and had a greenish-looking brass button exposed in the band of his shirt." The "greenish-looking brass button" to which she referred was most likely the button commonly worn by Parham's workers. His disheveled look could probably be attributed to the fact that he was mid-way in his journey from Houston to Los Angeles. More importantly, this account describes the fact that when he was asked to pray before the evening meal, he did so "with a good deal of fervor." These might be viewed as what Alma White considered to be his best characteristics.

The description did not end here, however. Alma White went on to make a scurrilous attack on Seymour. She claimed that she had met "all kinds of religious fakirs and tramps" in her day, but that Seymour had "excelled them all." Even Seymour's time of prayer was written off as hopeless. "Before he had finished," she shivered, "I felt that serpents and other slimy creatures were creeping all around me." Why had he come her way? She thought she had an answer. God had sent Seymour her way, she claimed, because she needed to see "the person that the devil was going to use" in Los Angeles.

In reality, this account reveals much more about Alma White than it does about William J. Seymour. It was first published after Alma White and her husband Kent had separated. The reasons for their long separation were complex, though in one sense, they were simple—Kent White ultimately accepted the message of Pentecost, was baptized in the Spirit, spoke in tongues, and would not give it up. Alma White would not tolerate such doctrine or practice either in her home or in her church. Their separation began a life-long feud in which Kent and Alma White published vicious exchanges against one another. It should not be surprising to find her description of Seymour more than a little tainted.

2

REVIVAL COMES TO LOS ANGELES

༄

The news has spread far and wide that Los Angeles is being visited with a "rushing mighty wind from heaven." The how and why of it is to be found in the very opposite of those conditions that are usually thought necessary for a big revival. No instruments of music are used, none are needed. No choir, but bands of angels have been heard by some in the Spirit and there is a heavenly singing that is inspired by the Holy Ghost. No collections are taken. No bills have been posted to advertise the meetings. No church or organization is back of it. All who are in touch with God realize as soon as they enter the meetings that the Holy Ghost is the leader. One brother stated that even before his train entered the city, he felt the power of the revival.

THE APOSTOLIC FAITH

W HEN William J. Seymour arrived in Los Angeles in 1906 it was a bustling city of 238,000. It had more than doubled its population in the previous six years and was now growing by 3,000 residents every month. Each arriving train conveyed a batch of hopeful immigrants to the nation's seventeenth largest city. The area provided a promising array of possibilities that were creatively advertised by the region's many promoters. Local electric streetcar lines had recently been completed; the first such system to operate west of the Rockies. Property development boomed. The economic indicators pushed ever upward. It was raw, rugged, bawdy, and eclectic—a fertile seedbed for new ideas and new opportunities. It was a city full of dreams and ambitions. As one writer from the period put it, "Los Angeles entered the 20th Century in high gear."

Los Angeles gained great advantages from its strategic location on the west coast of the United States. By working with nearby Long Beach and San Pedro, it stood to become a major deep-water port with access to the entire Pacific Rim. By 1905 several transcontinental railroad lines also linked Los Angeles to the rest of the nation. The Southern Pacific, the Atchison, Topeka, and Santa Fe, and the San Pedro and Salt Lake Railroad that would eventually merge with the Union Pacific each had depots near the city's center. Locally, Henry E. Huntington's extensive streetcar line connected over a dozen outlying suburbs with the heart of Los Angeles. Known as the Pacific Electric Railway, it was among the best streetcar systems in the country.

Housing developments grew rapidly as "booster" magazines such as *Sunset* and the Pacific Electric's *P. E. Topics* painted tantalizing word pictures of the region. They spoke of vast citrus groves with sweetly scented blossoms and bountiful fruit, gentle breezes and swaying palm trees in a temperate climate, a rising skyline as business converged on the city, and a water supply guaranteed to meet the region's needs for a century or more. When these maga-

A view of Broadway, looking north from East 4th Street in 1907

zines began to include large photographs of recently constructed parks, lush gardens, and elegantly landscaped homes with long drives and paved streets and sidewalks, immigrants came in increasing numbers. By 1906 the downtown area of Los Angeles featured modern hotels, broad boulevards, electric lighting, and large windows. No house in the city was further than three blocks from a streetcar line, and thus from the heart of the city.

The number of churches in the city grew as well, from 180 churches in 1905 to 254 by 1907. Numerous tent and street meetings also dotted the landscape, especially around East Seventh Street between Spring and Broadway. While the Catholic church was the oldest denomination in the region, it was no longer the majority church. Near *La Placita*, the plaza near what is now Olvera Street that was the historic Mexican center of the city, Our Lady of the Angels served the needs of the Latino community. The Cathedral of St. Vibiana, a mile south of the plaza, catered more to the upper-class Anglo faithful. But Protestant churches outnumbered Catholic by a wide margin.

A view of Spring Street looking north from East 4th Street in 1907

The Methodists and Presbyterians had arrived early. After the Civil War they had been joined by Episcopalians, Congregationalists, Southern Methodists, Baptists, members of the Christian Churches (Disciples of Christ), Unitarians, Seventh-day Adventists, Mormons, Lutherans, and followers of Christian Science. A substantial spiritualist community also called Los Angeles home. The Methodists and related Wesleyan holiness churches, however, dominated the scene.

In May 1906 over thirty Protestant congregations formed the Los Angeles Church Federation, pledging to work toward "good government" by supporting a slate of political candidates. They opened a "coffee club" at Third and Main Street, including a public restaurant and private dining areas for use by Christian businessmen. The club as a whole provided Christian businessmen with a place to develop relationships and consummate deals with each other over a meal. It also provided an employment service.

While many Los Angeles residents had migrated from the upper Midwest, a substantial number had also come from the South. Most Angelinos were White. A large group of Europeans, especially Scandinavians, Germans, and Russians, had settled in Los Angeles within the previous twenty years. By 1906 fourteen German-speaking congregations and neighborhoods dotted the city. Swedish, Norwegian, Danish, Italian, Russian, Polish, Spanish, and Chinese congregations also rubbed shoulders in the metropolis.

Los Angeles's largest racial minority was its African American community, comprising fifty-four hundred people—many of them well-educated, professional, middle-class home owners. African Americans were generally integrated into the life of the city. By 1907 some held positions in the city's police and fire departments. Others served as doctors, dentists, pharmacists, veterinarians, lawyers, teachers, and building contractors. Even the city's "deputy assessor and tax collector" was an African American. Children from the community attended fully integrated public schools. The primary African American churches were First African Methodist Episcopal Church and Second Baptist Church. Half of the African American population attended one of these two churches, and at least ninety percent of black Angelinos belonged to a Christian church of some sort.

Of the three thousand or so Mexicans and Mexican Americans who made Los Angeles their home, the majority had arrived only recently. Recruited to work on various railroad projects for a dollar a day, they frequently lived in railroad cars or railroad camps provided by the Southern Pacific. When the railroad eventually ceased to need them and cast them off, they survived in squatter camps or shantytowns, lacking even the most basic of necessities. They erected shelters from scavenged wood, canvas, stones, gunny sacks, and sheet metal on overcrowded plots of land lacking water and sewer services. With neither gas nor electricity, they cooked on open fires. Disease such as measles and diphtheria ran rampant through these camps. Clearly, their inhabitants constituted the poorest class in the city.

Finally, between 1903 and 1912 several thousand Russians and Armenians arrived in the city, refugees from Russia's increasingly repressive government. Unlike most Russians, they did not belong to the Orthodox church. They were Molokans, literally "milk drinkers," a name they received because they refused to fast from dairy products during traditional fast days. More importantly, they could be described as a "proto-Protestant" group, since they had been influenced by some of the sixteenth-century Reformers. They also had a special appreciation for the Holy Spirit. Many of them claimed that they had been directed to leave southern Russia through the gift of prophecy. They engaged in what was often described as ecstatic behavior, jumping and dancing; falling on the floor when they believed that they were possessed of the Holy Spirit to do so; and singing chant-like songs that strongly paralleled the "singing in the Spirit" (a multi-layered, harmony-rich singing in tongues that are unknown to the singers and are believed to be inspired by the Holy Spirit) at the Azusa Street Mission.

The subject of revival was in the air when William Seymour arrived. Since 1904 many Christians in Los Angeles had been hearing of a great revival in Wales. While many in the religious community were praying for revival in Los Angeles, the topic had proven to be a controversial one. The controversy had emerged when the prestigious First Baptist Church had decided in 1905 that their pastor, Joseph Smale, needed a rest. Originally from England, the Spurgeon College–educated Smale had ultimately immigrated to the United States. He had held three pastorates before coming to Los Angeles where he now led First Baptist Church. Smale chose to return to England to recuperate, but while he was there he developed a friendship with Evan Roberts, the leader of the Welsh revival. Upon his return to Los Angeles, Smale determined that First Baptist Church should lead Los Angeles into revival, and they would do so with prayer.

The Reverend Joseph Smale

Things seemed to go well at first. The people of First Baptist Church followed as Smale led them. He preached on the topic of revival, and he explained to his congregation how prayer had played the key role in the coming of the Welsh revival. He began a series of protracted meetings that ran every day of the week, in which he attempted to help his parishioners enter revival. Reports emerged that told of the breaking down of class and racial distinctions in these meetings. People were encouraged to act and pray in a spontaneous manner as the Holy Spirit directed. Smale encouraged his members to make public confession of their sin and to reach out to one another for the healing of their divisions.

Smale got in trouble with his board, however, over his firm insistence on the protracted meeting schedule. These meetings had continued for fifteen weeks when his board confronted him with an ultimatum: Either he would return things to the way they had been before he went to Wales, or he could leave. He chose the latter course, frustrated by the lack of vision he believed his board had shown for spiritual renewal at First Baptist Church.

For several days Smale was undecided on what to do. Over the next two weeks, however, some two hundred members from First Baptist Church came to his home and appealed to him to start a new congregation. They assured him that if he would do so, they would come. The congregation held an organizational meeting on September 22, 1905, adopted the name First New Testament Church, and approved a constitution. They seemed to anticipate the message that William J. Seymour would bring to the people of Los Angeles at the Azusa Street Mission. Their statement on "The Pentecostal Blessing" read as follows:

> We hold that it is the duty and privilege of the believer to know the Holy Spirit as "the promise of the Father" (Acts 1:4), elsewhere spoken of as "The Gift" (Acts 2:38), an experience distinct from regeneration. The disciples knew not the Holy Spirit as "the promise of the Father," or in other words as "the Gift" until the day of Pentecost, therefore we speak of the Spirit as "The Pentecostal Blessing," necessary to the believer's sanctification, his knowledge of the fullness of God and his anointing for service.
>
> Scripture References.—Isaiah 11:2; Luke 24:49; John 20:21–22; Acts 1:8; Romans 8:2; Galatians 5; 1 Cor. 2:9–12; 2 Cor. 3:18; Ephes. 1:17 to Ephes. 2:1–6; Ephes. 3:16–19; 2 Thess. 2:13; 1 John 2:20–27.

By September 24 Smale had leased a leading theater, Burbank Hall, at 542 South Main Street—a lease that would run until August 1907.

Over the next several months, Smale advertised First New Testament Church as a "fellowship for evangelical preaching and teaching and Pentecostal life and service." Clearly, Smale had come deeply under the influence of the rhetoric and the vitality of the Welsh revival. He sounded like revivalists before him when he asserted that the miraculous had departed from the church through the centuries because the church had departed from the faith. By March 1906 he could be found urging his congregation to "grasp the very glory of God, and bring it to earth." What that would produce, he contended, was a church in full communion with God, reflecting "all the splendors of the first Pentecost." Smale fully expected the charisms mentioned in 1 Cor. 12:8–10 to appear among his people.

The congregation caught Smale's vision, and for several months they prayed that these gifts might appear among them. Their services, offered morning, afternoon, and evening, lasted as long as five hours. During this period, Frank Bartleman, the man who would ultimately chronicle the work of the Azusa Street Mission, became an active participant in Smale's church. He sang Smale's praises abroad, believing that First New Testament Church was on its way to revival.

Elsewhere in the city, First Methodist Church member Florence Crawford later reported, "the young men in the First Methodist Church were holding all night prayer meetings." This was an unprecedented activity in Los Angeles; to Crawford, it illustrated how deeply the city's people were sensing their own spiritual need. "God was laying it on the hearts of the people to pray for the outpouring of the Spirit." It was into this expectant context that William J. Seymour came.

Seymour's Arrival and the Beginning of Revival in Los Angeles

When William J. Seymour arrived in Los Angeles on Thursday, February 22, 1906, he came into a situation about which he knew very little. He had received an invitation from Mrs. Julia W. Hutchins to assume the pastorate of a small holiness congregation located at 1604 East Ninth Street, near the corner of Ninth and Santa Fe. It was a classic storefront mission of some twelve hundred square feet, leased by Mrs. Hutchins and separated from the corner billiard parlor by a single wall.

Since its founding, the church had met for services each Sunday afternoon and on Tuesday, Friday, and Sunday evenings. Mrs. Hutchins had started the congregation to demonstrate her evangelistic and administrative skills to the Holiness Association of Southern

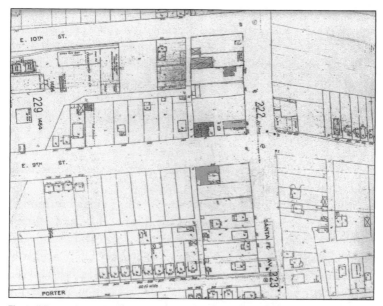

The building on the northwest corner of 9th and Santa Fe housed a billiard parlor and Mrs. Hutchins's congregation. The Catley family, later members of the Azusa Street Mission, lived on the northwest corner of the intersection.

California. She wanted to go to Liberia as a missionary under their auspices. The leaders of the Holiness Association were favorably impressed with her work and published her story in their periodical, *The Pentecost*. The editor suggested that she and her husband, Willis, were worthy of financial support for such a mission.

When Mrs. Hutchins decided she would prepare to go to Liberia, she began a search for her successor. She had asked a number of different individuals to preach there since she founded the congregation, but she was looking for someone who was neither a "self-appointed leader" nor "harsh and denunciatory." When she asked the members of her congregation for suggestions, Miss Neely Terry, who had been to Houston in 1905 where she had heard Pastor Seymour preach, recommended him to the group. After hearing from Terry, the group prayed, and Mrs. Hutchins sent the invitation for Seymour to come.

Seymour would later write that he came to Los Angeles at the request of "the colored people," because they wanted him "to give them some Bible teaching." He had sat at the feet of a number of Wesleyan holiness teachers over the previous half dozen years—among them Martin Wells Knapp, Charles Price Jones, and Charles Fox Parham. He had held evangelistic meetings in Texas and Louisiana. He had provided interim leadership to a small congregation in Houston. He was now ready to begin his ministry in earnest. It was time to put into practice what he had learned at the feet of others. He had come "to take charge"—that is, to become the permanent pastor of this little mission.

Some have assumed that following Seymour's initial sermon at the mission, Mrs. Hutchins locked the door on him and refused him further access. That is probably not the case. Seymour began preaching there on Saturday evening, February 24. He probably conducted the regularly scheduled services on Sunday, February 25; Tuesday, February 27; and Friday, March 2. In addition, if Seymour kept to the schedule Mrs. Hutchins had in place, he would have held afternoon prayer meetings at 3 P.M. each day in which the faithful prayed for the "endument of power." Furthermore, Shumway, who interviewed Seymour, notes that Seymour preached on a variety of subjects there. They included regeneration, sanctification, baptism in the Spirit, "the anointing of the Spirit," and speaking in tongues "as a sign that the Baptism of the Spirit had taken place." He also gave considerable attention to the subject of "faith healing." Seymour almost certainly did not unload this entire set of teachings in a single sermon. It is much more likely that he addressed each of these issues in a separate service.

In fact, Mrs. Hutchins and William Seymour shared much the same theological position. It was only when the newly arrived preacher introduced the subject of speaking in tongues and its relationship to the baptism in the Spirit that the founding pastor became upset. Seymour argued that baptism in the Holy Spirit was something that came to people who had already been converted and sanctified. Most holiness people, including Mrs. Hutchins, equated baptism in the Spirit with sanctification, and they did not see the ability to speak in tongues as connected to it at all. According to Seymour, baptism in the Spirit did not impart purity; it brought empowerment for ministry. For Seymour to suggest that Mrs. Hutchins's experience was in some way lacking was news to Mrs. Hutchins. It sounded similar to the "third work" theology that most holiness people had already rejected as heresy. That "heresy" held that salvation, sanctification, and baptism in the Spirit were three separate works of grace. Seymour did not teach that the baptism in the Spirit was a work of grace. He taught that it was merely an empowering encounter with the Holy Spirit that was evidenced by speaking in tongues. But it came only to those who had been saved and sanctified.

Mrs. Hutchins was concerned to preserve holiness orthodoxy among those she had brought into the Holiness Church. As a result she probably concluded, following the Sunday morning service on March 4, that she could no longer allow Seymour to confuse her flock. By the time the evening service was scheduled to begin, she had already alerted the president of the Holiness Church Association, the Rev. J. M. Roberts, to her "problem." When Seymour arrived for the evening meeting along with the African American couple, Edward S. and Mattie Lee, they found that Mrs. Hutchins had locked the door and refused to admit him. Not knowing what to do, Seymour returned to the Lees' home. Shortly after this incident, Mrs. Hutchins and the holiness association called a special meeting. A number of holiness pastors and leaders were present, and Seymour was asked to explain his doctrinal position.

Seymour may have preached a sermon or simply engaged his questioners in discussion at that meeting, but he was given the opportunity to explain what he believed and he did so clearly. For their part, the holiness leadership claimed that sanctification and the baptism in the Holy Ghost were the same thing. Seymour remained unconvinced that they had been baptized in the Spirit, because they had not spoken in tongues. In the end, President Roberts made two decisions. First, he told Seymour that he could no longer preach his doctrine of the baptism in the Spirit in the Holiness Church. Second, he told Seymour that he was pleased with the fact that Seymour was seeking the baptism in the Spirit and he hoped that he would be successful in his quest. Seymour remembered Roberts as saying, "When you receive it, please let me know, because I am interested in receiving it too."

Following the decision rendered by Roberts, Seymour could no longer serve at the Ninth and Santa Fe mission. He continued to stay with the Lees, who lived near the corner of Union and West First Street (now Beverley Blvd.). Lee was a janitor at the First National Bank, but he had held a variety of jobs in earlier times. He had even been a preacher in Fresno before moving to Los Angeles. During his stay with the Lees in the early days of March, Seymour and the Lees would pray together. Others from the Ninth and Santa Fe mission joined them, as did Frank Bartleman. When the group outgrew the Lees' house, the prayer meeting moved to the home of another African American couple, Richard and Ruth Asberry, at 214 (now 216) North Bonnie Brae Street, about two blocks away. While Richard Asberry was then employed as a janitor at the Wilcox Building in downtown Los Angeles, he had earlier worked for the Pullman Pacific Car Company and had purchased at least two lots with a vacant lot between them, each with a house and a smaller cottage behind it, on North Bonnie Brae Street. The meeting at the Asberry home may have begun as

Richard Asberry

Ruth Asberry

early as March 12, but it was certainly going on by March 19. It would continue until further notice.

As the prayer meeting grew, other African Americans joined Seymour, the Lees, and the Asberrys. William "Bud" Traynor, a young railroad worker, and his mother, Sallie, joined them. They were also staying with the Lees. William Henry and Emma Cummings and their three sons and two daughters joined them. Mr. Cummings was a plasterer. Miss Jennie Evans Moore, who lived directly across the street from the Asberrys, joined the group as well. She had worked as a domestic and cook for a variety of Los Angeles businessmen. In 1906 she was employed as a masseuse. Thus, the core group at the Asberry home comprised about fifteen African Americans, including five children. Seymour was invited to explain once again his position on baptism in the Spirit. Those who were gathered in the home soon came to accept his teaching and to pray that they might receive that baptism. To help him minister to these people as he and they sought to be baptized in the Spirit, Seymour contacted two friends in Houston, Lucy Farrow and Joseph Warren. He invited them to join him for meetings at the Asberry home.

As these African American friends waited for Farrow and Warren to arrive, they went about their ordinary duties during the day, gathering in prayer each evening. Others joined them from time to time. Frank Bartleman attended the meeting on March 26, and he returned again on March 28 with "Mother" Wheaton, a nationally famous evangelist who ministered in prisons across the country.[11]

Emma Osterberg, a recent Swedish transplant from the Chicago area, attended fairly regularly during this time. In late March, she testified about the meetings to the congregation at the Full Gospel Tabernacle at Sixty-Eighth and Denver. She urged the congregation, which was led by her son, Arthur Osterberg, to join her there. Embarrassed by his mother's public prompting, Arthur drove to the Asberry home with his board members, "Brothers Worthington, Weaver, and Dodge." He concluded that the people gathered there were truly spiritual. His encounter with this group led him to undertake a personal two-week study of the book of

Acts in which he came to accept Seymour's position. The holiness sector of the city was soon abuzz with word of the Asberry meetings and the new teaching.

During his breaks in the basement of First National Bank, Edward Lee often prayed. One day he claimed that the apostles Peter and John appeared to him in a vision. As they stood in front of him, "they lifted their hands to heaven and they began to shake under the power of God and began to speak in other tongues." Edward Lee shook, too, and he didn't know what was wrong with him. When he returned home, he told Seymour what had happened, claiming, "I know now how people act when they get the Holy Ghost." That evening, Lee shared his experience with the prayer meeting. And they were encouraged to continue their quest.

Shortly thereafter, Edward Lee believed that he was ready to receive this baptism in the Spirit. At the dinner table, he asked Seymour to lay hands on him. At first Seymour was afraid to do so in light of his understanding of 1 Timothy 5:22, which says, "Lay hands suddenly on no man." Later in the evening he laid his hands on Lee "in Jesus' name," and Lee fell to the floor as though he were dead. Mattie Lee was so frightened that she screamed and asked him what he had done to her husband. Seymour began to pray, and eventually, Lee got up—more convinced than ever that Seymour was right.

On Friday, April 6, the members of the prayer meeting decided to take the issue one step further by adding fasting to their discipline of regular prayer. They planned a ten-day fast, during which they would study Acts 2:1–4 and pray each evening until they had the same experience described in this text. They meant business!

Meanwhile, in nearby Glendale, Pastor Elmer Kirk Fisher was getting ready to resign the pastorate of Calvary Baptist Church. He had led this congregation for less than a year and had been preaching a series of sermons on the Holy Spirit after reading R. A. Torrey's book on the subject. When some of the people began to give "demonstrations of joy" in his services, his deacons prevailed upon him to change his preaching emphasis. It may be that they had

Joseph Smale and First Baptist Church in Los Angeles in their minds, and they didn't want similar problems at Calvary Baptist Church. Just two days after the folks at the Bonnie Brae Street prayer meeting decided to begin their quest in earnest, Fisher resigned from his pastorate in Glendale. He quickly made his way to Smale's First New Testament Church in Los Angeles, where he was welcomed and became part of Smale's staff.

Lucy Farrow and Joseph Warren arrived in Los Angeles that same weekend. Around 6 P.M. on Monday, April 9, Edward Lee came home from work, not feeling well. He had, after all, been fasting for three days. When he arrived at home, he found that Lucy Farrow had arrived before him. He was excited to see her, since Seymour had promised she would be able to give them more light on the subject. He asked her to lay hands on him right then, in anticipation that he would be baptized in the Spirit. Farrow refused, suggesting that the Lord would tell her if and when she should do it.

Edward Lee, Lucy Farrow, Mattie Lee, her unnamed brother, and William Seymour were now all present. As they sat around a table, Edward Lee complained to Seymour that he didn't feel well and that if he were going to be able to attend the evening meeting, Seymour should lay hands on him and pray for his recovery. Seymour came around to Edward Lee and asked Lucy Farrow to join him in prayer. She and Seymour prayed for his physical recovery, and, seeing Lee's genuineness, Farrow announced that the time was right to pray for his baptism in the Spirit. When they laid hands on him, he fell to the floor and spoke with tongues. Only the distress of Mattie Lee and her brother cut short the moment. Edward Lee got up and returned to the table. He and Seymour were "overjoyed" by what had taken place. It was now time to tell the others.

The group walked the two blocks to the Asberry home, reaching there just before 7:30 P.M. A number of people had already arrived and were waiting expectantly for the meeting to begin. All of them were African American. They filled the "double parlor," with a few people in adjacent rooms. Seymour began the meeting, first leading them in a song. The group offered three prayers and then gave their testimonies. This first part of the meeting may have taken a half hour or more. It was now time for Elder Seymour to speak, and he announced, as was expected, that he would be using Acts 2:4 as his text. He began to tell them about what had happened to Edward Lee only an hour before their arrival. No sooner had he completed the story when someone in the group began to speak in tongues. As Shumway told the story in 1914, "The whole company was immediately swept to its knees as by some mighty power." They began to pray, and before the evening was over, several others had spoken in tongues as well. Among them was Jennie Evans Moore.

Shumway notes that Jennie Moore quickly made her way to the piano and "improvised a melody, with accompaniment, to which

This photograph was taken about the time of the meeting in 1906. About 1910 the address was changed from 214 to 216 North Bonnie Brae Street, in accordance with the city's plan. In 1914, the Asberrys remodeled the house, removing the bay window feature on the right, thereby adding a bit more space to the living room, and building a solid façade on the front porch to the height of the railing. In 1985, under the leadership of Dr. Art E. Glass, Pentecostal Heritage, Inc. purchased the house. In 1997, the deed to the house was given to the First Jurisdiction of the Church of God in Christ. Under the leadership of Bishop Charles Blake, the house has been renovated, restoring the interior to its original beauty.

she sang in her new ecstatic 'tongue.'" Willella Asberry, who was in the kitchen, flew into the parlor to see what was happening. "Bud" Traynor jumped to the front porch, where he shouted out the news to nearby neighbors.[12]

Over the next three days the Asberry home became the focus of attention within the various networks of Los Angeles Wesleyan holiness people. As Frank Bartleman observed, "The news spread like fire, naturally." By the next day, the Asberry home was filled with genuine seekers and curious onlookers alike. People gathered outside, straining to hear through open windows those who were now receiving their baptism in the Spirit and speaking in tongues. The Asberrys turned their front porch into a platform from which those who chose to do so could preach or lead others in singing or testifying. The pulpit looked out over an ever-increasing crowd of people in the yard and street below who could not enter the house because it was so full.

This was no quiet demonstration; it was full of noisy manifestations, shouts, speaking in tongues, moaning, and singing in tongues that undoubtedly would have frightened any uninitiated within audible range. Fortunately, the neighborhood was lightly populated, with houses spaced on alternate lots filled with sympathetic friends. In any case, the meetings were soon forced to move: just as things were heating up, the weight of the excited worshippers on the front porch caused it to collapse. While no one was injured in this relatively minor mishap, the eager crowds clearly needed to find a more suitable space for their worship. On Thursday, April 12, after a long evening spent in prayer, William Seymour finally received his baptism in the Spirit, falling on the floor as though dead and then speaking in tongues.

The Founding of the Azusa Street Mission

As Seymour and his flock thought about their next move, someone mentioned the now vacant building on Azusa Street. As A. C. Valdez put it, it was "a boxy, two-story, wooden building which, except for a tall Gothic window on the front of the second floor, looked like the general store in many a small, western town."[13] William Seymour and his new congregation negotiated a lease with First African Methodist Episcopal Church for their old facility just before Good Friday, April 13, 1906. It would cost them eight dollars a month.

When Seymour took possession of the former church at 312 Azusa Street, it was a mess. The one photograph that exists from earlier days indicates several things. First, the building had a rather steeply pitched roof. Second, the original sanctuary had been on the second floor. Third, an external staircase had originally stood at the front of the building like an inverted "V" that provided immediate entry to the sanctuary. Fourth, the building had been constructed with wood-framed Gothic style windows, including ornamental tracery lines curving across the tops of the window panes that

This is the only known photograph of the building at 312 Azusa Street. It shows the Stevens AME Church choir standing on the external staircase that gave access to the sanctuary. At the top right, it is possible to notice the pitched roof that originally topped off the building. It is possible to observe the tracery windows.

stood above and on either side of the doorway at the top of these stairs. All subsequent photographs show a rather dirty building, much as A. C. Valdez described it. How had this come to be?

When the former congregation moved out in early 1904, First AME Church decided to undertake some remodeling. They intended to build some walls in the old sanctuary on the second floor, yielding a long central hallway from front to back with rooms of varying sizes on each side of the hall. These they wanted to rent as a series of apartments. The basement, which comprised the entire ground floor, had been used to house the horses of worshippers during services. It would remain unfinished, with its low ceiling, open studs and joists, and dirt floor. Within a month of the congregation's vacating the building and before they could begin the job, an arsonist went through the downtown area lighting fires. At 1:00 on the morning of March 10, 1904, a livery stable was burned near Sixth and Olive. Thirty-five horses died, and the adjacent Engleside Hotel had to be evacuated. While firemen were

The FOR SALE sign is visible at the upper corner of the mission. Below it is the door through which most parishioners entered. In the foreground is the rear of the "tombstone" shop, known as the Brown and Ford marble and granite works.

fighting that fire, the arsonist set a second blaze. This one burned Kratz's Mill and Feed Company to the ground on the corner of Fifth and San Pedro. Shortly after 4:00 A.M., the church became the third target. Firefighters did their best to save the structure, but the roof was burned completely off and the building was deeply marred with charred wood and water damage. One newspaper declared it a complete loss.

Following the fire, First African Methodist Episcopal Church took the existing building, put a new, flatter roof on, and divided the second floor according to its plan. The windows on each side of the original second floor entry were removed and replaced by standard double-hung windows. The V-shaped staircase was removed, and another staircase was built at the rear of the building. A local carpenter, perhaps a member of First AME Church who had been making the repairs, used the ground-floor basement for the storage of building equipment and lumber. Whether it was a lack of funds or a lack of interest in the project, the building remained incomplete when Seymour's group leased it in April 1906. Nothing cosmetic had been done to cover the smoke and water damage. One can easily understand why the building was often described as "old," a "tumble-down shack," or a "barn" located in the "slums." None of these descriptions was really accurate, but the place was a disaster. If they were going to worship in this building, Arthur Osterberg, who was volunteered for the cleanup job by his mother, had his work cut out for him.

Easter was upon them, and cleanup began immediately. Osterberg quickly organized the work crew—a racially mixed group including African American members of the Asberry prayer meeting, both men and women, a few white friends of the Osterbergs, and several Mexican laborers employed at the McNeil Construction Company where Osterberg worked during the week. They expected to open the doors to the public on Easter Sunday, although they may have met at the church as early as the night after Seymour spoke in tongues.

Together, the work crew cleared space on the ground floor sufficient for twenty to forty worshippers. Osterberg ordered a large wagon to haul the junk away. They scattered straw and sawdust on the dirt floor. The walls were made of rough lumber with exposed studs. Eventually they would whitewash these walls. For now, they cleaned out the many spider webs and scrubbed the windows. For a church, the ceiling was very low, standing between eight and nine feet high. It was strung with a single line of incandescent lights. When services began at the mission, men often stood on their seats to hang their hats from nails on the beams above them. Redwood planks supported by nail kegs became the first pews in the mission. By the end of the week, however, people had also brought an odd assortment of kitchen chairs, benches, and backless stools.

The seats were arranged in a square, facing the center of the building. Pastor Seymour would oversee things from that vantage point. A commercial wooden packing crate used to ship shoes from the manufacturer to the dealer was covered with a single piece of cotton cloth to serve as the mission's pulpit. Space was left in the center of the room for the construction of an altar. Joseph Warren set up a makeshift altar, a board between two chairs, but Osterberg argued that it was inadequate. He approached his employer, Mr. McNeil, a Roman Catholic, and asked for a small donation of lumber so that he could build a proper altar. McNeil agreed to the donation, and Osterberg proceeded to construct a slightly elevated platform in the center of the room as well as some benches for kneeling. Osterberg later jokingly called it his "Catholic altar."

The inside walls were important for the congregation as well. From the beginning, a mailbox was hung inside the door. No offerings would be taken in this mission. People were taught to tithe and to give freely and generously. They took their instruction seriously. They were on their honor to leave their donations for the support of the ministry in this mailbox. As people began to be delivered from various habits such as tobacco or liquor, and as others began to be healed, they left their crutches, braces, old smoking pipes, and the like against the walls. These souvenirs or testimonies to deliverance and healing became staple fixtures in the Pentecostal churches that would follow, and they closely paralleled the use of *milagros*, charm-like representations of various body parts that have been healed, in the popular religious expression of Roman Catholic Latino piety. Finally, by September 1906 a sign hung on one wall. "Mene, Mene, Tekel, Upharsin," it read "in vivid green letters with the Ns and Ss upside down."[14]

The original sanctuary on the second floor, now divided into rooms connected with a central hallway, would serve a variety of needs. It would provide a room and a small kitchen where Pastor Seymour would live, one or two offices in which the staff could meet and work, and a room where those who desired to be healed could receive special prayer. A long, narrow prayer room was set aside for those seeking to be baptized in the Spirit. It was outfitted with three long California redwood planks placed on a series of backless chairs. This room was also apparently used for "Children's Church" on Sunday afternoons.

That first Good Friday evening following the outpouring of the Spirit at the Asberry home, April 13, Jennie Evans Moore was busy serving a dinner party for a couple who were entertaining an attorney. While they were eating, the woman of the household addressed Jennie. Moore was so overwhelmed with "joyful praise" that she responded in tongues. This scared the entire party, and Moore immediately retreated from the dining room. She was quickly joined by one of the guests who, on behalf of the woman of the house, encouraged her to leave and get some rest. At first, Moore protested that she was not really that tired. But as she reflected further, she realized that they thought she was "losing her reason." So she excused herself and quickly left.

On Easter Sunday morning, April 15, Jennie Moore and Ruth Asberry worshiped at First New Testament Church, where Smale preached on the subject of "The Resurrection." During his sermon he told the congregation about his recent trip to Palestine, and he described his visit to the empty tomb. He went on to claim,

It matters much to human welfare that Christ rose from the dead. He was a representative character. As the eternal Son of God and nothing else, He could never have been despised and crucified. He chose to be manifested to take away human sin. When He was taken down from the cross His honors began as an accepted sacrifice for sin. On the third day the demonstration was given. He was raised for our justification.

At the conclusion of the sermon, Pastor Joseph Smale gave the worshippers an opportunity to share a few testimonies. Jennie Moore stood up and told the congregation about the meetings that had been taking place at the Asberry home. She went on to announce that "Pentecost" had come to Los Angeles, and she concluded her testimony by speaking in tongues. The place was electrified! Some were so frightened they jumped for the doors. Others shouted praises. One or two had been to Seymour's meetings at the Asberry house, and they, too, began to speak in tongues. Before things could get too far out of hand, Pastor Smale stepped in and closed things down creatively, but sensitively. He had, after all, preached that such things were possible. Now he would be forced to come to terms with them in his own congregation.

Frank Bartleman watched as the congregation left. They gathered in clusters along the sidewalk, he wrote, trying to make sense of what they had just seen. That afternoon, Bartleman went out to the Asberry home. There he found a small group of people, as he put it, "taken up with God."

Two days later, the *Los Angeles Daily Times* decided to send a reporter to this new mission on Azusa Street. The reporter attended the Tuesday evening, April 17 service and wrote up his findings, clearly hoping to entertain his readers with his ridicule. On Wednesday morning, April 18, the newspaper proclaimed its discovery in the first of many articles describing the meetings—"Weird Babel of Tongues."

These people, comprising "colored people and a sprinkling of whites," claimed to be able to speak in tongues and understand it. "Such a startling claim has never yet been made by any company of fanatics," wrote the reporter, "even in Los Angeles, the home of almost numberless creeds." Those who woke to this report in their morning papers no doubt shook their heads in dismay at the strangeness of the events it described. An "old colored exhorter" with "his stony optic fixed on some luckless unbeliever" who "yells his defiance and challenges an answer"? An "old colored mammy" who swings her arms wildly about while uttering "the strangest harange [sic] ever uttered"? A "buxom dame" so overcome with excitement she almost faints? "A gurgle of wordless prayers" that is "nothing less than shocking"? A neighborhood that has become "hideous" because of the "howlings of the worshipers"? And a "rabbi" named Gold who claims to have been healed and converted to the group's teachings? What was the world coming to?

The city's attention was soon forcibly focused some three hundred and fifty miles to the north. At 5:13 a.m., the ground shook and the city of San Francisco crumpled and burst into flames. For the next four days tremors rocked the city, buildings collapsed, fires burned out of control, and people died. Until April 18 such a calamity had seemed very distant—unthinkable within the safe borders of America! To be sure, on August 27, 1883, the Pacific volcano known as Krakatoa had blown its top with a destructive force that had killed over one hundred thousand people. On April 9, 1906, only the week before the San Francisco earthquake, Mt. Vesuvius had erupted, causing extensive damage. And earthquakes of the magnitude of San Francisco's quake would soon shake Valparaiso, Chile, producing a tidal wave akin to the one that flooded southern Asia on December 26, 2004. The wave would inundate the city, killing thousands of Chileans. But this earthquake was different: disaster had come to California!

About noon the next day, two smaller tremors shook Los Angeles, and those who were already alert to the tragedy of San Francisco now wondered what was in store for them. Alfred G. Garr, pastor of a holiness group called the Burning Bush, surveyed the city. "Our church building trembled and heaved . . . while in other parts of the city of Los Angeles, windows were broken and chimneys were thrown down." Garr wondered aloud, "Will cities and individuals take heed after seeing such horrible displays of the omnipotence of the great God?" He was afraid he knew the answer: "No!"

Frank Bartleman was attending the noon meeting at another holiness ministry, Peniel Hall, 227 South Main Street, when these tremors hit. "The floor began to move with us," he wrote. "A most ugly sensation ran through the room." "We sat in awe. Many people ran into the middle of the street, looking anxiously at the buildings, fearing they were about to fall. It was an earnest time." That evening, accompanied by "Mother" Elizabeth Ryder Wheaton, he attended the Azusa Street Mission for the first time.

Thus was the potentially provocative article about a small African American congregation buried, the next day, by events that appeared on the surface to be much more profound. Many had died, and the indomitable San Francisco was in flames. People were fleeing in unprecedented numbers. While many would cross the bay to Oakland, many others would make their way to Los Angeles. Over the next several weeks, the enormous tragedy of San Francisco and the attempts by various groups and agencies in Los Angeles to aid their northern neighbors swallowed up all available news space.

As after any natural disaster, people wanted answers. "Why did this earthquake happen?" people wondered. Many times those who raise these questions turn to their spiritual leaders for answers. We do not know the topic of Pastor Seymour's sermon the Sunday following the earthquake, but we may safely conclude that he mentioned that tragic event.

Over the following weeks, many Los Angeles pastors claimed to see the hand of God in the earthquake. Some suggested that God was addressing—even judging— the people of San Francisco. Others tried to disabuse their people of such ideas. The Rev. Robert Burdette, pastor of Temple Baptist Church, quickly announced that he didn't believe that this was some kind of judgment for "any sinful nature of the city." A. C. Smither, pastor of the First Christian Church, and C. C. Pierce, of the Memorial Baptist Church, explained the earthquake in purely naturalistic terms. The famous pastor of First Presbyterian Church, Frank DeWitt Talmage, spoke more strongly yet. "To talk about it being a punishment is all rot." And he encouraged his congregation not to rush to judgment themselves.

Frank Bartleman boiled at the idea that any preacher would deny God had spoken through this earthquake. Three weeks before, Bartleman had written a tract he titled "The Last Call." He told how the people of Noah's day (Gen. 6—7; Matt. 24:37–39) had been warned of impending doom. Now, Bartleman had argued, the world stood at the brink—"some tremendous event" was "about to transpire." He predicted that the Spirit would soon be poured out and then the Lord would return. He challenged his readers to respond to God's warning.

On Saturday evening, April 21, Bartleman began work on a new tract. He titled it simply "The Earthquake!!!" The next day, Bartleman marched into First New Testament Church armed with ten thousand copies of the previous tract, "The Last Call." He began handing these to workers who quickly scattered them throughout the city. That Sunday, Pastor Smale was away. Elder T. C. Horton presided at the morning service and Evangelist John Boyd took the evening service. In the First New Testament Church *Bulletin* for Monday, Pastor Smale had asked his flock to pray "that all the people and work of this New Testament church may be baptized in the Holy Ghost."

When Bartleman read the reports of sermons preached in Los Angeles that Sunday, his anger was further provoked. "The preachers became a mighty instrument in the hands of Satan to drown [God's] voice," he would later write, "as they labored to convince the people that the quake was not a direct agency of God. Only earthquake ground." While people worked "strenuously to rule God out of it," he went on to claim, "they secretly cursed Him in their hearts for it." Shortly thereafter, Bartleman predicted, these same people would thank God for destroying the old city, so that "they might build a nice San Francisco, earthquake and fire-proof"—and, he added cynically—"God proof."

Bartleman continued to work on his earthquake tract until after midnight on Tuesday, April 24, and then at 7 A.M. he raced to the printing office with an order of twenty-five thousand copies. Within days he had ordered another twenty-five thousand copies. In Oakland, William F. Manley, head of the "Household of God," a holiness group formed by John J. Scruby and William F. Manley that took Ephesians 2:19 as the theme for its work together, was so taken with it that he printed another fifty thousand copies for distribution in the East Bay, where thousands had fled following the earthquake. By May 11, Bartleman's tract had been printed one hundred twenty-five thousand times!

"The Earthquake!!!," printed on two sides of a single page, was not particularly profound. In it, Bartleman asked, "What does God have to do with earthquakes?" Then he listed Bible verses mention-

ing earthquakes, reminded his readers that Los Angeles had received a warning, and called them to be reconciled with God. The tract raised the ire of many pastors and ordinary people alike. Bartleman, true to time-honored practice, distributed them in bars and brothels, on streetcars and in businesses—anywhere he could find an open hand. He claimed that a specific policeman was assigned to hunt him down, and that a conductor threatened to throw him off of his streetcar if he didn't stop giving them to passengers. He concluded, with obvious pride, "I have never written a tract that had so much influence."

So here was a fact not lost on those who frequented the Azusa Street Mission: *The Los Angeles Daily Times* had first publicized their meetings on the same day that the earthquake had destroyed San Francisco. This convergence they quickly interpreted—and proclaimed—as an apocalyptic sign that people needed to get ready for the imminent return of Jesus Christ. Later in the summer an African American woman from Pasadena named Mary Galmond reportedly prophesied at the mission the imminent destruction of Chicago, Los Angeles, and Pasadena. This apocalyptic claim was published both in the organ of Manley's Household of God and in a secular Los Angeles newspaper, giving it wider distribution and further credibility among Manley's readers.

Joseph Smale had been absent from his pulpit the Sunday following the earthquake, but he addressed the subject in his first Sunday sermon following his return. He made it clear that he did not believe in a wrathful God, but rather a loving one. And he called a number of local pastors to task when he implored,

> Do not tempt God by saying that it is its geographical position or the geological formation of the land upon which it is built. It is my solemn conviction that the only thing which has saved Los Angeles is the intense and abounding prayer life of many of the Lord's intercessors in this city.

The problem with a simple rationalistic approach to the subject, he observed, was that,

By explaining the recent event on lines of rationalism, we are exposed to the charge of worshiping a God of love who is indifferent to his creatures, or a God who is mastered by his own laws and cannot deliver from peril those whom he loves.

We repudiate the rationalistic position. We believe God was in the earthquake and we believe in God as a God of love, and we can see in the truth that he is a God of love an argument for his presence in the earthquake.

Smale was not alone. *The Los Angeles Herald* announced that the San Francisco earthquake had served as a "wakeup call" to many who had been converted among the Salvation Army, the Volunteers of America, and at local Rescue missions during the week following the earthquake.

While the city of Los Angeles focused its energies on news of the earthquake and then on efforts to move beyond the disaster, services at the Azusa Street Mission continued apace. The mission now offered a regular schedule of services. On Sunday morning the service was scheduled to begin at 10 A.M., though people often came a nine or earlier to sit quietly or to kneel and pray. Though the mission listed a beginning time for the afternoon service, it was often nothing more than a continuation of the morning service. The evening services always began at 7:30 P.M. and soon were scheduled every evening. Each weekday morning a prayer and Bible study convened, either downstairs or in the "upper room"— the prayer room where seekers travailed to be baptized in the Spirit. William Seymour or another person such as Hiram Smith, a former Free Methodist pastor, led these meetings.

The Times had first covered an April 17 meeting held during the mission's first week of services. When journalists returned in mid-June, they were surprised to find how fast the mission had grown. By the Sunday evening service on June 10, less than two months after the mission's opening, reporters described the congregation as "composed of whites and blacks" numbering "several hundred people" with "scores of faces peering in from "the windows."" The number of worshippers would continue to rise, and by mid-July the press commonly reported regular attendance figures of five hundred to seven hundred people. Arthur Osterberg would later state that as many as fifteen hundred people attended the mission on most Sundays in 1906. Obviously a building of only twenty-four hundred square feet cannot hold such numbers at a single event. But Osterberg's estimate may not be very wide of the mark. People worshipped at the mission around the clock; many came for a service and then left, leaving spaces for others to enter; some moved upstairs to spend time in prayer; and scores more stood outside, listening through the windows. This was the beginning of a revival that would have far-reaching consequences.

As the press rediscovered the revival, some complained about the coverage. It was generally, even overwhelmingly, negative. But it had its bright side as well—in the first edition of the mission's newspaper, *The Apostolic Faith*, the editor observed,

> The secular papers have been stirred and published reports against the movement, but it has only resulted in drawing hungry souls who understand that the devil would not fight a thing unless God was in it. So they have come and found it was indeed the power of God.

Many of the people who visited the Azusa Street Mission between April's earthquake and June's renewal of press interest came from local churches. This sort of stirring in the churches seems to happen any time people become aware of some place where a revival has been reported. One need only think of the revival in Toronto, Canada, that became known as the "Toronto Blessing," or the revival in Pensacola, Florida. Many Christian visitors to those revivals came to see for themselves what they had read about in various secular and religious newspapers. Some came as genuine seekers. Others, engaged in various sorts of ministry, came to see if the revival at the Azusa Street Mission could be somehow transferred to their own fields of operation. Of the roughly five hundred names of people that I have collected who visited the mission during the years 1906–1909, fully one-third were pastors and evangelists.

So many members from First New Testament Church came to Azusa Street that Bartleman claimed Joseph Smale had to visit the mission to find his own congregation. While that is clearly an over-statement, Smale and his congregation were deeply touched by what was happening at the Azusa Street Mission. While Smale agreed with Seymour on the need for baptism in the Spirit, he dif-fered from the Azusa Street pastor on the relationship between baptism in the Spirit and speaking in tongues. Smale viewed tongues as a gift or charism governed by the descriptions and regu-lations found in 1 Corinthians 12—14, not as an evidence of baptism in the Spirit. "Thousands of the Lord's dear people have been bap-tized in the Holy Ghost and in fire who never received the gift of tongues," he argued. But from June 22 onward, Smale was willing to make space for his members to exercise the gift of tongues, to prophesy, to exorcise demons, to pray for the sick, and to expect miracles in First New Testament Church. Thus, in many respects, Smale's congregation almost immediately joined forces with the Azusa Street Mission in this revival. And like the worshippers at the Azusa Street Mission, Smale viewed the revival as a sign of the imminent return of the Lord Jesus Christ.

The press covered the revival with relentless attention through-out the summer months, continuing to ridicule the mission in many of its reports. Pastors of the established churches repre-sented by the Los Angeles Church Federation now raised serious questions. They believed that what was taking place at 312 Azusa Street was nothing more than out-of-control fanaticism. Many of their parishioners had begun expressing concern about the revival, placing pastors who opposed the revival under increasing pressure to respond. Some chose to address the Azusa Street phenomenon in their sermons, repeating the charge of fanaticism against Sey-mour and his work and assuring their people that they didn't need what Seymour claimed God was doing.

About July 15, 1906, the Los Angeles Church Federation author-ized its president, the Rev. Edwin P. Ryland of Trinity Methodist Episcopal Church (South), to visit the Azusa Street Mission. He did so, praising their evangelistic zeal, but he was quoted as saying that he feared "certain of the enthusiasts might lose their reason through over zeal and become dangerous." As a result, the federation decided to develop a plan to counter the revival's successes. Leaders called a meeting of members for the evening of July 24 to map out their strategy.

That week the press revealed that the daughter of a prominent Los Angeles physician and surgeon and hospital president, Miss Lillian Keyes, had begun not only to speak but to write in tongues. Dr. Henry S. Keyes had been a member of the board of First Baptist Church when Smale was pastor, and he had been among Smale's closest allies at First New Testament Church. The fact that he supported his daughter's activities and viewed them as genuine spiritual phenomena given by the Holy Spirit must have caused many readers to consider the claims of the revival anew. As a result of the interview with Dr. Keyes, another newspaper published a detailed description of a service at First New Testament Church under the title "Queer 'Gift' Given Many." Indeed, Pastor Smale displayed a remarkable tolerance for a wide range of charismatic manifestations in his congregation, especially given that he himself had not experienced any of them.

Pastor Joseph Smale proved the ideal mediator between the Azusa Street Mission and the Los Angeles Church Federation. While he did not belong to the federation because he didn't believe in formal cooperative efforts between churches, his sympathies lay in both directions. He decided to advocate for the revival and challenge the federation by writing an open letter to its members.

On the evening of July 23, the night before the federation was to meet, Smale's letter was published in the *Los Angeles Express*. In it, the First New Testament Church pastor predicted that a "great Pentecost" would soon envelop the churches of Los Angeles, and he made a plea for toleration. He then set forth the following seven recommendations to the federation.

- The churches need a fearless ministry who are willing to preach the Word of God boldly.
- The churches need to be called to a renewed prayer life.

- The churches need to tighten their membership standards and admit to membership only the "godly."
- The church needs to step back from its arrogance and identify with the offense and suffering of the cross.
- The churches need to move beyond their sectarian divisions to a shared position of submission to the Lordship of Jesus Christ.
- The churches need to stop competing with one another for primacy of place.
- The churches must allow the Holy Spirit freedom to move.

The federation met the next evening at its coffee club at Third and Main, claiming that its agenda did not include the "enthusiasts" who spoke in tongues. It attempted to distance its members from public criticism for standing against the growing revival at the Azusa Street Mission, which had now spread not only to First New Testament Church but also to churches in nearby Pasadena and Whittier. Thus, the federation claimed to focus solely on its member churches' own, "orthodox" revivalistic methods. At the end of the meeting the Los Angeles Church Federation had set the following agenda for its churches:

- The churches of the federation would implement a regular program of street meetings for which permission from the Police commission would be sought. They acknowledged that the Azusa Street Mission and First New Testament Church had taught them the value of such things. The first such meeting was scheduled for July 30.
- The churches of the federation would form "Prayer Bands" to pray for revival in the city. This plan moved the historic Protestant churches beyond their current mid-week services to embrace an additional prayer meeting one night each week and it encouraged the members of these churches to commit themselves to the personal discipline of times of "secret prayer" throughout the week.
- The churches of the federation would cooperate with one another in dividing the city into geographical districts. They

would canvas these districts on a regular basis and share the
names with member congregations for follow up.
• The churches of the federation would work toward a city-
wide evangelistic campaign, if possible, to be held in March
1907.

The fact that the actions of the Azusa Street Mission, the First
New Testament Church and its pastor Joseph Smale, and the Los
Angeles Church Federation received such public notice shows that
within three months, the revival begun at Azusa Street had already
profoundly affected Los Angeles churches. At the time, the press
and public recognized the federation's new agenda as clear evidence of this impact. In other words, although President Ryland
tried to separate the federation from the debate about the Azusa
Street revival, the press quickly saw that agenda as a direct
response to the revival. The public would not be fooled by the rhetoric of federation leaders.

What is surprising is that Frank Bartleman, who was best situ-
ated to tell this story, failed to pen a single word about the impact
of the Azusa Street Mission or First New Testament Church on the
Los Angeles Church Federation. And the mission itself remained
almost silent on the matter, only noting, in the second issue of its
Apostolic Faith newspaper, that "in California, where there has been
no unity among churches, they are becoming one against this Pentecostal movement."

3

LEADING THE AZUSA STREET REVIVAL

A lanky, black wench took the center of the stage. The most noticeable things about her were her neck and mouth. Her neck was remarkable for its length, and her mouth for its width. When she opened that mouth there was nothing to do but dodge or be engulfed by the undertow. She was the orator of the evening, and "felt de han' of Gawd laid on heh hea't to preach to de shepa'ds."

"Ah read fum de thuty-foth chapte' of Zekel."

She read from the "thuty-foth chapte' of Zekel" for about an hour and a half. She would read one line and expound it until she had told all she could think of, and then read another line. She concluded her oration to the shepherds.

Warns the Shepherds

"An' you shepa'ds, you pasto's, you'd bettah feed youh flock on de Holy Ghost o' they won't feed you. If you all don't git right wid Gawd you won't have no mo' congregation and you'll have to go out and go to wuk."

Los Angeles Herald

WHEN MOST PEOPLE think of Azusa Street, they think about it as an "event." The revival that took place at the mission was an "event" to which people went. Thousands of people attended the revival but most of them took part in it for only a short period of time. They may have attended only a single meeting or perhaps a series of meetings over a week or two. Because this was such a common pattern, most of those who wrote about the revival failed to look beyond the "event" character of what they had observed to see the larger, ongoing, ecclesial nature of the mission. The Azusa Street Mission was after all, a local congregation that hosted and nurtured this revival for three years. It was first and foremost an African American congregation that grew out of a cottage prayer meeting on North Bonnie Brae Street. It had an African American pastor, and for the first couple of months at least, African Americans comprised the majority of the congregation.

This congregation was different from most black congregations in Los Angeles. From the beginning, Pastor Seymour envisioned it becoming a multiracial, multiethnic congregation. In keeping with that vision, the mission quickly attracted—and for an extended period of time, it welcomed and maintained—a membership that was broadly representative of various racial and ethnic groups: blacks, whites, Latinos, Asians, and Native Americans. "The work began among the colored people," the mission reported. "Since then multitudes have come. God makes no difference in nationality, Ethiopians, Chinese, Indians, Mexicans, and other nationalities worship together." It became one of the most racially inclusive, culturally diverse groups to gather in the city of Los Angeles at that time. It included people from all classes. It held the attention of the highly educated alongside the illiterate. It had something for new converts as well as for seasoned professionals in ministry. Even so, worship at the mission was undoubtedly heavily flavored by the dominantly African American character of its founding core membership.

Like most congregations, the Azusa Street Mission published a doctrinal basis that outlined what the congregation believed. It had a voting membership. And it had a duly elected board of trustees. In September 1906 it began to publish a newspaper called *The Apostolic Faith* that would ultimately number fifty thousand copies per issue. On March 9, 1907, the congregation incorporated with the State of California under the name Apostolic Faith Mission. The following month, on April 12, the congregation ended its lease with First African Methodist Episcopal Church when Pastor Seymour purchased the building at 312 Azusa Street for fifteen thousand dollars. The mission offered regularly scheduled services and daily Bible studies. Its leaders planned an aggressive evangelistic outreach program, coordinated cottage prayer meetings, held weekly training sessions for leaders as they came into the revival, facilitated a four-month long "camp meeting"[15] that drew thousands, and provided a weekly children's church.

Many have seen the revival as a spontaneous "event." But neither the many pastoral programs nor the far-flung missionary effort of the mission's people ran themselves. It took sustained, coordinated effort to facilitate a revival of this size while at the same time serving the needs of a growing congregation. William Joseph Seymour was the person responsible for recruiting and overseeing a staff sufficient to the task. He was "de shepha'd" of the Azusa Street flock.

As the opening quotation makes clear in the graphic language of that day, the question of what constituted appropriate leadership was high on the mind of at least one African American woman who preached at the mission in September 1906. Undoubtedly she had in her sights the various pastors, evangelists, and church leaders who had come to the mission merely out of curiosity—those who were resistant to the message of the mission. She warned that if they didn't "git right wid Gawd"—that is, if they didn't catch the vision and provide appropriate leadership for their own congregation that was consistent with the message of "Azusa Street"—their people would soon leave them and they would have to find other employment. From her perspective, what constituted good leadership was their ability to feed their flocks on "de Holy Ghost."

In this chapter I will tell the story of those who were responsible for leading the Azusa Street Mission and show how they did it. We will begin by looking at Pastor Seymour. What did he believe? How did his beliefs and experiences as an African American help to mold his understanding of Pentecostal leadership? We will then look at the people with whom Pastor Seymour surrounded himself. What gifts did they bring that enriched the lives of those they touched at the mission? How did this leadership team function at the mission? How did they help to further the revival? How did they empower the members of the congregation to undertake their work?

Leading by Example

From the beginning, William Joseph Seymour was the acknowledged leader of the Azusa Street congregation. He had brought the
Apostolic Faith message to Los Angeles when he arrived in February 1906. He had proclaimed it to the members of the Ninth and
Santa Fe congregation. He had shared it with Edward and Mattie
Lee and with those who met for prayer at the Asberry home. He
had prayed with them until they had been baptized in the Holy
Spirit. And when they received that baptism, he became their pastor by acclamation. While several people have written about Pastor
Seymour, they haven't said much about Seymour as a leader. Further study of the many sources surrounding the mission and its
activities, however, has made it possible to present a more complete picture of Seymour as leader.

The Reverend William J. Seymour at middle age

The Bible translator Adolphus S. Worrell visited the Azusa Street Mission toward the end of the summer of 1906 and then published the following description of Pastor William J. Seymour.

The writer has not a single doubt but that Brother Seymour has more power with God, and more power from God, than all his critics in and out of the city. His strength is in his conscious weakness and lowliness before God; and so long as he maintains this attitude, the power of God will, no doubt, continue to flow through him.

Worrell reflected the thoughts of many when he penned these words. Many others who wrote about Pastor Seymour also enlisted adjectives such as "humble," "quiet," "soft-spoken," "unassuming," and "gentle" in their descriptions of him.

The Chicago pastor William H. Durham, who traveled to Los Angeles in February 1907 to seek his "Pentecost," described Seymour, "the leader of the movement under God," in similar terms. "He is the meekest man I ever met," Durham began,

He walks and talks with God. His power is in his weakness. He seems to maintain a helpless dependence on God and is as simple-hearted as a little child, and at the same time is so filled with God that you feel the love and power every time you get near him.

Durham seems to be giving Seymour's spiritual leadership high marks—an assessment that emerges again in the Chicago pastor's description of the Azusa Street Mission itself.

The first thing that impressed me, was the love and unity that prevailed in the meeting, and the heavenly sweetness that filled the very air that I breathed . . . I never felt the power and glory that I felt in the Azusa Street Mission.

The evangelist Glenn Cook echoed Durham's early evaluation of Pastor Seymour. He, too, cast his vote for Seymour as the meekest man that he had ever met. It is not surprising, then, that during the heyday of the revival, the congregation at the Azusa Street Mission held Seymour in such high regard. He was a humble man, and he led his people out of a spirit of gentleness.

Seymour's demeanor was unusual for a Christian leader in the holiness movement at that time. Many holiness leaders seemed to thrive on conflict and confrontation. William J. Seymour seems to have taken the opposite tack—one of gentleness, humility, weakness, and graciousness. The fact that he was meek did not mean that he was weak, but his meekness contributed to what was a rare and disarming style of leadership. When necessary, Seymour was quite capable of providing clear, decisive direction or a well-reasoned apology for his beliefs and actions. Where he differed with many holiness leaders was in the way he lived out his belief in the equality of every person who gathered for worship at the mission. He invited them to a space made sacred both by the presence of God and by Seymour's commitment to take seriously whatever gifts the people brought to share. He made it clear that it was an open space. And he allowed his people to express themselves even when he disagreed with them. It did not matter whether they were old or young, rich or poor, black or white, male or female, lay or clergy. Seymour took them all seriously and thereby empowered them within the space he seemed to enlarge just for them.

The feisty evangelist Glenn Cook later wrote a testimony that explained why he had first attended the Azusa Street Mission. It provides us with a great example of how Seymour's graciousness shaped his ministry. Cook went to the mission to set Seymour and his followers straight. So far as he was concerned, Seymour was preaching heresy and the manifestations that took place at the mission were not of God. "I was not alone in this effort," he recalled. As the evening progressed, many took the floor to testify or provide some exhortation. Finally it was Glenn Cook's turn. He began by telling the people that they were all wrong. The longer Cook railed against Seymour and his people that evening, the more he became convicted in his own heart that Seymour was right. Before he was through speaking, he was on his knees asking for forgiveness and praying to receive what Seymour was preaching: the baptism in the Spirit. Speaking for critics who had experienced something similar, Cook later recalled that Pastor Seymour would simply "sit behind that packing case [the pulpit] and smile at us until we were all condemned by our own activities."

Such a leadership style might not have been easy for most people to embrace, especially those who tended to dominate through sheer force or bravado in other contexts, or those for whom the exercise of power was how they conceived of ministry. Perhaps Seymour had learned the type of humility and submission he exercised at the mission from the societal norms to which he was subject as an African American. It would have been extremely difficult for a black man to lord it over a white man at that time. But then again, Jesus was a gentle leader, directing with soft words, and Seymour was a man who spent much time in prayer with his Lord.

Before arriving in Los Angeles, Seymour had committed himself to the personal discipline of spending five or more hours each day in prayer. In those first weeks following his arrival in Los Angeles, Seymour had increased this prayer time. Even after the mission came into being, with all of its urgent demands on his time, Seymour continued a regimen of prayer. Frank Bartleman observed that "Brother Seymour generally sat behind two empty shoe boxes, one on top of the other [which served as the mission's pulpit]. He usually kept his head inside the top one during the meeting, in prayer. There was no pride there." His time spent in prayer likely contributed to his clear sense of calling and purpose, shaping him into a leader open and vulnerable to others.

Pastor Seymour's lack of selfishness set him apart from many around him. He believed that God was doing something new, and he wanted simply to be used in that new thing. When others looked at the revival, they, too, wanted to be part of it. Some took part by moving in and attempting to take over. While most of them did not challenge Seymour's leadership in the mission, they did challenge him by holding meetings nearby. Los Angeles was a growing city and it would have been possible to begin other Apostolic Faith congregations in many parts of the city. Most competitors, however, stayed within four to six blocks of the Azusa Street Mission. Frank Bartleman started his Eighth and Maple Church about six blocks from the mission. Pastor Elmer Fisher led a September, 1906, off-shoot of First New Testament Church, later known as the Upper Room Mission, at 107 $^1/_2$ North Main Street, just four blocks from the mission. (It later moved to 327 $^1/_2$ South Spring Street, about the same distance from the Azusa Street Mission.) At first Fisher's ministry drew very few from the mission, but by 1908 it had attracted many of the whites who had in earlier days attended Azusa Street. Other similar churches joined Bartleman's and Fisher's. But in every case, Pastor Seymour valued the new ministries as allies. Before long, he was hosting weekly "leadership meetings" at the mission.

Leading through Training

As the revival grew, it was inevitable that new works would emerge. Lesser leaders might have complained that other congregations were being formed too near the mission and siphoning off members. Seymour celebrated the spread of the revival to other congregations regardless of where they were established. *The Apostolic Faith* published a running account of this expansion into First New Testament Church, the Russian Molikan community, the Eighth and Maple Mission, the Upper Room Mission, the People's Church, and among the Nazarenes in Elysian Heights and at the Vernon Mission. Seymour invited prayer on their behalf, published testimonies provided by their leaders, preached in their churches, and invited their participation in leadership at the Azusa Street Mission even on occasions when he was absent. Whenever new preaching points, cottage prayer meetings, or congregations emerged, he advertised their meetings.

Seymour envisioned a series of Apostolic Faith missions springing up that would work in concert with the Azusa Street Mission. He invited emerging leaders within the congregation as well as competitors outside the doors of the mission to participate in the revival with him. He embraced their gifts and sought to expand the influence of the revival by providing coordination for their efforts. He viewed them as fellow-workers.

From Seymour's perspective the city was a sufficiently large mission field to need these other churches. But he also made clear that he wanted these churches to have a continuing relationship to the Azusa Street Mission. He worked toward that end by establishing special meetings designed for their leaders, held each Monday morning at the Azusa Street Mission. These leaders came together for prayer, mutual support, counsel, Bible study, and both short- and long-term strategic planning. Regular participants included Upper Room Mission pastor Elmer K. Fisher; William H. Pendleton from the Eighth and Maple Mission; Rev. and Mrs. Charles Kent, formerly Nazarene pastors, who established a mission on Fifty-first Street; and A. H. Post, who by July 1906 had established a Pentecostal work in nearby Pasadena.

The Azusa Street revival spread swiftly to all points in the greater Los Angeles area, assisted by a growing interurban trolley system. Most participants did not yet own automobiles; instead they walked or rode the streetcar, which took them to within half a block of the mission. It is not surprising, then, that the streetcar system would become part of the mission's evangelistic outreach plans. Ultimately, new missions and preaching points sprang up at the end of each streetcar line, in Long Beach, Pasadena, Anaheim, Whittier, and Monrovia.

By fall 1906 a number of leaders were coming to these meetings. These included Edward McCauley, an African American preacher who led the work in Long Beach before going as a missionary to Monrovia, Liberia; the Rev. A. H. Post, working with the Household of God in Pasadena; and Henry S. Prentiss [alternate spelling Prentice], an African American evangelist who gained notoriety in the press for his direct and outspoken preaching. The group must have numbered about two dozen people, including the mission's primary staff people.

A simple, profound announcement of the group's message appeared in the January 1907 issue of *The Apostolic Faith*.

We must give God all the glory in this work. We must keep very humble at His feet. He recognizes no flesh, no color, no names. We must not glory in Azusa Mission, nor in anything but the Lord Jesus Christ by whom the world is crucified unto us and we unto the world.

We stand as assemblies and missions all in perfect harmony. Azusa stands for the unity of God's people everywhere. God is uniting His people, baptizing them by one Spirit into one body.

The leadership meetings continued through at least April 29, 1907, and it is likely that they continued well beyond that time.

Leading through Planning

Messengers watched all the trains to receive the holiness people who arrived from every point of the compass at all hours night and day, and escorted them at once to the wonderful meeting.

W. B. GODBEY

While Pastor Seymour valued spontaneous actions as possible interventions of the Holy Spirit in the midst of the revival, he was also convinced of the value of planning. Several features in the revival reflect this. First, a team of "messengers" met various trains when they arrived in Los Angeles. When in 1909 the widely acclaimed holiness preacher, W. B. Godbey, visited Los Angeles, he was impressed to find Azusa Street messengers greeting out-of-towners interested in the mission's meeting. Leaders of the "Toronto Blessing" in the 1990s did something similar when they stationed messengers at the Toronto airport to meet the crowds of incoming passengers who wanted to visit that revival.

Second, Seymour and his staff coordinated outreach efforts from the mission. By November 1906 Florence Crawford was designated "state director," and Glenn Cook was "assistant state manager" of the Apostolic Faith movement. Crawford and Cook extended the influence of the mission by holding meetings along the west coast of the United States as well as in Oklahoma and Indiana. Local businesswomen Phoebe Sargent and Jennie Evans Moore were each appointed to the position of "city missionary," overseeing work throughout Los Angeles and its outlying communities. The mission also recruited preachers and others who could support these officials' work in nearby communities; workers took the Pacific Electric streetcars to meetings held in those communities. In the case of nearby Monrovia, the mission paid for streetcar tickets so members of the Holiness Church in Monrovia who wanted to attend a meeting or two at the Azusa Street Mission could do so. In nearby Whittier, when four people were arrested for disturbing the peace on Sunday, October 7, 1906, word soon reached the Azusa Street Mission, and fifteen more workers were

"Canvas tabernacle and big week-day congregation at Arroyo Seco campground of the 'holy rollers,' with which people of Highland Park are finding fault.... On these grounds, through Divine grace, members of the sect say they expect eventually to erect permanent buildings for use in promotion of the faith!" This caption appeared below one of only two known photographs stemming from the 1907 camp meeting held by the Azusa Street Mission. The camp meeting took place in what is now Arroyo Seco Park, near the 110 Freeway (Los Angeles to Pasadena) and Avenue 60 in Highland Park. The area was, and still is, shaded by a substantial grove of Sycamore trees. The camp meeting began June 1 and officially ran to September 1, 1907.

quickly recruited "to take the place of the four." The meetings apparently continued unabated.

A third feature of the revival that demonstrated planning began on Monday morning, April 22, 1907, when Rachel Sizelove, Clara Lum, and R. J. Scott attended the Monday morning leadership meeting and raised the subject of a possible camp meeting. Others present encouraged the three, and a camp meeting committee was formed. Advertising for the event began immediately in The Apostolic Faith. Florence Crawford's husband, Frank, a local real estate agent and developer, helped the group lease fifteen acres in the arroyo that ran between Pasadena and Los Angeles, adjacent to what is now the Pasadena Freeway in Highland Park. A stream of fresh water flowed through this acreage, and it was covered with sycamore and oak trees in abundance. By Saturday, June 1, 1907, the camp meeting had begun.

Articles in the local press, although ridiculing and criticizing the camp meeting, demonstrated that it was well planned. One reported that "the Holy Rollers' tents extend along both sides of the arroyo for a distance of perhaps half a mile. There are hundreds of them. The tents themselves are well kept and comfortably furnished. In them live Negroes and whites, side by side." It went on to complain that "there are hundreds of 'Holy Rollers' here encamped, and hundreds of little children, scores of them already obsessed by this curious mental disease, masquerading as religion."

Such criticisms continued throughout the summer, but R. J. Scott, who was responsible for overseeing the organization of the camp that summer, made it clear to reporters that a team of people took responsibility for the ongoing sanitation and order that was so evident within the camp. What may be most significant about the mission and the 1907 camp meeting is the fact that Pastor Seymour gave others free rein to lead its meetings. He himself never led a service at the meeting throughout its June-to-September run. In fact, he never even attended the camp meeting. During those same months, Pastor Seymour visited Houston, Texas, and Zion, Illinois, and he participated in other parts of the revival as it began to break out in Minneapolis, Indianapolis, and Virginia. During this absence he had complete trust in his people and in this cooperative effort in which Frank Bartleman, William Pendleton, Elmer Fisher, Edward Lee, and the staff of the Azusa Street Mission all participated.

One final example of Seymour's leadership through planning came in the publication of a more or less regular newspaper, *The Apostolic Faith*. This was a cooperative effort for which Clara Lum took primary editorial responsibility, editing the paper and undoubtedly writing many of the articles (though always anonymously). Glenn Cook, who had ties to a local newspaper, probably oversaw printing and distribution. But the paper was a product of the mission, and it required a staff of people to research stories, respond to inquiries, and address and mail each issue. The newspaper became a powerful vehicle for furthering the revival, but it was highly dependent upon the mission's staff.

Leading through His Staff

Within weeks of the beginning of the Azusa Street Mission, seasoned workers began to arrive. Many of them were local people who came from other congregations in the region. Among the earliest to arrive at the mission were Glenn A. Cook, G. W. Evans, Hiram Smith, Clara Lum, and Florence Crawford. Once they were baptized in the Spirit, they were invited to become part of Seymour's leadership team. Others included Jennie Evans Moore, Sister Prince, Mrs. May Evans, Mrs. Phoebe Sargent, and Thomas Junk. About the beginning of August 1906 this group of people posed for a historic photograph with Pastor Seymour. Several of them held specific portfolios in the work of the mission. Others volunteered their time. This was the inner circle of Azusa's leaders.

For a short time, then, Pastor Seymour surrounded himself with this very capable, interracial staff of women and men. Together they provided the planning and forethought required by the revival. It was they who commissioned a significant number of missionaries and evangelists, and supported a rescue mission in Los Angeles. They coordinated workers who traveled on the streetcar

Featured in this photograph from left to right standing are: Phoebe Sargent, G. W. Evans, Jennie Evans Moore, Glenn A. Cook, Florence Louise Crawford, Thomas Junk, Sister Prince. Seated from left to right are Mrs. May Evans, Hiram W. Smith with Mildred Crawford on his lap, Elder William Joseph Seymour, and Clara Lum. This photograph must be dated sometime between mid-July and early August 1906.

system to predetermined sites. They communicated with these workers, keeping tabs on the progress of their work and encouraging them to think of the Azusa Street Mission as their connective center. They accepted invitations to speak and hold meetings in other cities in congregations that wanted to identify with the revival. In a sense, they laid out the plans that might have developed into a new Pentecostal denomination with the Azusa Street Mission at its core. Pastor Seymour clearly helped to define this interracial mission and its message, but he did not do it alone.

The things that occurred at the Azusa Street Mission in 1906 quickly attracted the attention of many veteran holiness and evangelical preachers, evangelists, and Christian workers. That fact in itself may explain the success of the revival as well as anything else. William Seymour took advantage of these veterans' presence at the mission and recruited them to aid him. With such talent available, the potential for confrontation and competition between these leaders and Elder William J. Seymour was great. Several of them were strong personalities, and in one or two cases they could be typified as rather selfish.

The Rev. Hiram W. Smith, a former Methodist minister, provided wisdom and spiritual counsel to the revival by serving as a "deacon" and a "devotional leader" at the mission. His maturity and ministerial experience may have endeared him to Elder Seymour, for in the early days of the mission when workers were given credentials to enter ministry under its auspices, he and Pastor Seymour were the two who signed the credentials.

Glenn A. Cook arrived at the mission shortly after it began. Following his 1901 conversion he had joined the Metropolitan Church Association, a radical expression of the Wesleyan holiness movement that was known for its demonstrative worship style. Within a year he had become a creative apologist and preacher for the group. From 1902 onward he contributed articles to and printed the association's paper, *The Burning Bush.*

When the Azusa Street Mission opened in April 1906, Cook was holding meetings in a tent on the corner of East Seventh and Spring Streets. It was early July when Cook went to the Azusa Street Mission to criticize its leaders for teaching that speaking in tongues constituted the Bible evidence of baptism in the Spirit. After he became convicted of his error (in the midst of his speech!), he received tongues. Pastor Seymour and others laid hands on him, setting him apart to serve as the mission's business manager. In December 1906 he was made Assistant State Manager of the Apostolic Faith Mission.

Cook oversaw the handling of mail received at the mission. In 1906 he was among those who corresponded with inquirers. During the summer of 1906 he held meetings in the holiness church in Monrovia, a small town twenty miles northeast of Los Angeles. He also preached at the People's Church that stood within blocks of the Azusa Street Mission. In January 1907 he traveled to Indianapolis on behalf of the mission, where he held a series of meetings at the Union Gospel Tabernacle before returning to Los Angeles.

Originally from western Oregon, **Florence Louise Crawford** was converted in Los Angeles around 1900. As a young woman she had been prominent in her town's social scene, frequenting the theater, hosting card parties, and enjoying ballroom dances. It was while she was on the dance floor, she later wrote, that God first addressed her. Three times she heard the words "Daughter, give *me* thine heart." This incident led her to contact a friend, who prayed with and for her, and led her to make a profession of faith. After presenting herself for baptism at First Methodist Episcopal Church, she joined the church and quickly became a "class leader." Crawford threw herself fully into church and rescue work, and became active in the Women's Christian Temperance Union (WCTU). In 1906 she attended the county convention of the WCTU as a delegate from Highland Park, where she lived with her family.

Rescue work appealed deeply to Mrs. Crawford. She counted among her friends the sheriff of Los Angeles, as well as many of that city's detectives and policemen. She often visited the local prisons and slums, and worked closely with the juvenile court. She became friends with many local pastors who from time to time opened their pulpits for her to make appeals for aid in her rescue work. Her work also brought her into contact with the city's various social and civic clubs engaged in volunteer work. Out of her concern for young people, she joined the local chapter of the National Congress of Mothers, founded in 1897 and known today as the Parent-Teacher Association (PTA).

In April 1906, shortly after the Azusa Street Mission opened its doors, Crawford attended a service there. She met with Pastor Seymour after the service, and he told her that she needed to be sanctified. This experience Crawford received within days, and a week later, as she later related, "the Holy Ghost came down from Heaven and fell upon my life, and baptized me with the Holy Ghost and fire, [and] spoke through me in another language."

Crawford brought several gifts to Seymour's staff. Her rescue work and her obvious public speaking skills made her valuable to the unfolding work of the mission. She became one of the leaders who helped set mission policy. In November 1906 she was appointed state director of the Pacific Coast Apostolic Faith Mission.

Mrs. Phoebe Sargent was the wife of a successful home builder. In 1904 she owned and operated the Elysian Hospital, a sanitarium. This suggests that Sargent had excellent business, administrative, and people skills. A former member of the Los Angeles Holiness Church, she carried the title "City Missionary" at the Azusa Street Mission.

Following her baptism in the Spirit at the Bonnie Brae meeting, **Jennie Evans Moore** used her gifts in music. She could often be found leading singing at the mission. Like Phoebe Sargent, Moore served initially as a City Missionary. It is likely that the two worked together in the mission's evangelistic ministries. These would have ranged from praying with people at the mission altar, to coordinating street meetings such as those held at Second and San Pedro, to organizing the far-flung outreaches that spread the mission's work and fame throughout Southern California.

Others in the 1906 photograph also contributed to the regular work of the mission, although they are not mentioned on the mission's letterhead. **Dr. G. W. Evans** and his wife May, the first white woman to speak in tongues under Seymour's ministry, were both experienced in ministry. They participated regularly at the leaders' meetings and undoubtedly helped to pray with people who came to the altar. They would ultimately leave the mission to take news of the revival to Northern California.

Sister Prince also appears in the famous portrait of early mission leaders. She was described as a "Mother in Israel." Even Frank Bartleman, who did not generally waste time building up the reputations of others, noted that Prince was "well known and reverenced among us." He described her as "a colored lady . . . a very ordinary woman, as natural talents go, but intensely pious and of childlike faith (of great quality, however)."

As an African American woman with a significant "spiritual" reputation, she may well have been the first woman recognized at the mission, in accordance with African American and early Pentecostal church tradition, as a "church Mother"—one sought out by newer or younger believers for prayer and advice. In keeping with the tradition of "church Mothers," she probably also offered advice to Pastor Seymour.

Of all the people in that photograph, **Thomas Junk** is the most elusive. It is not entirely clear why he was chosen or what role he played at the mission. He had probably had some experience in ministry before coming to the mission. In 1907 Junk worked with the ministry team that Florence Crawford led in a series of evangelistic meetings from Los Angeles to San Francisco. Once the team reached the San Francisco area, however, Thomas and Mrs. Junk left. They moved on to Seattle, where Junk led a congregation before going to northern China as an independent Apostolic Faith missionary.

Each of these people—Hiram Smith, Glenn Cook, Florence Crawford, G. W. and May Evans, Thomas Junk, Phoebe Sargent, Sister Prince, and Clara Lum (see below)—served as a member of the mission's credentials committee. When people came wanting to serve as missionaries and evangelists, this committee examined them. Once they approved and licensed candidates, they laid on hands and prayed over them.

The final person in the photograph—seated next to William J. Seymour, pencil in hand—is **Clara Lum**. She filled multiple roles at the mission, and her substantial contribution must be singled out. She may have held the second most important role in the organization from its beginning until she left the mission in 1908: secretary to Pastor Seymour.

Lum first came to the Azusa Street Mission about the last week of May, 1906. Shumway says that she had served for a period of time as a servant in the home of Charles F. Parham, an interesting intersection if it can be proved. Before coming to Los Angeles, she had worked in Shenandoah, Virginia, with a paper called *The Missionary World*. While those who knew her described her as quiet, unassuming, and highly focused on her writing and editing work, she was clearly excited about what had happened to her in these meetings. She was baptized in the Spirit in one of the mission's earliest outreach meetings in Whittier and reported that she had received the "gift of healing and casting out devils." With these gifts it is likely that she spent time in the mission's upstairs healing room and praying with those who came for salvation.

With her well-developed journalistic abilities, Clara Lum played a major dual role at the mission. First, she put her stenographic skills to work recording many of the oral testimonies as well as a few of the sermons given at the mission. And second, she edited and published the mission's newspaper, *The Apostolic Faith*.

Many wrote to the mission, and handling that correspondence was a huge undertaking. Some letters came in response to the workers who went out and testified to events at the mission; an increasing number came from those who read *The Apostolic Faith*. In 1906, while Glenn Cook saw to it that all inquiries received a written response, Clara Lum selected excerpts from letters and read them aloud during some of the services. This allowed the congregation to see how the revival was spreading. Lum also selected excerpts from those letters to publish in the *The Apostolic Faith*, thereby including in the Azusa Street fold many of the readers from around the world.

Lum was also responsible for compiling the various regional mailing lists from the addresses people gave when they wrote for copies of the newspaper. This was a huge task that, together with folding, rolling, and addressing copies of the newspaper for mailing, required a sizeable contribution from a volunteer labor force. "All the work at the Mission is done freely," *The Apostolic Faith* reported.

By January 1907 *The Apostolic Faith* office was receiving as many as fifty letters a day, and the staff tried to answer each one personally. Mrs. Ida May Throop helped in this task. Some time after May 1906 Mrs. C. J. Hagg and the missionary-evangelist Mae Field Mayo also served in this capacity. By December 1906 Mary P. Perkins had joined the newspaper staff. Most of the time it required at least two people working full time to keep up with the correspondence. Even then, their responses were often late, a tardiness apologized for in the pages of *The Apostolic Faith*.

The letters sent to the mission varied in content but fell into several categories. Some writers requested more information on the mission's teachings. Others asked to be placed on the mailing list of *The Apostolic Faith*. Since the newspaper was given freely

upon request and the mission was looking for ways to build its circulation, those who requested the paper often received multiple
copies for distribution. Repeatedly, however, they were advised to
be good stewards and make sure that the papers they received were
read and passed on to others.

Beginning in October 1906 a third group began sending testimonies of what God was doing in their own lives or churches. As
the movement spread and evangelists and missionaries went out
from the mission, the mission became a kind of clearing house for
their correspondence. They wrote letters to fellow workers with
whom they had lost contact, sent them in care of the mission, and
the mission forwarded them. This constituted a fourth type of correspondence for which the mission became responsible. *The Apostolic Faith* even advertised this service.

A fifth category of correspondence involved offerings. We can
not determine how much money came in from those who were
interested in the mission's ministry, or who gave in response to
occasional pleas that were published in *The Apostolic Faith*. Azusa
Street functioned along the "faith mission" line, never officially collecting offerings. Its newspaper was published on a self-supporting
basis, though the mission refused to charge for it. Instead, readers
were constantly reminded of the needs associated with the production of such a paper, and the editor often suggested that some
might like to make a contribution by sending cash or U.S. postage
stamps. Many did.

Then there was the group of letters that came with requests.
Sometimes they were simple requests for people at the mission to
pray for some individual to receive salvation or sanctification or the
baptism in the Spirit. At other times, they requested prayer for
healing. Many people would enclose handkerchiefs, small pieces of
cloth, or aprons in an envelope, with a request that the mission
staff pray over these items and return them so that they might be
applied to someone suffering from a particular illness. Sometimes
the mission received testimonies that such prayers had been effective and the sick one had been healed.[16]

The office staff seems to have taken these requests very seriously. The staff viewed all that they did as "ministry," as a service to others. "The offices are places of prayer and power," *The Apostolic Faith* reported, "and the power of God comes down on the workers as they fold the paper." When the mailing had been prepared, the workers would "lay on their hands and pray over them" before sending them out. As a result, Rachel Sizelove claimed, "many were healed when they received the paper, so strong was the faith."

With the help of others, Reuben Clark, a retired Civil War veteran, folded and mailed papers full time. Mr. Thomas (Tommie) Anderson, a former drug addict, helped from at least January 22, 1907, until mid-year. By the following January he was in Winnipeg, and later he served as a missionary with the International Church of the Foursquare Gospel in Latin America. They were joined by other unnamed volunteers who aided in spreading the message of the mission.

Something that has never been noted before is the fact that much of this group had left the Azusa Street Mission by early 1907. The photograph was taken around August 1, 1906, and it has often been treated as representing "the staff"—as though this particular group stayed together. But that was not the case. By September 1906 the Evanses could be found on the road with Florence Crawford, holding meetings along the central coast of California, in the San Francisco Bay area, and on into Woodland, California, where they stayed. Thomas Junk and his wife (unnamed) joined the Evanses and Crawford until they reached the Bay area, then moved on to Seattle. After Mrs. Junk died, Thomas Junk sustained a relationship with the Azusa Street Mission through correspondence. By late December 1906 Glenn Cook traveled to Indianapolis where he conducted meetings for several months among a growing congregation of people. The Sargents moved on to the Church at Eighth and Maple, where their close friend and former pastor, William Pendleton became their pastor once again. Thus the only members of this group that remained to work with Seymour in 1907 were Jennie Evans Moore, Sister Prince, Hiram Smith, and Clara Lum.

Leading with Volunteers

Some, like Pastor Seymour, Glenn Cook, and Clara Lum, worked full time for the mission. Others worked part time. Even the full-time staff worked on a faith basis with no guaranteed salary, and the majority of workers at the mission were entirely volunteers. The staff featured trained volunteers who worked at the altar or in the rooms set aside for those who were seeking to be baptized in the Spirit or physical healing. They also led people into salvation or sanctification. A staff of volunteers folded and mailed the newspaper. Several others sorted the mail, helped build the mission's mailing lists, and wrote responses on behalf of the mission.

The mission's many workers possessed organizational skills, practical skills, and spiritual skills. They took responsibility for many of the congregation's activities. They planned for the future while they took care of present necessities. They helped prepare other upcoming leaders. They recruited other able staff persons. They preached, taught, prayed, ministered, evangelized, recorded, wrote, published, publicized, paid the bills, traveled, and founded churches. They were attempting to build a new network of Apostolic Faith believers. In short, they handled all of the details and incidentals to facilitate both the ongoing life of a local congregation and the "event" that would become known as a worldwide revival. Furthermore, they took as their tools the latest in communication instruments—from periodicals to telephones—and they plotted their strategies using the most up-to-date mode of transportation, the streetcar.

The life of the Azusa Street Mission transcended its walls. Many volunteers in the congregation were actively involved in neighborhood evangelization. Some held home Bible studies in which they prayed with those who wanted a deeper encounter with God. In my research of the two hundred or so longer-term members of this congregation, I placed on a map tacks representing their home addresses. They tended to cluster in several neighborhoods. One group clustered around the mission itself, another near the house on North Bonnie Brae Street, a third one in the Armenian neighborhood between Temple and Sunset, another in the downtown area south of the mission, another between Santa Fe and the railroad tracks near Lenard Street, and still another in Highland Park. The existence of these clusters strongly suggests that some of these people shared the message effectively with their neighbors.

These people did not work only their neighborhoods; some of them also led downtown street meetings. Their favorite locations included the corner of East First and San Pedro, and the corner of East Second and San Pedro a half block from the mission. Others chose East Seventh and Spring or East Seventh and Broadway. Sometimes groups of street evangelists would meet at the mission, then board a streetcar to a nearby suburb like Whittier, San Pedro, or Long Beach, where they would hold street or tent meetings. Most of these evangelists were not clergy, but they had a testimony to share, they were excited to share it, and they wanted to spread the message. In one case, when four of them were arrested and held for disturbing the peace on Whittier's streets, word came back to the mission and a group of fifteen quickly took their place. At times hundreds of the faithful took streetcars to the beach for well-organized baptismal services. And from June 1 through the end of September 1907, the mission ran a camp meeting in the great Arroyo Seco, halfway between Los Angeles and Pasadena. All of these activities, which made use of the streetcar system, required planning and coordination.

Leading through the Exposition of Scripture

Pastor Seymour was a student of Scripture. He was not a highly educated man, and he did not make any pretensions to learning. If he approached his task in simplicity, he was nevertheless sure of what he believed. This is evident from the sermons that he preached. He drew repeatedly from all four Gospels, Acts, Romans, 1 Corinthians, Ephesians, Hebrews, and the book of Revelation. In the excerpts we have from the sermons he preached, he either quoted from or alluded to nineteen of the New Testament's books. His familiarity with the Old Testament was less developed, but he

This was one of several publicity photographs of the Reverend William J. Seymour. These photographs probably date from about 1906, shortly before Charles Parham came to Los Angeles. In this instance, he is pictured as reading a Bible.

drew heavily from Genesis, Exodus, 1 and 2 Kings, 1 Samuel, the Psalms, Isaiah, Joel, and Zechariah. At one level he could be described as a literalist in his interpretation of most texts. He accepted Bishop Ussher's literalist dating system, which placed creation in 4004 B.C. But in keeping with his Wesleyan holiness training, Seymour also employed typology in several of his sermons. One example of this is a sermon he preached on "Rebecca: Type of the Bride of Christ," based on Genesis 24.

While much of his preaching reflects the impact of the holiness movement on his formation, Seymour did not hesitate to voice his own opinion on a subject even if it contradicted others around him. When he was called upon to explain himself, he was quite capable of doing so and doing it well. But when pushed to take a defensive posture, he was equally willing to engage in self-criticism and undertake further study on a subject that he felt needed it. His willingness to be self-critical and reflective meant that his teaching in general—and especially, later on, his understanding of the boundaries of legitimate spiritual experience—was subject to the answers he received when he studied the Scriptures.

From the start the Azusa Street Mission occupied experimental territory. What was happening at Azusa Street was new. There were no recent books that gave instructions on how to establish a Pentecostal church or how to lead and disciple Pentecostal believers. Other than selected passages from Acts, 1 Corinthians 12—14, Romans 12:1–8, Ephesians 4:1–16, and 1 Peter 4:7–11, very few texts yielded help on topics such as the baptism in the Holy Spirit or the gifts ("charisms") of the Holy Spirit. And there was no one in Los Angeles more experienced than William J. Seymour to show Azusa Street participants the way or tell them when they had gone too far.

With the exception of Charles F. Parham, who was in Texas at the time, there was no one else to whom Pastor Seymour could go for further instruction. He could not turn to the pastors of the historic churches in Los Angeles. Most of them did not believe that the spiritual experiences and gifts recognized at Azusa Street were even possible any longer. Their theological positions were in place, and for the most part these positions did not allow room for such things. No one in the area had had any experience with such phenomena as speaking in tongues. In fact, many local pastors viewed these things as evidence of fanaticism, or as demonic—either way, a potential danger to society. William J. Seymour and his workers found themselves on their own as they interpreted their experiences. They were pioneers.

For Pastor Seymour to lead this revival under such circumstances meant that he had to manifest certain personal qualities if he was not to become overbearing. He had to be personally vulnerable. He had to be tentative with his initial conclusions. He had to provide safe space for his followers to experiment, setting them free to learn their own lessons—sometimes alone. He had to provide a forum for various members of his congregation to make their case or to demonstrate their charism in the context of the worshipping community, without fear of recrimination. Judgments ultimately had to be rendered. But all of this experimentation had to be done under the eye of one who was firm yet flexible—who was willing to stake a claim regarding a position taken but generous enough to allow for mistakes to be made that would ultimately contribute to the spiritual growth of the flock. One clear example of this can be demonstrated in Seymour's assessment of a phenomenon known as "writing in tongues."

Before people spoke in tongues at the Asberry home on April 9, 1906, it is doubtful that anyone in Los Angeles other than William Seymour and his friends Lucy Farrow, Joseph Warren, and Edward

Lee had witnessed such a thing. As Seymour's flock began to experiment with this phenomenon, however, they sought answers to a number of questions. Were tongues a gift, a sign, an evidence, or something else? Did these tongues come in human languages, and if so, how could those languages be identified? If they were not human languages, what were they? Were they some form of angelic speech? Was this merely some kind of humanly contrived ecstatic behavior? Should speaking in tongues be viewed as a psychological phenomenon, a linguistic one, or a theological one? Could they be faked? During this period of inquiry, sooner or later someone was bound to wonder whether the Holy Spirit could not also empower someone to write in tongues. After all, if tongues were supposed to be some kind of language, and all other languages could be reduced to a written form, why couldn't the same be true for utterances in "tongues"? So the Azusa Street faithful began to experiment.

For a time the idea that a person could both speak and write in tongues caught the imagination of people at the mission. As early as 1901 one of Charles Parham's students, Miss Agnes Ozman, had written in "tongues" in Topeka, Kansas. Examples had even been reproduced in the Topeka, Kansas, newspaper. Now the phenomenon began to appear in Los Angeles. Even the *Los Angeles Daily Times* carried an example of it, complete with an alleged "interpretation." And when people left the mission to evangelize in other cities such as Salem and Portland, Oregon, local newspapers reported that the phenomenon continued. At the Azusa Street Mission, *The Apostolic Faith* announced experiments along these lines with a note of optimism. "The Lord has given the gift of writing in unknown languages, also the gift of playing on instruments," it proudly announced.

About the same time, however, a spiritualist was giving public demonstrations in Southern California of what was being called "psychography." This phenomenon involved a person concentrating on a board, allowing a purported spirit to channel through the person's mind and produce a written script on the board. Seymour, who had undoubtedly witnessed appeals to spirits among those who practiced Hoodoo in Louisiana, searched the Scriptures for

HAND-MADE CHICKEN TRACKS ON PAPER.

This facsimile of Dr. Keyes' effort to "write in tongues" was run in the *Los Angeles Daily Times*. An interlinear translation or interpretation into English is present as well, signed by Mr. LeNan. At the bottom of the page is a note signed by the Hindu, Baba Bharati, declaring it not to be one of the languages with which he was familiar. Many of the earliest Pentecostals thought that they could write in tongues. The *Topeka Daily Capital* featured an attempt by Agnes Ozman to do so in January 1901. The Salem and Portland, Oregon, papers reported that M. L. Ryan and Mildred and Florence Crawford claimed to be able to write in tongues. In fact, M. L. Ryan, who was right handed, believed that Jesus was left handed since Ryan seemed to be able to write in tongues only with his left hand. This phenomenon did not continue to develop at the Azusa Street Mission once Seymour searched the Scriptures and found no precedent for it.

guidance. In the end he reported that he could find nothing in Scripture to justify the practice of writing in tongues, in which the pen functioned like the *planchette* (a small pencil/pointing device on casters) used by spiritualists to produce automatic writing or determine hidden messages on a Ouija board. "We do not read anything in the Word about writing in unknown languages," The *Apostolic Faith* soon after announced, "so we do not encourage that in our meetings."

You can see the gentleness of the decision. While others might continue with their experiments in this phenomenon, this statement effectively ended further experimentation of this sort at Azusa Street. Seymour made clear that Scripture would be the norm for Pentecostal practice, and the mission would not support practices not found in Scripture or practices found to be contrary to Scripture. Seymour had learned something from his study of Scripture and he passed it on to his followers.

In January 1908 Pastor Seymour published a sermon titled "To the Married." In this teaching based on 1 Corinthians 7, he set forth his understanding of the nature and use of Scripture.

> The Corinthian church was one of Paul's most gifted Churches, and just as it is today, where a church is very gifted, the only safeguard from deceptive spirits is by rightly dividing the Word of God to keep out fanaticism. We may let down on some lines and rise on others, but God wants everything to be balanced by the Word of God.

After citing 2 Timothy 1:13–14 and 2 Timothy 3:14–16, Seymour went on to say that "God wants us to search and compare scriptures with scriptures." Later in the same sermon he repeated this principle, noting that it would counter confusion, deception, and wrong teaching. Frank Bartleman agreed—as far as he was concerned, at the Azusa Street Mission "the Word of God itself decided absolutely all issues."

Although several strong personalities were involved in the practice of writing in tongues, Pastor Seymour was determined to allow the Scriptures to be the final arbiter in all disputes. He had created a climate in which anyone able to lead in a prayer, give a personal testimony, sing a song, manifest some charism, or exhort the saints was allowed to do so. And people took full advantage of that freedom.

Having given this much freedom to the congregation, Seymour had to take a firm position, but he also had to let others challenge him on this position. Pastor Seymour clearly had to be personally secure, and he had to have confidence in the position he adopted.

Leading through Preaching

Seymour preached regularly at the mission, although this was not his primary contribution to the revival. He willingly and regularly shared the preaching ministry with others. Both women and men rose to the occasion, including Glenn Cook, Frank Bartleman, Elmer Fisher, W. B. Godbey, William H. Durham, A. A. Boddy, and many others. Several witnesses have left descriptions of Seymour's preaching style. One participant wrote of a service in which Seymour preached from Luke 4:1–19, "with demonstration of the Spirit and power, the saints drinking in the Word with shouts of praise and victory." Another wrote of a "short fiery talk on some of the words of Isaiah" that Seymour gave before closing with an altar call (the preacher's invitation to the congregation to come forward and pray at the altar). On some occasions Seymour was described as speaking softly, while on others he was described as speaking with a strong voice.

One reporter told of a sermon that lasted about twenty minutes. He called it "a jumble of Scripture and shouting," in which Seymour "preached hell-fire and a lake of burning brimstone for the wicked and predicted pestilence and trouble on the earth which could only be avoided by joining the Holy Jumpers." It is easy to see that Seymour drew from the biblical tradition to make his points. Passages such as the Olivet discourse in Matthew 24–25 might have formed the basis for such a sermon. These verses paint the troubling picture of apocalyptic events that will surround the coming of the Son of Man, complete with the consequences facing those who do not repent and ask God for forgiveness. A reporter who had already decided to ridicule the mission could easily have construed an altar call based on this apocalyptic passage as less an invitation to join the mission than a threat against those who failed to heed Seymour's wishes.

Another person described Seymour as yelling a sermon defiantly, challenging his hearers to respond. On another occasion, Seymour reportedly preached for over an hour and a half. The reporter describing that sermon ridiculed Seymour for confusing the term "irrigation" with "navigation" when he tried to develop an illustration rooted in California's agricultural experience. Baptism in the Spirit causes a person's soul to bubble forth and overflow, argued Seymour, in the same way that California's irrigation system causes water to overflow from large canals into the dry fields of the central valley to cultivate lush produce.

To my knowledge, no complete copy of a single Seymour sermon exists. We probably owe to Clara Lum the few excerpts from his sermons that have survived. As a stenographer and as the editor of *The Apostolic Faith*, she did publish excerpts from a dozen or so of Seymour's sermons. She identified them with the name "W. J. Seymour" or the initials "WJS" in many—but not all—cases. At least part of one excerpt was published twice under two different titles, and one of these appeared without any identification of its author. This strongly suggests that a number of other pieces published in *The Apostolic Faith* without an author identification may be attributable to Pastor Seymour. This is especially likely where two or three items strongly resembling excerpts from sermons preached at the mission appear in a row, with only the last one carrying Seymour's name.

What is equally interesting is what the excerpts reveal about Pastor Seymour's preaching style. Some of these excerpts clearly employ language that suggests they are verbatim recordings of an oral presentation rather than a written message. And they represent two features common in African American preaching.

The first of these we see in a *Los Angeles Daily Times* reporter's observation that Seymour held a "miniature Bible from which he reads at intervals one or two words—never more." This is a common method by which African American preachers work their way through the text, and it is evident in a short excerpt of a Seymour sermon titled "The Holy Ghost and the Bride."

> We read in Revelation 22:17, *"The Spirit and the bride say come."*
>
> Oh how sweet it is for us to have this blessed privilege of being a co-worker with the Holy Ghost. He inspires us with faith in God's word and endues us with power for service for the Master. *Bless His dear name!*
>
> Every man and woman that receives the baptism of the Holy Ghost is the bride of Christ. They have a missionary spirit for saving souls. They have the spirit of Pentecost. *Glory to God!*
>
> *"And let him that heareth say, come; and let him that is athirst, come; and whosoever will, let him take the water of life freely."*
>
> Oh what a blessed text. The bride of Christ is calling the thirsty to come to Jesus because this is the work of the Holy Ghost in the believer. He intercedes for the lost; He groans for them.
>
> The Spirit also calls the believer to come to Jesus and get sanctified. He points the sanctified to Jesus for his baptism with the Holy Ghost. When you are baptized with the Holy Ghost, you will have power to call sinners to Jesus, and they will be saved and sanctified, and baptized with the Holy Ghost and fire. *Amen!*

In this excerpt we can see the quotation from Revelation 22:17 (a) in the first part, and from Revelation 22:17 (b–d) in the second part. What follow each part of the quotation are Seymour's reflections—expansions based not so much on detailed analysis as on how Pastor Seymour sees the text applying to what he desires to share with his people.

Other excerpts reveal a second practice common in African American preaching. Within the African American tradition, preaching always takes the form of a dialogue with the congregation. The preacher makes a statement or a comment, conveys an image, or tells a story, and the congregation responds by speaking back to the preacher. This is commonly identified as the "call and response" form. Through the years it has characterized not only black preaching but also much Pentecostal preaching. The form likely found its way into non–African-American Pentecostal preaching from the African American practice. In Pastor Seymour's case, he seems to have primed his hearers by speaking back to himself—in a sense, indicating where he anticipates responses from members of his congregation. We see an example of this in the previous excerpt, as well as in an excerpt from a sermon titled "The Holy Spirit Bishop of the Church."

> It is the office work of the Holy Spirit to preside over the entire work of God on earth—John 10:3. Jesus was our Bishop while on earth, but now He has sent the Holy Ghost,
>
> *Amen,*
>
> to take His place, not men—John 14:16; 15:26; 16:7–14.
>
> *Praise His holy name!*
>
> The Holy Ghost is to infuse with divine power, and to invest with heavenly authority. No religious assembly is legal without His presence and His transaction. We should recognize Him as the Teacher of teachers.
>
> The reason why there are so many of God's people without divine power today, without experimental salvation, wrought out in their hearts by the Blood, by the power of the blessed Holy Spirit, is because they have not accepted Him as their Teacher, as their Leader, as their Comforter. Jesus said in His precious Word that if He went away He would send us another Comforter. The need of men and women today in their lives is a Comforter.
>
> *Praise our God!*
>
> We have received this blessed Comforter, and it is heaven in our souls. We can sing with all our hearts:
>
>> What matter where on earth we dwell
>>
>> On mountain top, or in the dell,
>>
>> In cottage or a mansion fair,
>>
>> Where Jesus is 'tis heaven there.
>
> *Bless His holy name!*

May God help every one of His Blood bought children to receive this blessed Comforter,
Glory to His name! Hallelujah! Hosannah to His omnipotent name! Oh, He is reigning in my soul! Hallelujah!
I just feel like the song which says:

> Oh spread the tidings round
> Wherever man is found,
> Wherever human hearts
> And human woes abound,
> Let every Christian tongue
> Proclaim the joyful sound,
> The Comforter has come!

The various exclamations of praise that Seymour employed—"Bless His holy name," "Hallelujah," and the like—invited others to respond as well. Such exclamations can be found woven throughout many of his sermon excerpts, and some of them appear distinctive to him. When these same phrases appear in unsigned articles in *The Apostolic Faith*, they may serve as clues that these articles also originated in an oral form, and quite probably with Pastor William J. Seymour himself.

Leading through Doctrinal Boundaries

Seymour used his sermons to instruct his people on important aspects of their faith. Beginning with the first number of *The Apostolic Faith*, Seymour saw to it that the statement outlining the beliefs of the mission was published in every issue. In addition, this statement of faith was printed up as a small, one-sided flyer and handed out to those who requested it. At least one news reporter wrote that he had received a copy. The bottom line of this sheet was signed simply "W. J. SEYMOUR, Azusa Street."

The statement has four sections. The first is a preamble defining the "Apostolic Faith Movement." The movement stands for "the restoration of the faith once delivered unto the saints." This language, based on Jude 3, had first been employed by Charles Parham,

The Apostolic Faith Movement

Stands for the restoration of the faith once delivered unto the saints—the old time religion, camp meetings, revivals, missions, street and prison work and Christian Unity everywhere.

Teaching on Repentance—Mark 1: 14, 15.
Godly Sorrow for Sin, Example — Matt. 9: 13. 2 Cor. 7, 9, 11. Acts 3: 19. Acts 17: 30, 31.
Of Confession of Sins—Luke 15: 21 and Luke 18: 13.
Forsaking Sinful Ways—Isa. 55: 7. Jonah 3: 8. Prov. 28: 13.
Restitution—Ezek. 33: 15. Luke 19: 8.
And Faith in Jesus Christ.

FIRST WORK.—Justification is that act of God's free grace by which we receive remission of sins. Acts 10: 42, 43. Rom. 3: 25.
SECOND WORK.—Sanctification is second work of grace and the last work of grace. Sanctification is that act of God's free grace by which He makes us holy. John 17: 15, 17.—"Sanctify them through Thy truth; Thy word is truth." 1 Thess. 4: 3. 1 Thess. 5: 23; Heb. 13: 12; Heb. 2: 11; Heb. 12: 14.

Sanctification is cleansing to make holy. The Disciples were sanctified before the Day of Pentecost. By a careful study of Scripture you will find it is so now. "Ye are clean through the word which I have spoken unto you" (John 15: 3; 13: 10); and Jesus had breathed on them the Holy Ghost (John 20: 21, 22). You know, that they could not receive the Spirit if they were not clean. Jesus cleansed and got all doubt out of His Church before He went back to glory.

The Baptism of the Holy Ghost is a gift of power upon the sanctified life; so when we get it we have the same evidence as the Disciples received on the Day of Pentecost (Acts 2: 3, 4), in speaking in new tongues. See also Acts 10: 45, 46; Acts 19: 6; 1 Cor. 14: 21. "For I will work a work in your days which ye will not believe though it be told you."—Hab. 1: 5.

Seeking Healing.—He must believe that God is able to heal.—Ex. 15: 26: "I am the Lord that healeth thee." James 5: 14; Psa. 103: 3; 2 Kings 20: 5; Matt. 8: 16, 17; Mark 16: 16, 17, 18.
He must believe God is able to heal. "Behold I am the Lord, the God of all flesh; is there any thing too hard for Me?"—Jer. 32: 27.
Too many have confused the grace of Sanctification with the enduement of Power, or the Baptism of the Holy Ghost; others have taken "the anointing that abideth" for the Baptism, and failed to reach the glory and power of a true Pentecost.

The Steps unto Heaven —Conviction, deep and pungent; Repentance; Surrender; Godly Sorrow; Restitution.
Conversion; Pardon; Regeneration; Washing of Regeneration; Conception; Witness; Baptism by Immersion (single); Censecration, in sentiment or promissory, in reality, forsaking all, for a hundred-fold; Sanctification, from inbred Sin and from inbred Disease; Born of God; Witness; Anointing of Holy Ghost that abideth; Baptism of Holy Ghost— Pentecost; Gift of Tongues; Sealing the Saints; Refining Fire; Earnest of our Inheritance. Redemption — Dead Raised; Living Changed in a moment; the one, true, Glorious Church set in order; Adoption; Perfect Bodies; GLORIFICATION.

The blood of Jesus will never blot out any sin between man and man they can make right; but if we can't make wrongs right the Blood graciously covers. (Matt. 5: 23, 24.)

We are not fighting men or churches, but seeking to displace dead forms and creeds of wild fanaticisms with living, practical Christianity. "Love, Faith, Unity" is our watchword, and "Victory through the Atoning Blood" our battle cry. God's promises are true. He said: "Be thou faithful over a few things, and I will make thee ruler over many." From the little handful of Christians who stood by the cross when the testings and discouragements came, God has raised a mighty host.

W. J. SEYMOUR, Azusa Street.

then subsequently adopted by Seymour. But it is important language for understanding both the Azusa Street Mission and the larger Pentecostal movement, which understand themselves as restoring an ineffective or a compromised church to its former state. Restorationism pervaded the U.S. during the nineteenth century. Groups as diverse as the Disciples of Christ/Christian Churches and the Church of Jesus Christ of Latter Day Saints (both nineteenth-century innovations) understood themselves as representing a much needed restoration of true Christianity. Others sharing this emphasis included the Millennial Dawn or Jehovah's Witnesses, the Seventh-Day Adventists, and the Apostolic Faith movement.

Restorationists believe that at some time in the history of the church—usually, it is said, around the time when the church emerged from "persecuted sect" status to become the Roman Empire's state religion—genuine Christianity was lost. They often, though not always, associate this loss with the rule of the emperor Constantine. Restorationists have generally taught that now, at last, God has begun his final intervention on the human stage to bring about the full restoration of the church. Each group has heralded its own vision of how God is restoring his church—the Disciples of Christ proclaiming non-sectarianism; the Mormons, Joseph Smith's new "revelation"; and holiness and Apostolic Faith groups, the outpouring of the Holy Spirit.

Most people within the holiness movement—and especially those in the Apostolic Faith—came to believe that God's intervention began with the emergence in the sixteenth century of Martin Luther, who restored the teaching of justification by faith. God then moved the church's restoration forward through John Wesley, with his emphasis upon sanctification. The list would frequently continue with other names—like the Quaker, George Fox, or the founder of the Salvation Army, General Booth—but names vary depending upon the group. In the case of the Apostolic Faith movement, this theory of history was soon connected with Joel's prophecies describing loss and restoration (Joel 1:4, 2:25) and with the "early and latter rain" (Joel 2:23).

The lead article in the second issue of *The Apostolic Faith* [Los Angeles, CA] clearly established the mission's commitment to restorationism. "The Pentecostal Baptism Restored," confidently announced its headline. "The Promised Latter Rain Now Being Poured Out on God's Humble People," continued the subtitle. "All along the ages men have been preaching a partial gospel. A part of the gospel remained when the world went into the dark ages." "Now," the article proclaimed, "He is bringing back the Pentecostal baptism to the church."

The second section of the statement of faith outlined the three basic teachings of the Apostolic Faith movement. The first point was that salvation came about through justification by grace through faith in Jesus Christ. This was the classic Protestant position on justification. The second point was that subsequent to

This visual aid read in a counterclockwise direction, helped Aimee Semple McPherson explain various stages in the history of the Church. "Sister," as her followers called her, was committed to a Restorationist reading of history based upon Joel 1:4 and 2:25. She preached her sermon, "Lost and Restored" annually, supported by a group of actors. Those who represented the New Testament Church and those who represent the Church before the throne of God at the end of time are viewed as "The Perfect Church." The actors were robed in white. Those representing the "Dark Ages" were robed in black.

salvation, a second work of grace known as sanctification was not only possible, it was part of God's plan for every Christian. In this work, Christians were made holy. In fact, the "sin nature"—that is, one's propensity always to sin—was thought to be eradicated in this crisis experience of grace. This statement clearly placed the mission within the holiness camp. The third element concerned the baptism in the Spirit. This baptism was not described as a "third work" of grace, but rather as a "gift of power upon the sanctified life." Furthermore, those who received this gift of power would receive the same evidence that the disciples had in Acts 2, when they spoke in new tongues. Only the inclusion of this element in the statement of faith separated the mission from the majority of Wesleyan holiness people around it.

In the third section of the statement, the reader is introduced to the fact that the mission believed healing was available through prayer. This section also spells out a concern aimed at certain people in the holiness movement. It notes that many people in the Wesleyan holiness movement had confused the work of sanctification with baptism in the Holy Spirit. Identifying these two things was, in the eyes of the mission, an error.

In the final section of the statement, Seymour provides a list of what he calls "The Steps unto Heaven." The list includes many technical, theological terms used in the study of systematic theology to describe various aspects of salvation and the Christian life from the moment of conversion through the return of the Lord and the onset of his eternal reign. Salvation and forgiveness come, this section clearly states, through the atonement accomplished only through the shedding of Christ's blood. The Azusa Street Mission strongly emphasized the doctrine of the atonement based on the death, burial, and resurrection of Jesus Christ and the shedding of his blood on the cross.

The existing excerpts from Seymour's sermons reveal that Pastor Seymour preached on a number of topics consistent with the mission's doctrinal statement. Some of them would have been sermon topics popular with the Evening Light Saints, the Wesleyan holiness people, C. P. Jones, C. H. Mason, and Charles Parham. Seymour preached sermons with titles such as "The Precious

Atonement" and "River of Living Water," which deal with salvation. "The Way into the Holiest" and "Sanctified on the Cross" deal with sanctification. One sermon, "Behold the Bridegroom Cometh," points to the Second Coming of Jesus Christ. But the bulk of extant sermon excerpts clearly attributed to Seymour treat "baptism in the Holy Spirit."

Leading through Church Discipline

People within the African American church tradition as well as the larger Wesleyan holiness movement were often expressive in their worship style. Noise was not a problem for them. Their worship could be very loud and exuberant, though typically it was conducted in a fashion deemed orderly. Orderliness, of course, was measured not only by guidelines found in Scripture (1 Cor. 14), but also by cultural criteria. In our next chapter, we will hear about many of the manifestations that were ruled "in order" at the Azusa Street Mission but that might have been understood as "out of order" in another Christian congregation. The Azusa Street Mission may have been the most expressive and vocal congregation in Los Angeles at its time. Occasionally extreme behavior and disorderly manifestations required Pastor Seymour to discipline those who crossed from order into disorder. When he did so, he typically continued to be both gracious and soft-spoken.

Some eyewitnesses remembered Seymour placing a gentle hand on someone's shoulder with the words, "Brother. That is the flesh." The "brother's" action ceased. Others noted correction that came through a look or the intervention of his "calm, strong voice" indicating that it was time to move the service along. I once worshipped in a large black Pentecostal congregation in the Bahamas that was led in this manner. The pastor sat in a large chair on the platform, holding a microphone in his hand. People would begin to sing and shout and dance. The pastor would simply observe what was taking place until he thought it was beginning to get out of hand. Then he would intervene with a simple word, "People," softly at first, then gradually louder. "People." "People!" By the third time he said, "People," the congregants had settled quietly back into their seats and the service moved on. They knew that he held the reigns of order in the congregation.

In the early days of the revival at the mission, Seymour later recounted, "we all used to break out in tongues." In later days, he noted, everyone had "learned to be quieter with this gift." Some may have worried that he was in danger of "quenching" the freedom of the Holy Spirit, but most of them agreed with his position. Even so, there was always room for the occasional "waves" of blessing in which everyone would speak in tongues together. When the preaching began, however, those "waves" would cease. As Seymour wrote, "we want to be obedient to the Word, that everything may be done decently and in order without confusion [1 Cor. 14:40]."

Pastor Seymour believed that effective leadership required a commitment first and foremost to the authority of Scripture. He also believed it was necessary to trust his people to do what was right. He demonstrated that trust repeatedly. He committed himself to embrace the ministry of this community of believers even as he ministered to them. Seymour understood his role in leadership as one of empowering his people for the work of ministry. Just as he had something to offer them, so they had something to offer to him. Ministry flowed in both directions. As a result, his people treated him with respect, love, and open signs of affection. The hugs and kisses this African American pastor accepted even from white women and men in his congregation illustrate his willingness to be vulnerable; they also show the mission faithful's strong commitment to him and to his interracial vision. This was not always understood by outsiders, however. Members of the local press were scandalized by such freedom across racial and gender lines. In their attempt to turn public opinion against him, they reported these activities in glaring headlines.

In July 1906 one newspaper announced, "Religious Fanaticism Creates Wild Scenes." Accompanying this headline were such delectable subtitles as, "Holy Kickers Carry on Mad Orgies," and "At All Night Meetings in Azusa Street Church, Negroes and Whites Give Themselves Over to Strange Outbursts of Zeal." Not to be outdone, another newspaper excitedly cried out, "Women with Men Embrace." Others joined in: "Whites and Blacks Mix in a Religious Frenzy." "Wives Say They Left Husbands to Follow Preacher." "Disgusting Scenes at Azusa Street Church." In summer 1907 one paper raised the specter of "Crazed Girls in Arms of Black Men." Seymour had to deal with these criticisms, and he did so by providing guidelines.

Some people at the mission undoubtedly crossed the line of acceptable behavior. Empowerment had its limits. Just because someone had found spiritual fulfillment at the mission did not mean he or she could unilaterally put an end to previous commitments. "At the height of [one] meeting," a reporter claimed, "a rather prepossessing white woman...testified that she [had] left her husband and children in order to follow the Negro." It is difficult to know exactly what stood behind this testimony and others like it. Some critics of the mission charged it was a nest of "free lovism"[17] or painted William J. Seymour as a marriage breaker.[18] But these claims do not fit Seymour's explicit statements. He expressed deep concern for the sanctity of marriage, a theme that shows up in excerpts from at least two sermons related to marriage. But stories continued to circulate in the Los Angeles press that some women had deserted their husbands in order to spend their time pursuing or spreading the revival.

One reporter complained that Seymour offered no public rebuke to such behavior, and that the people in the mission seem not to have been offended by the testimonies of desertion. Seymour may have given no public rebuke because he understood that most of these women were not speaking in literal terms. They were not guilty of desertion; they were worshipping at the mission because in one sense, their devotion to the Lord was more important to them than anything else at that moment, including their families. The Azusa Street pastor may also have believed it was better to speak to these women privately than embarrass them in public.

In at least one case, a woman did leave her husband to pursue full-time ministry. As a result, Pastor Seymour eventually spoke to the issue at the mission without identifying anyone by name, and his words were published in *The Apostolic Faith*. "Wives have left husbands and gone off claiming that the Lord has called her to do mission work and to leave the little children at home to fare the best they can." One can only wonder whether he had Florence Crawford in mind when he said this, for she left her husband and children in Highland Park and carried the revival on the road. By 1908, her children had joined her in Portland, but she never returned to her husband. But the problem could easily cut the other way, with men deserting their families. Some viewed Frank Bartleman as guilty of this. Pastor Seymour would have none of it. "Dearly beloved, let us respect homes and families," he counseled. When people made their marriage vows, said Seymour, God expected them to keep those vows. Not even an appeal to Luke 14:26, a difficult text in which Jesus said that the person who did not "hate his father, and mother, his wife, and children, his brethren, and sisters, yea and his own life also, he cannot be my disciple," would be sufficient to justify their actions.

The most significant and far-reaching challenge to William J. Seymour's leadership during this period came in November 1906 from Charles F. Parham. As the Azusa Street revival spread from Los Angeles to the smaller suburbs surrounding the city, Seymour wrote to Parham and invited him to come to Los Angeles and lead "one great union revival" beginning at the Azusa Street Mission. With great anticipation, Pastor Seymour advertised Parham's arrival. When Parham arrived, however, he disagreed with some of what Seymour was doing—not least, the full racial integration of the congregation and the roles Seymour had allowed Glenn Cook and others to play. Parham did not approve of the methods they used when they worked with people around the altar. He judged them fanatical. Parham attempted to take over the mission and stop the work of those Seymour had recognized as leaders. Seymour was forced to dismiss Parham before he damaged the work irreparably, but Parham stayed in town long enough to establish a small, competing congregation just blocks from the mission. He appealed to the press not to pay further attention to Seymour's work, but to turn their eyes to him as the true leader of the Apostolic Faith movement. As Parham's aides advertised his meetings first in Los Angeles and then in nearby Whittier, they made strident claims:

We conduct dignified religious services, and have no connection with the sort which is characterized by trances, fits and spasms, jerks, shakes and contortions. We are wholly foreign to the religious anarchy, which marks the Los Angeles Azusa street meetings, and expect to do good in Whittier along proper and profound Christian lines.

When questioned about Parham shortly thereafter, the mission answered in the pages of *The Apostolic Faith*, "He is not the leader of this movement of Azusa Mission." The response continued,

We thought of having him to be our leader, and so stated in our paper, before waiting on the Lord. We can be rather hasty, especially when we are very young in the power of the Holy Spirit. We are just like a baby—full of love—and were willing to accept anyone that had the baptism with the Holy Spirit as our leader. But the Lord commenced settling us down, and we saw that the Lord should be our leader. So we honor Jesus as the great Shepherd of the sheep. He is our model.

Frank Bartleman may have had a point when he called Pastor Seymour the "nominal leader in charge." He wrote,

The Mission had no pope or hierarchy. We were "brethren." We had no human programme. The Lord Himself was leading. We had no priest class, nor priest craft....We did not even have a platform or pulpit in the beginning. All were on a level. The ministers were servants, according to the true meaning of the word.

Bartleman really makes the point that Pastor Seymour provided the "space" for ordinary people to make their contributions. But that provision of space was not accidental. It was planned. It is to the use of that space in the Azusa Street worship services that we now turn our attention.

4

WORSHIP AT THE AZUSA STREET MISSION

෨න

Surrounded by your glory, what will my heart feel?
Will I dance for you Jesus, or in awe of you be still?
Will I stand in your presence, or to my knees will I fall?
Will I sing "Hallelujah"? Will I be able to speak at all?
I can only imagine. I can only imagine.[19]

As we turn our attention to the subject of worship at the Azusa Street Mission, we should understand the circumstances surrounding that worship. The Azusa Street Mission began as a largely African American congregation that people of many other ethnic and racial groups joined, though Bartleman rightly reported that at times the crowd was predominantly white. The building in which they met was "tucked away" in a transitional neighborhood. It was nothing to look at—little more than a poorly whitewashed, burned-out shell with makeshift essentials. On its sawdust-covered dirt floor sat a collection of nail kegs and boards, and an assortment of discarded chairs. Because it lacked insulation and air conditioning, and its ground floor was built of rough-sawn studs with only the outside lumber as walls, during the summer months the building grew intensely hot. With so many perspiring bodies jammed together in such close quarters, the air became so foul at times that, as one reporter sniffed, it was "necessary to stick one's nose under the benches to get a breath of fresh air." At least one visitor insisted that the health department close the mission down because its lack of ventilation was a "violation of the sanitary laws."

To make matters worse, through much of that first summer of 1906 the place was plagued by flies! One reporter painted this graphic picture: "The temple of the Holy Rollers was a stable not so long ago, and the big lazy flies, separated from the friendly horses, still haunt its dim recesses in a disconsolate sort of way and alight sickly on neck and faces, refusing to budge until they are rudely slapped off." Another cowered, "Swarms of flies, attracted by the vitiated atmosphere, buzzed throughout the room, and it

This photograph of the Azusa Street Mission highlights in graphic relief its rustic character. Please note that the inverted "V" stairway, which led to the original sanctuary on the second floor is missing. The tracery windows have been replaced, although it is possible to see a vague outline above the upper right hand window on the Mission's front wall. The roof, which was quite steep, is now flat. The sidewalk is a wooden affair that drops off rather steeply at points, into an unpaved street. Women sometimes complained about the mud in the streets during the rainy season. The man at the front corner of the Mission is likely Pastor Seymour, with his Bible tucked in his arm. This photograph probably dates from late 1906 or early 1907.

was a continual fight for protection." Still another complained that while some prayed, others slapped away the persistent "stinging flies."

In spite of all of these problems—the substandard facilities, intense heat, lack of ventilation, and swarms of flies—people came by the thousands. Many of them came because they believed that God was doing something new in that place and they wanted to be a part of it. And many of these went away satisfied that their quest had been rewarded.

Worship is what we do when we encounter God. The words of the worship song with which I began this chapter imagine a future encounter with God in heaven. Yet all of the responses described in those lyrics could be found among the thousands who worshipped at Azusa Street. The intensity of their encounter with God led many at the mission to respond in ways that before their encounter, they could "only imagine." It was a life-changing moment, a transformative time that produced a range of responses. There were those who, "surrounded by [His] glory" at the mission, broke into dance. Others jumped, or stood with hands outstretched, or sang or shouted with all the gusto they could muster. Others were so full of awe when they encountered God that their knees buckled— they fell to the floor, "slain in the Spirit." Some spoke, rapid-fire, in a tongue they did not know, while others were struck entirely speechless.

In 1978 Samuel Terrien wrote a thought-provoking book titled *The Elusive Presence*.[20] I believe it has some bearing on such responses. After reviewing the ways the people of ancient Israel encountered God, Terrien concluded that their encounters were generally of two types. Those who lived far from Jerusalem and the temple gathered from time to time at various sites or shrines in order to hear the Scriptures read. They encountered God primarily through the *ear*. They encountered God when he spoke to them at Sinai (Exod. 20:1–17). They came to *hear* God through the words of the Torah (Deut. 6:4–9; Josh. 8:34) when it was read to them, or through the words of the prophets when they spoke. These people's response to that encounter with God was to live and to act according to what they had heard. They went about doing good in the name of Yahweh.

On the other hand, those who lived in or near Jerusalem and gathered regularly in the temple encountered God primarily through the *eye*. As the worship service unfolded in that majestic place, as incense burned and priests chanted, while choirs sang and cymbals crashed, they could close their eyes and in their minds they could envision God, who sat in their midst on his glorious throne. Either they were awed by God's holy presence much as Isaiah was at the time of King Uzziah's death (Isa. 6:1–13) or they responded to Yahweh's presence with exuberant praise as did the psalmists. Within the temple at Jerusalem, there were choirs and orchestras, trumpets, tambourines and cymbals, singing, clapping, shouting, and dancing.[21] Worship in the temple was anything but boring! It involved the senses of sight and sound, of touch and smell.

In spite of the differences in the ways they encountered God, there is no question that both groups encountered God. One group *heard* God while the other group *saw* him. One group may have stood or sat silently as God spoke, while the other burst into what some might describe as ecstatic worship in response to God's presence among them. But the important thing to remember is that they seem to have encountered and responded to God in very different ways—ways that may have seemed foreign to or even mutually exclusive of each other.

The divine encounter that people experienced at the mission had a profound effect upon them and the ways they responded to it. Worship at Azusa Street was often more like the worship that took place in Jerusalem than it was like the worship of the rest of Israel. For that matter, it was more like the worship that took place in Jerusalem than it was like the worship that took place in most other Christian congregations in 1906 Los Angeles. While most congregations in Los Angeles could be viewed as encountering God through their spiritual "ear," the people of the Azusa Street Mission clearly encountered God through their spiritual "eye."

Many people at Azusa Street responded to God's presence in

much the same way that David did when he brought the ark of the covenant back to Jerusalem (2 Sam. 6:12–23; 1 Chr. 15:25–29). David led Israel's worship with sacrifices, accompanied by an orchestra of lyres, harps, bronze cymbals, tambourines, trumpets, and castanets. He did not respond to the presence of God in a silent, "reverent," meditative, awe-filled, intellectual mode such as could be found at Los Angeles's First Methodist, or First Presbyterian, or First Congregational Church. David's worship of his Lord was not simply or even primarily cerebral. The expression of worship, the response to the Lord's presence that came from David as he "danced before the Lord with all his might," rose from his very soul. It was primal! It was passionate! It was exuberant! It was filled with emotion and feeling! It touched his whole body, from head to toe. It was not limited only to his mind. Indeed, it was quite like the worship that many African American slaves enjoyed when left to themselves, with dance and shout, rhythm and song, possession and falling.

One obvious lesson to be drawn from the incident of David dancing before the Lord, however, was that his wife, Michel, did not understand his response. She despised him for it. Similarly, William J. Seymour may have led his congregation to "dance" before the Lord with all their might, but many local pastors and reporters despised him for it. The possibility of public ridicule, then, could be added to the list of things that might have kept people away from worshipping at the Azusa Street Mission.

This does not mean that people at the mission never enjoyed more silent, "reverent" times of worship—sensing the presence of God moving among them and being still and reflective. They did. Many services began with people quietly entering the mission, finding a personal space, kneeling, and pouring out their hearts before the Lord, often in whispers. There were many times when, as Frank Bartleman reminds us, a kind of "holy hush" fell across the congregation. And there were many times when worshippers were so overcome in their encounter with God that they were left completely speechless, with nothing more than moans or groans or even silence (some called it trance) to express their feelings.

This cartoon was published in Los Angeles, California, at the top center of page 1, just below the masthead of *The Evening News*, July 23, 1906. The title, "Summer Solstice Sees Strenuous Sects Sashaying" is clearly a tongue-twister intended to ridicule speaking in tongues. July 22 was the summer solstice, the longest day of the year. The cartoon characters demonstrate the derogatory names being hurled at the people of the Mission. The language of "tongues" surrounding the woman at the lower left, ranges from Oopsquee [Pig Latin] to *e pluribus unum* [Latin] with ditties and noises as well. The poem at the bottom of the cartoon takes a shot at the extensive role that women legitimately played in the Azusa Street meetings, based upon the Mission's understanding of Joel 2:28–29. The reference to Paul, on the other hand, is to 1 Corinthians 14:34a "Let your women keep silence in the church," the position of most traditional churches at that time. This cartoon not only ridiculed the Mission, it acted as a form of free advertisement as well.

Not every manifestation or phenomenon at the Azusa Street Mission came from the Holy Spirit, however. Churches that encourage congregational participation in the service through times of personal sharing and testimony; that allow for personal emotional expression such as crying, shouting, or laughing; that recognize claims to giftedness and provide space for the exercise of some of the more spectacular charisms such as speaking in tongues or prophesying; and that claim a tangible, immanent presence of God in their midst in much the way that Azusa Street did, often attract people in need. Some come and find healing. Others come to manipulate, to make themselves seem important, or even to take control. Pastor Seymour and much of his congregation were well acquainted with what they understood to be things done "in the flesh." It was a balancing act that Seymour led—one in which fanaticism and wildfire were not likely to displace genuine worship, but the danger was always present, and it was often most present in spectacular screams or gyrating gymnastics. Such activities had to be weighed in their context to be judged properly, but mission leaders indeed weighed and tested them before they accepted them.

In this chapter I will draw upon some long-forgotten news articles as well as the words of some participants at Azusa Street in order to give us a sense of what the services were like there. What was it that drew people to this humble place, in spite of all the hurdles they had to overcome? What took place in the services facilitated under Pastor Seymour's leadership at the mission? How did those who worshipped there respond to the presence of God among them? How did it affect what they did once they left?

The Uniqueness of Azusa Street's Meetings

Like most other Christian congregations in Los Angeles, the Azusa Street Mission offered regular services. These services differed from those offered by the majority of Los Angeles' congregations in two respects. First, Azusa Street's services ran seven days a week. To be sure, Sunday was the biggest day, but hundreds attended services throughout the week. Services were scheduled daily at 10 A.M., at 3 P.M., and again at 7:30 P.M. But as one person observed, "Meetings continue every day with seekers at every service." Second, as this observer added, "the three meetings run very near together." Despite the posted schedule, the services at the mission often ran into one another not only hour to hour, but day to day—melding, almost, into one long, three-year service through the course of the revival. People simply lost track of time as they entered into the presence of the Lord. The African American preacher Mother Cotton, for example, described what in her mind had become a single, seamless meeting, running "for three years, day and night, without a break."

Looking at the basic outline of the mission's worship life, it would be difficult to conclude that the services were anything other than ordinary Christian services. The mission acted in accordance with its published statement of beliefs, a statement largely consistent with those of other churches within the Wesleyan holiness tradition. It practiced Christian baptism by immersion in water using the traditional Trinitarian formula. It offered the Lord's Supper regularly, sometimes accompanied by the washing of the "saints'" feet in the manner of many Anabaptist and Wesleyan holiness congregations. It embraced strict standards of "holiness," viewing many things practiced by the wider culture as "worldly" and thus to be avoided. It engaged in evangelistic and missionary activities, and it provided opportunities for visitors to encounter God in fresh ways.

While the mission valued and celebrated spontaneity, every service also included the predictable. There were public prayers, singing, testimonies, preaching or teaching from the Bible, and time spent around the altar or in one of the upstairs rooms in personal prayer. Like most Christians, members of the Azusa Street Mission believed that God could heal the sick. But they did not invoke such abstract doctrines as providence or divine sovereignty to support this belief. Instead, they viewed these explanations as being, all too often, excuses for those with "too little faith." All one needed, they believed, were simple childlike faith and persistent prayer to a loving God who cared greatly about the physical and spiritual suffering of individuals.

The one teaching that set the mission apart theologically from most other Los Angeles congregations was its doctrine of baptism in the Holy Spirit. But several major cultural differences, some with important theological implications, also separated the mission from many other congregations. The first was the freedom it granted all people, regardless of race, gender, or station in life, to be treated as equals. Anyone could play an active role in worship; no one was ruled out by virtue of gender, color, class, or previous condition of servitude. That was not the case in most other churches, which left the liturgy to the professional clergy.

The mission also proved culturally distinctive in its assessment of which actions were and which were not consistent with good church "order." The mission allowed enormous leeway in its judgment of legitimate emotional expressions in worship, although that was not altogether new, nor was it without limits. Many of the expressions approved at Azusa Street could also be found within traditional African American centers of folk worship—especially in the rural South—though they were largely absent from the more sophisticated black congregations of Los Angeles. These congregations, it appears, were more interested in assimilating to the area's dominant Anglo culture than they were in preserving the older communal ways of their African American heritage.

This cultural distinctive caused many to call the mission "the old negro church." More than one reporter complained of "scenes that duplicate those of the negro revival meetings of the South." One reporter went so far as to say that he was surprised that "any respectable white person would attend such meetings," because their worship so closely resembled African American worship. But this didn't seem to stop some whites, the reporter continued, from "casting in their lot with the negro ranters." Such factors have led historian Eileen Southern to claim, and I think rightly so, that all Pentecostal worship in the United States is in some sense the direct "heir to the shouts, hand-clapping and foot-stomping, jubilee songs, and ecstatic seizures of the plantation 'praise houses.'"[22]

While the mission was led by an African American pastor, dominated by an African American membership, and heavily influenced by African American worship patterns, it quickly developed into a multiethnic and multiracial congregation. It would be unfair to claim that the *only* influence that played a role at the mission was the African American one—non–African-Americans did bring their own gifts and experiences. The revivalist camp meeting tradition so prevalent among whites (as well as blacks) on the American frontier clearly contributed much to the mission's music, preaching, and prayer life. The more radical worship services in various Wesleyan holiness congregations in Los Angeles had given plenty of room for the white folk that participated in them to shout or to fall on the floor as they were "slain in the Spirit." Recent Russian and Armenian Molokan immigrants already practiced the unusual jumping and chanting also found at the mission.

Worship at the Azusa Street Mission differed in this: when expressions from this variety of cultures were brought together in one place, something new transpired that traditional Christians in Los Angeles—indeed, the city as a whole—was ill prepared to embrace. This was a revival unlike any other the city of Los Angeles had ever seen. No wonder some perceptive skeptic had written, on the day the mission received its first notice in the *Los Angeles Daily Times*, "Another new religion, in Los Angeles, of course." This certainly seemed a new phenomenon—this seemingly uninhibited mixture of African Americans, Latinos, Armenians, Russians, Swedes, Germans, Italians, Chinese, Japanese, Native Americans, and other ethnic groups who found space among them for the bountiful presence of ecstatic manifestations such as speaking in tongues, prophesying, claims of dreams and visions, trances, healings, exorcism, and falling "in the Spirit."

Worship through Prayer

I saw, too, that they had a wonderful spirit of prayer upon them; I never had seen such people to pray. Such liberty and unction in prayer, and such continuance in prayer; and that, not merely at

public meetings and altar services; but in cottage prayer meetings, in all-nights of prayer, and in the smaller gatherings of two
and three, how remarkably have I found the spirit of prayer and
intercession upon them.

GEORGE B. STUDD

ANYONE who reads the accounts of worship at the Azusa Street
Mission will conclude that prayer was probably the centerpiece of
the revival. It is the medium through which all other activities at
the mission must be viewed—from singing to personal testimony
to preaching to time spent at the altar before and after any service. Pastor William J. Seymour provided the norm for the whole
revival when he reportedly sat with his head tucked into the
makeshift pulpit, praying, while other things went on about him.
William J. Seymour was a man of prayer. He dedicated himself to
pray for hours each day prior to the coming of the revival, and
while he attended many of the meetings held under his leadership, he attempted to continue this discipline of prayer. Prayer
and meditation on the Scriptures gave him the thoughts he
desired to share in his sermons. Prayer—especially spontaneous
and boisterous prayer—seemed to bathe all the events of the
revival.

While prayer played an extremely important role in the worship life of the Azusa Street congregation, very few of the participants have left any kind of journal recording their prayer lives,
and even fewer have done any reflection on the role that prayer
played. That is one reason the testimony left by Frank Bartleman
is so significant: he did both. On the other hand, Pastor Seymour
did neither, so far as we know. We do not know how long he
prayed each day once the revival began. We do not know whether
he prayed in tongues for any extended periods. We do not even
know what role praying in tongues played at the mission—
whether it was seen as providing any intercessory role, or
whether it was simply viewed merely as "evidence" of baptism in
the Spirit, as means of "spiritual song," and as gift that required
interpretation. Most theories Pentecostals now hold about the

role of tongues in the Christian life, they developed since the revival. But one thing is clear: prayer played a central role in the revival. Most reports show this amply.

On one occasion the police intervened at 1:30 A.M. to close down a service so noisy that it was preventing the neighbors from sleeping. The next evening, the service began with a "lengthy prayer" that was "offered up in the hope that the guardians of the public quiet might be pardoned for their grievous sin." A reporter chuckled as two patrolmen, listening to the prayer, "nudged one another" when they heard it.

We see just how important prayer was to the revival in the special rooms its leaders set apart for certain types of prayer. The altar at the center of the sanctuary on the ground floor shows us that the mission considered prayer necessary in matters related to salvation, sanctification, and baptism in the Spirit. The "upper room" was provided for those who wished to pursue their baptism in the Spirit in what can only be described as "tarrying meetings," that is, extended sessions of prayer that might last anywhere from several hours to several days. The room set aside for prayer on behalf of the sick and infirm also illustrates the mission's commitment to prayer, as does the presence of "altar workers" at mission worship services.

Charles Parham condemned these altar workers when he visited the mission. He described them as "over-zealous, ignorant helpers" who had laid hands on those who were seeking their baptism in the Spirit, jerking their chins, massaging their throats, and telling them to repeat certain sounds over and over or faster and faster until they spoke in tongues. "We cannot afford to be deceived in this. O, how many have been deceived by the Azuza [sic] mess," Parham later groused,

and by those workers who get the poor seekers to yell "glory, glory," until they can no longer say it in English, but in a half hypnotized condition, they cry, "glug, glug," or some other peculiar sound, and one more is counted to have his Pentecost, when only worked into a frenzy.

Pastoral problems in such practices may seem obvious now, but as Parham watched these well-meaning altar workers, he concluded that their mechanical techniques did nothing but elicit counterfeit results.

Parham was further piqued by Seymour's failure to segregate worshippers by race or gender, either at the altar or in the "upper room" where people tarried together in prayer. While a placard nailed to the wall of the upper room commanded, "No talking above a whisper," the commotion caused by the shouts, groans, and pleas of the writhing wrestlers-with-God would have drowned out virtually any conversation. Men and women of all "colors" gathered together there, beseeching God for their baptism in the Holy Spirit. Worshippers exchanged "holy kisses" and hugs across both gender and racial lines.

Parham was scandalized by these things. He could not tolerate seeing a black man aiding a white woman in prayer, especially when it involved any form of touching. In their ecstatic state, he claimed, they engaged in unseemly activities that no person in his or her right mind would tolerate. As he later recalled it,

> men and women, whites and blacks, knelt together or fell across one another; frequently, a white woman, perhaps of wealth and culture, could be seen thrown back in the arms of a big "buck nigger," and held tightly thus as she shivered and shook in freak imitation of Pentecost. Horrible, awful shame! Many of the missions on the Pacific coast are permeated with this foolishness, and, in fact, it follows the Azuza [sic] work everywhere.

Whatever we might think of Parham's racial stereotypes or even of his criticisms, we can see that multitudes were intent upon praying at the mission. On the first anniversary of the outpouring of the Spirit on the faithful at the Asberry home, Seymour set apart three days of "fasting and prayer" at the mission with the hope that it would provide "more power in the meetings." The Lord answered, *The Apostolic Faith* claimed, as souls were slain all about the altar the second night. We have felt an increase of power every night. At this writing in the office, the power in the meeting is felt. The heavenly anthem is heard and the shouts and praises of the saints. All the afternoon there has been an altar service and souls coming through. A brother came this morning saying God had showed him that self was creeping in. Another said God had been showing him the same all night. The workers all got down before God and the power fell. This is the way of victory to go down before God. The great need is prayer.

As the New Year began in 1908, prayer was still on the mind of the staff, though the editor of the mission's newspaper thought it important to remind the reader that prayer and the study of Scripture went hand in hand. "O may God help us all this year to keep prayed up and read up and sung up. If there is too much reading of the Word without prayer, you get too argumentative, and if you pray too much without reading you get fanatical," she wrote.

Prayer seems to have been a constant concern among the mission staff. Clara Lum reported, "There is a spirit of harmony and unity in the office work. We feel the power of God as we write off these blessed reports. The offices are places of prayer and praise and the power of God comes down on the workers as they fold the paper." The staff gathered regularly in the dining room of a small cottage that stood behind the mission on the Azusa Street property. During the first year, Lucy Farrow, who had also been a professional cook, used the cottage to prepare and serve meals to the staff. People were healed, slain in the Spirit, and baptized in the Spirit there. "The dining room is a blessed place," Lum wrote. "The power comes down so upon the workers that we can scarcely eat. We sing, speak in tongues, and praise God at the table."

Prayer for healing also became a staple of the mission. People were healed "every day" in both the main worship space and the upstairs room set apart for the sick. *The Apostolic Faith* recorded one incident in which a man identified only as a "rough Indian," an indigenous man from Mexico, laid his hands upon Mrs. S. P. Knapp when she complained of having consumption. Before the service ended, she testified of her healing. The next day her father, Mr. Frank Gail, wrote to the mission expressing his conviction that she had been healed through the prayer of this otherwise nameless "Indian."

"Last November in the Azusa Mission," testified Mrs. A. L. Tritt, a visitor from Montana, "one of the saints laid hands on me and prayed for my healing, and the Lord has healed me of that awful disease eczema. O, hallelujah! It pays to believe in the whole Gospel." Such testimonies of God's healings through the laying on of hands became regular fare at the mission. A portion of some services was given over to excerpts from letters of those who had been touched by reading *The Apostolic Faith*, read aloud by Clara Lum. These times only served to strengthen the resolve of many to continue to pray. G. B. Cashwell testified that when he came into a service where Clara Lum was reading these excerpts to the people, "I began to speak in tongues and praise God."

Prayer for healing was not always done through the laying on of hands; sometimes it came through the instrument of anointed handkerchiefs. *The Apostolic Faith* reported that one of the women who had participated in the meetings on North Bonnie Brae Street, the African American Sallie Traynor, prayed over such a handkerchief when a woman brought it into the healing room. "The Spirit came upon her in great power and she prayed in tongues, and kissed the handkerchief three times, as the Spirit seemed to lead her. It was sent with a prayer and the brother was immediately healed."

Prayers answered through such instruments inspired the mission's regular worship life. *The Apostolic Faith* recorded that testimonies to these healings often led to periods of praise. "As I laid the handkerchief on my forehead," wrote Viney McNall, "I received such a clear witness that the work was done. . . . O how I praise God for the great Physician that can cure all manner of sickness." "Received the handkerchief all right and God sent two distinct waves of power over us," wrote a woman identified only as S. A. from Morrisburg, Ontario. "All glory be to God who does the work," commented the editor. "She has taken no medicine, but is healed by faith. Hallelujah!" Mrs. A. L. Werhan of Lamont, Oklahoma, wrote, "Dear ones in Christ: I write to tell you that God healed me before the handkerchief got back to me. I praise His dear name forever." And Mrs. M. J. Wilson of Portsmouth, Virginia, wrote, "Glory to God for the blest handkerchief. I was healed before it got here. I felt the prayers of the saints as God healed me. As I took the handkerchief out of the letter, it seemed that the Lord poured out a blessing on me."

When the mission congregation heard of these and other testimonies sent in by people around the country, they felt attached to an ever-growing movement of revival. Such testimonies also gave them a reason to continue to pray and to worship God for who he was as well as for what he was pouring out upon them. Mission faithful often prayed together, though few of their prayers were recorded. And as one reporter wrote, "No one in particular led in prayer. They all prayed. They all made different prayers and the confusion of tongues had the tower of Babel backed off the boards." To the outsider, it must have seemed like the situation described by the apostle Paul in 1 Corinthians 14:23.[23] Still, J. H. Sparks would write, "Sunday evening [April 5, 1908] found the house packed from door to door and such a volume of praise as went up to the shining courts; it seemed the angels and archangels must have rejoiced together with us." Glenn Cook concurred, "We were saturated with the spirit of love and prayer and the days passed all too swiftly." Frank Bartleman concluded, "There was a presence of God with us, through prayer, we could depend on."

Worship through Song

And of their spirit of praise, worship and adoration, I will only say that though I have lived and laboured with spiritual workers and very prayerful people in many places for twenty years, I have never seen such praise and such worship as amongst these Pentecostal people—never.

GEORGE B. STUDD

WHEN the mission opened its doors to the public in April 1906, it had no hymnals, and for several months it included no musical instruments. *The Apostolic Faith* proudly reported that no instruments were needed! The people were content to sing with nothing more than the rhythmic accompaniment of hands clapping or slapping against thighs, or feet stomping, and the rich harmonies produced as different ones sang out in parts.

Individuals, most often African American women, simply led out in song, drawing from the repertoire of hymns and songs they had learned in their various home churches. They did so spontaneously, when they believed that the Spirit was moving upon them to do so. As one reporter wrote, "Someone happened to want to sing a song and started it. Every one followed. If one didn't want to sing the song then on the program he sang some other one. It was all the same." As one reporter described a July 1906 service, "Another negro started 'I am washed in the blood,' and a genuine camp-meeting time followed, with clapping of hands and stomping of feet."

Little separated the worship at the Azusa Street Mission from that of many African American and Wesleyan holiness groups when it came both to the forms that the music took and the selection of the hymns sung. Not only did they use the same basic style of singing, they sang many of the same songs. Among the favorite hymns given voice at the mission was Francis Bottome's "The Comforter Has Come!" set to music by William J. Kirkpatrick. Bottome had written this hymn as a reflection on Jesus' promise recorded in John 14:16. It quickly became a kind of theme song, sung at virtually every meeting.

The Comforter Has Come!

O spread the tidings round, wherever man is found,
Wherever human hearts and human woes abound;
Let ev'ry Christian tongue proclaim the joyful sound:
The Comforter has come!

The long, long night is past, the morning breaks at last,
And hushed the dreadful wail and fury of the blast,
As o'er the golden hills the day advances fast!
The Comforter has come!

Lo, the great King of kings, with healing in his wings,
To ev'ry captive soul a full deliverance brings;
And through the vacant cells the song of triumph rings;
The Comforter has come!

O boundless love Divine! How shall this tongue of mine
To wond'ring mortals tell the matchless grace divine—
That I, a child of hell, should in His image shine!
The Comforter has Come!

Sing, till the echoes fly above the vaulted sky,
And all the saints above to all below reply,
In strains of endless love, the song that ne'er will die"
The Comforter has come!

Refrain

The Comforter has come, The Comforter has come!
The Holy Ghost from heav'n, the Father's promise giv'n
O spread the tidings 'round wherever man is found
The Comforter has come.

Many of Azusa Street's worshippers had sung this hymn as holiness believers. Now they read its words with new eyes, reinterpreting the message based on John 14:16. Now they celebrated not so much the comfort as the empowerment of the Spirit.

Other favorite songs featured the blood of Jesus. Among them were songs such as "Under the Blood," "The Blood Is All My Plea," "Are You Washed in the Blood?" "Saved by the Blood of the Crucified One," and "Hallelujah! 'Tis Done.'"

In a 1974 interview Lawrence F. Catley told of singing "This Is Like Heaven to Me" and "Where Jesus Is, 'Tis Heaven There" at the mission. Then he broke into a rendition of

Oh, the blood, the blood, the blood done sign my name.
Oh, the blood, the blood, the blood done sign my name.
Oh, the blood, oh, the blood, the blood done sign my name.
Oh, the blood done sign my name.

"They used to get 'happy' over that song," he laughed.[24]

The mission faithful sang "All I Need," by C. P. Jones. Other favorites included "Beautiful, Beckoning Hands," "God Be with You 'Til We Meet Again," "Heavenly Sunlight," and "Where the Healing Waters Flow" by holiness hymnist, preacher, and healing minister R. Kelso Carter. Martha Neale, a woman who attended the 1907 Apostolic Faith camp meeting in the Arroyo Seco, reported that on June 15, 1907, the saints gathered at the mission's camp meeting sang "The Name of Jesus Is So Sweet." Henry Prentiss made it clear that they all knew "Oh, How I Love Jesus." Lillian Garr and Florence Crawford sang, "Jesus, Savior, Pilot Me" as a duet during one service.

The Apostolic Faith also printed a number of songs that were probably sung at the mission. F. E. Hill, the former pastor of the Second Church of the Nazarene in Los Angeles, contributed a song titled "Baptized with the Holy Ghost." Another song featured in the mission paper was "Jesus Is Coming"—written by F. A. Graves with music by Thomas Hezmalhalch. Graves had been part of Dowie's Zion, Illinois, experiment and Hezmalhalch had held more than one meeting there. The mission, which emphasized the Second Coming, supported this new hymn as a way of conveying an important doctrinal and pastoral reminder to the faithful.

Bessie Cummings, a young African American girl who left the Azusa Street Mission with her family in May 1907 to pursue foreign missionary service in Liberia, was playing the piano when she invited her mother to join her. Bessie began to sing while her mother recorded, with pencil and paper, a reflection based on Mark 16:15. Mrs. Cummings then wrote a verse of her own, and together they completed yet another song titled "Jesus Is Coming." It was published in *The Apostolic Faith* after the two of them, Emma and Bessie, sang the composition at the mission. "The words and music were both from heaven," an anonymous reporter wrote, "and it is inspiring to hear it sung."

Newer music that emerges in any generation is often difficult to integrate with the hymnody that has preceded it. Martin Luther's attempt to introduce a new and truly German hymnody into

Germany's Protestant churches raised the eyebrows of those reared on the Latin mass. New England Puritans resisted the hymns of Isaac Watts when he first wrote them, some charging him with heresy for changing the ways they sang (they had limited their singing to the words of the Psalter). Much the same could be said of the hymns of John and Charles Wesley when they put words to the music of British folk tunes at the end of the Methodist Revival.

It is always difficult to maintain the balance between carrying the tradition of the church forward through music and reshaping that tradition for a new generation. Frequently those who fight to keep things the way they think they have always been are ignorant of past church hymnody. As well, they often either cannot embrace the forward-looking vision necessary to communicate the tradition to the next generation or will not make the necessary transition to accommodate the needs and interests of the young. On the other hand, those who sacrifice the essence of the tradition on the altar of relevance jeopardize the very source of their own spiritual life—and risk breaking continuity with the past, producing yet another gospel!

The often astute Frank Bartleman reflected thoughtfully on the nature of the "music war" that resulted among some at the Azusa Street Mission. Every new revival has a tendency to produce changes in the music of the church, he observed. That is to be expected. The Azusa Street revival was not exceptional at this point. The mission's faithful sang traditional hymnody, learned new hymns and choruses, and even embraced the new form that became known as "singing in the Spirit" (harmonious singing in tongues).

Bartleman did see plenty of room for innovation both in the songs that were sung and the way the singing took place, even though his personal preference was for a continuation of the spontaneous worship and song that he saw modeled at the beginning of the Azusa Street revival. He vehemently condemned any worship singing ordered by the intervention of some leader who would direct the "song service," because he believed such intervention resulted in worship that was forced or contrived. From his perspective, it was like invoking a law that all people must attend church under sanction, and then expecting them to worship God freely of their own accord.

Bartleman was convinced that some of the leaders of the revival were actually quenching the Spirit because they moved from hymns in the corporate memory or "singing in tongues," to singing from published hymnals and pre-selected songs led by designated song leaders. From his perspective, these practices were nothing more than human attempts to control people who would prefer to embrace the spontaneity of the Spirit—indeed, they looked to him like attempts to control the Spirit himself. "It was like murdering the Spirit, and most painful to some of us," he complained. Then he lamented, "the tide was too strong against us." Of course, Bartleman was attacking more than the wills of the mission leaders when he criticized the mission's music. But he was surprisingly open to the newer music, provided that the tunes were not particularly "jazzy." These were, after all, songs given to the faithful by the Holy Spirit.

"Singing in the Spirit"

There was a most remarkable incident of the sweetest singing I ever heard by about half a dozen women, all in unknown tongues, in which at intervals one voice would die away in very plaintive strains, while the others carried on the song. Then the former would break out in rapid strong language, filled with unction, and others would give tones as of singing in the distance. This was most enchanting, and filled with tender love.

This singing was led by Miss [Jennie Evans] Moore, who never could sing before, until she was baptized with the Spirit.

WILLIAM F. MANLEY

"SINGING IN THE SPIRIT" received the nearly unanimous praise of all who heard it. Frank Bartleman repeatedly gave his imprimatur to this unique manifestation. It went by various names—"singing in the Spirit," "singing in tongues," the "heavenly anthem," the "heavenly chorus" or the "heavenly choir," and the "chorus of 'tongues.'" The faithful believed that this music was inspired completely by the Holy

Spirit; they found a scriptural basis for it in the apostle Paul's words of
1 Corinthians 14:15, "I will sing with my spirit, but I will also sing with
my mind." Charles Parham, on the other hand, saw nothing spiritual
about it. He snorted that it was nothing more than "a modification of
the Negro chanting of the Southland."

I have been struck by how similar the mission's singing in
tongues was to the descriptions I have read of the "Negro chant"
prevalent in the African American "praise houses" during and
after the time of slavery. I would not be surprised at all to find that
singing in the Spirit is deeply rooted in the African American past
as it emerged at the mission. Whatever it was, however, this Spirit-
inspired singing often emerged without words, or else in languages that the congregation did not understand—that is, in
tongues. It was as spontaneous an intervention as anyone might
imagine. At times it was sung to familiar tunes; on other occasions
new tunes seemed to be spontaneously generated. Even the skeptical press employed adjectives like "sweet," "plaintive," "ravish-
ing," "unearthly," "enchanting," and "rapturous" to describe it.

As early as the meeting in the Asberry home, Jennie Evans Moore
had sung in tongues. "On April 9, 1906," she would later write,

> I sang under the power of the Spirit in many languages, the
> interpretation both words and music which I had never before
> heard, and in the home where the meeting was being held, the
> Spirit led me to the piano, where I played and sang under inspi-
> ration, althought [sic] I had not learned to play.

Many reports single out African American women as the primary movers in this phenomenon, though singing in the Spirit was
limited neither to African Americans nor to women. One newspaper reporter sat spellbound as an African American woman began
to sing. "The Chorus of 'tongues,' while likewise unintelligible was
weirdly beautiful," he began.

> A colored woman with the voice of a Patti began singing in a
> tongue which probably never before was heard. Her voice was

joined by a contralto of great depth and richness, but singing another tongue. Others took up the chant, each after her own tune and 'tongues,' till the building was vocal with the tones of golden mellowness. They say that the Holy Ghost tunes their voices. During this manifestation several who had prayed for the coveted gift fell upon their faces in frenzied appeal and acted otherwise after the manner of persons obsessed.[25]

We do not know whose voice rang out like a "Patti" as hearts were poured out before God in song, but it might easily have been Jennie Evans Moore, since she played a continuing role in the musical life of the mission. "Singing in tongues" would become prominent at the mission, at times continuing for up to a half hour, though more usually for about half that time.

Although the mission faithful readily accepted this phenomenon, surprisingly few of its early participants reflected on its nature, meaning, or significance. The editor of *The Apostolic Faith* observed that "people are melted to tears in hearing this singing. It is the harmony of heaven and the Holy Ghost puts music in the voices that are untrained." A. W. Orwig, a former Methodist minister who visited the Azusa Street Mission where he was baptized in the Spirit, wrote,

It was not something that could be repeated at will, but supernaturally given for each special occasion and was one of the most indisputable evidences of the presence of the power of God. Perhaps nothing so greatly impressed the people as this singing; at once inspiring a holy awe, or a feeling of indescribable wonder, especially if the hearers were in devout attitude.

Many eyewitnesses were indeed awestruck by what they saw and heard when the faithful sang in tongues at the mission. Arthur Osterberg recalled,

We would all sing a song or chorus, and everyone would join in. Then choruses would break out here and there, and some would be singing in tongues and some in English—and the harmony was wonderful. Once in a while a soprano voice would leap out and you would hear it above the whole congregation. Then it would be mingled with other voices and it all formed a beautiful harmony. Then the singing would stop short and everyone would start praising the Lord, some speaking in an undertone in tongues, some clapping their hands in praise to God. No one who has ever heard a congregation singing under the unction of the Spirit could ever forget or mistake it.[26]

During the opening year of the revival, Frank Bartleman reflected on this spine-tingling phenomenon. "Sometimes," he wrote,

it is expressed without words, sometimes in praises to God. Often it is a chant by one or two, or more. But the greatest effect seems to be produced when suddenly in the meeting a dozen, or perhaps a score, will burst forth in the most beautiful chords, all in harmony, and all pitches of voice. . . . It is under direct inspiration of the Spirit, and can in no wise be produced at any other time. None can take part in this but those who have received their gift. They treasure it most sacredly. It is one of the most effective exercises of the Spirit in the present work. . . . It surpasses and defies the best trained choir of our land for harmony and feeling. This has been declared by most competent judges of voice culture. Besides this, the rapture the performer undergoes, especially when a number are singing in unison of spirit is beyond description. I speak this most humbly from personal experience. It is the very foretaste of the rapture that we soon shall realize when He shall call for us.

Twenty years later, while writing his memories of the revival, Frank Bartleman once again returned to the subject of "singing in tongues."

When I first heard it in the meetings a great hunger entered my soul to receive it. I felt it would exactly express my pent up feelings. I had not yet spoken in "tongues." But the "new song" captured me. It was a gift from God of high order, and appeared among us soon after the "Azusa" work began. No one had preached it. The Lord had sovereignly bestowed it, with the outpouring of the "residue of oil," the "Latter Rain" baptism of the Spirit. It was exercised, as the Spirit moved the possessors, either in solo fashion, or by the company. It was sometimes without words, other times in "tongues." The effect was wonderful on the people. It brought a heavenly atmosphere as though the angels themselves were present and joining with us. And possibly they were. It seemed to still criticism and opposition, and was hard for even wicked men to gainsay or ridicule. . . . In fact it was the very breath of God, playing on human heart strings, or human vocal cords. The notes were wonderful in sweetness, volume and duration. In fact they were oftimes [sic] humanly impossible. It was "singing in the Spirit."

"Singing in the Spirit" accomplished more than an expression of worship, however. It also provided a bridge that brought Russian and Armenian Molokans into the mission—among them the Shakarian and Mushegian families. These families arrived in Los Angeles in the 1905 emigration. The Molokans commonly practiced a kind of "sing-song" prayer, a form of vocal prayer and praise that resembled "singing in the Spirit." Walking down San Pedro Street in 1906, Demos Shakarian, grandfather of the Demos Shakarian who would later found the Full Gospel Businessmen's Association, and his brother-in-law, Magardich Mushegian, passed the Azusa Street Mission. As they drew near, they heard sounds of praying, singing, and speaking in tongues coming from the mission—expressions that they identified as similar to their own. The single phenomenon of "singing in tongues" convinced Demos to embrace the mission as a place his family could worship. From the moment he heard it, he concluded that "God was also beginning to move in America just as He had in their homeland of Armenia and in Russia."[27]

Worship through Testimony

The testimony meetings which precede the preaching often continue for two hours or more and people are standing waiting to
testify all the time. Those who have received the baptism with
the Holy Ghost testify that they had a clear evidence of sanctification first. Hundreds testify that they received the Bible evidence of speaking in a new tongues that they never knew
before.

ANONYMOUS

Ordinary people also contributed much to the worship life of the
mission through their interaction with one another—especially
during those times they shared their personal testimonies. These
times when people stood spontaneously at the mission to give testimonies of what God had done in their lives became a remarkable
feature of Azusa Street worship. The testimonies of the faithful
were not time-worn, tired retreads of something that had happened twenty or thirty years ago. They were new, vital vignettes—
glimpses into the lives of people who came to the mission. Many
visitors found themselves impressed enough with what they heard
in these times of testimony that they called them the highlight of
the meetings. People stood at the windows outside the mission just
to hear the latest tale of God's working. People stood in line for an
hour or more, eagerly waiting their turn. Many jumped to their
feet, one right after the other, for the privilege of telling the crowd
what God had just done in their lives. Their stories breathed excitement, and their voices rang with vitality. Sometimes testifiers could
be heard for blocks in every direction.

In mid-July 1906 a local reporter attended an evening service. As
he sat there, he took notes, trying to keep up with all the spontaneity and enthusiasm that infused the gathering he would describe.
Using ordinary words, he would try to give his readers something
of the feel of the meeting. In spite of the "objective" way the
reporter recorded the scene, it is impossible not to be touched by
the staccato sequence of people pressing their way to center stage
to tell their story of God's goodness to them. Obviously, the

account is written by a critic, but it gives a sense of the action as well as the substance that permeated the mission during his visit. Most pastors would be taxed by tracking the proceedings and leading the congregation where such interventions took place.

"A laboring man," began the reporter,

> told how he had been awakened at 2 in the morning, finding himself talking in an unknown tongue.
>
> As he spoke, a middle-aged negress arose on the outskirts of the circle. "The Lord has sanctified me. Praise His name," she shrieked, as she charged to the middle of the circle.
>
> "He called me and I am hyah, hyah, hyah." Dropping on her knees, she beat the floor with both fists and shouted, "Hyah! hyah! hyah! hyah! hyah!"
>
> A negress within the circle caught the head of the shrieking woman between both hands and putting her face close to the other, shouted in an unintelligible jargon.
>
> The first negress suddenly threw up both hands and fell on her back. Kicking her feet in the air, she screamed "Hallelujah!" until exhausted.
>
> The negress was followed by a white woman, gowned in a silk shirt waist suit. Her face gave evidence of education and refinement.
>
> The woman referred to herself as Sister Evans, and said she had been the first [white woman] to receive the gift of tongues. It came with the fire of the Holy Ghost after a 10 days fast. She gradually worked herself into a frenzy and concluded in a jabber.
>
> A long-haired young man leaped to his feet and asserted his possession of the gift of prophecy. He jabbered a prophecy in an unknown tongue and sat down.
>
> A negress came to the center with a warning of dire disaster. "But I've got my ticket and my trunk's packed. Hallelujah!" she concluded.
>
> An elderly white woman chanted a long "testimony" to a weird musical composition of her own.

"On the street of St. Irvah—in Kalamazoo—He gave me a tract—Salvation for you," she sang.

A negro boy, 9, got on a chair to praise God for "full and free salvation."

A white woman spoke in a clear and refined voice: "The blessed Pentecost has come tonight. Tum-a-luck, chup-a-buck, gok-a-luk, hum-a-tuck"—"Blessed are the pure in heart, for they shall see God," she translated.

The spirit began to move faster. A mulatto woman with a high pompadour and a white woman in a corner battled for supremacy. Another negro started, "I am washed in the blood," and a genuine camp-meeting time followed, with clapping of hands and stomping of feet, while a negress within the circle shouted "hong-kong" over and over.

In a moment of subsidence, a young man who looked like an early edition of Nat Goodwin got the floor and in the voice of a circus spleier [sic] told how the Lord had brought him to sanctification.[28]

The place must have snapped with electricity as the Spirit seemed to jump from one person to another. Many sat in the windows and scores of people stood in the front lobby, stepping on each others toes as they tried to see who was speaking next in this theater of the Spirit. "The room was crowded almost to suffocation. Men and women embraced each other in an apparent agony of emotion. Whites and negroes clasped hands and sang together," wrote one reporter.

One particularly picturesque description of a woman's attempt to participate in the service bears repetition in full.

A woman in the audience arose and sedately walked to the altar. She was probably 45 years old and could have poked a hole in the door of a steel safe with the point of her nose. Every bone in her face showed through the thin covering of skin. Her hair was drawn back over her forehead and tied in a hard, uncompromising knot on the back of her head. Her faded blue eyes were half hidden by enormous steel bowed spectacles.

With a ruler in her hand she would have appeared the typical old-maid school teacher that the comic magazines have made famous.

Inwardly the unregenerate trembled, fearing that she would spoil all the fun with a voice as sharp as her features.

"This is all foolish nonsense. Stop it this minute," was what was really expected of her.

But nothing of the kind occurred.

She shut her eyes and with hands behind her back opened her mouth.

"Ippy, Ippy, ippisit, ippley, catty catis, clak, claky."

She was interrupted by vigorous "Amens," but it didn't faze her. She was talking in the strange tongues that the Holy Rollers affect, but it sounded more like an old speckled hen had laid an egg in the corner of the barn and wanted everyone to know it.

If the old hen idea hadn't spoiled the effect of the thing it might have been awesome or tragical or pathetic or something else, but as it was it was simply ludicrous. It was evident she was terribly in earnest about it, though. She made her little speech in a few words, however, and without making any effort to translate it sat down again.

Another reporter described the session of testimonies he had witnessed the previous night, claiming that

these confessions came in the major part from women, and some of them talked at top speed until they became exhausted and fell prone on the floor.

Then there was a general round of "amens," pleasant smiles of satisfaction passed over the faces of the "congregation," and all eyes turned to the next confessor, who proceeded to fall into a trance as soon as the floor was hers. . . .

One "confessor" last night was a dignified mining man, well

dressed and well groomed. He wore diamonds that would have attracted attention in the lobby of the swellest hostelry in town, and the colored brethren did not fail to notice the sparklers in this little, one-story [sic] shack.

The miner told of his success, and then of his fortunate venture into one of the meetings a few nights ago, when he really realized the meaning of his wealth, etc., etc., until some one started to sing, and the prosperous man sat down.

Yet another testimony service ended rather abruptly. The only reporter to complain about "singing in tongues" looked on. He announced that

A buxom colored woman jumbled a few unheard-of words and translated them into Scripture. Then she burst forth in song.

Song! But it was without meter or melody and the words were senseless jargon.

As the weird shrieking increased in volume the cataleptic woman was seized by convulsive shudders. Both arms were now raised and at intervals her voice rose in a tremulous wail like the cry of the coyote. Her body swayed backward and whenever balance was lost dusky hands reached forth and steadied her.

The negro woman's "song" in the unknown tongue continued and a negro baritone joined in absolute discord. A dozen of the devout groaned and shouted. People in the rear of the hall rose to their feet and pressed forward. Pastor Seymour, colored, apparently scented trouble, and his calm, strong voice suggesting that the time for testimonies had come to a close, stilled the disturbance.

The "song" ceased.

Pastor Seymour brought the service to a general conclusion with a twenty-minute "discourse" before moving on to lead a time around the altar.

Worship through Preaching and Discussion

No subjects or sermons were announced ahead of time, and no
special speakers for such an hour. No one knew what might be
coming, what God would do. All was spontaneous, ordered of
the Spirit. We wanted to hear from God, through whoever he
might speak. We had no "respect of persons."

FRANK BARTLEMAN

Frank Bartleman's words set the stage for our understanding of the
role that preaching played in the Azusa Street revival. The mission
was unique in this regard. It was a place where preaching often
took place. But preaching was not always the centerpiece of any
particular meeting there. In many cases the centerpiece might be
an extended period of prayer, of praise through singing, or of testimonies, followed by an altar call that made the mission a center for
seeking the fullness of God. Many of the "sermons" were given by
lay people in the form of extended testimonies. On other occasions, Pastor Seymour or a visitor might provide the sermon.
These could run as short as fifteen minutes and as long as an hour
and a half.

Frank Bartleman told how he "gave a message" during his first
visit to the mission, April 19, 1906. Given Bartleman's reputation for
exaggerating his own importance at the mission, his "message"
may have been nothing more than an extended testimony, though
his account makes it sound like he preached a sermon. We don't
know exactly how long he spoke or what he said, but coming on
the heels of the San Francisco earthquake, it is a safe bet that it had
something to do with the message of either his just-completed
tract "The Last Call" or the tract he would write later that week,
"The Earthquake!!!"

After attending the May 10, 1908, afternoon service at the mission, George B. Studd complained that while the testimony meeting had been good, "Seymour seemed to throw away his message
(if he had one), threw it open for everyone to talk—and some
did, too." This happened, indeed, quite often. On some occasions

people were invited to interact with the sermon. On others they did it when they felt like it.

We must remember that Pentecostal worship was still in its infancy—a phase of experimentation. The mission was still testing out a number of beliefs and deciding which behaviors would be valued as "decent" and "orderly." Some of the worshippers would therefore naturally disagree with others over various issues—even confronting the preacher. Some, for instance, viewed speaking in tongues as a gift or charism of the Spirit and nothing more. Others viewed it as a charism, but also as the Bible evidence of their baptism in the Spirit. Some who attended the mission did not value tongues highly at all, while others imputed enormous value to the practice. Some viewed it as a language that pointed them to some foreign missionary field, while others saw it as more psychological in nature. How tongues should be used and regulated in the public meeting was also debated. And were these tongues real languages or were they something else? Was it possible to speak, sing, write, and even sign in tongues?—that is, could a deaf person use sign language as a means of speaking in tongues? The mission debated all these subjects, as leaders and congregation studied their impact in light of the Bible.

The mission also debated questions about the relationship between doctors, medicine (or such things as eyeglasses), and divine healing. One common point of contention concerned the ways in which various gifts or charisms came into play in a service. One person might claim, as an excuse to interrupt at will, "I can't control myself when the Spirit moves on me." Another might assert, "Self-control is a fruit of the Spirit, and thus, you can always control yourself until a more appropriate time if it is the Spirit who is moving on you." Still others debated who had the final say about what was said or done.

Given the exuberant activities within, the city of Los Angeles stationed one or two police officers outside the mission to guarantee that order was maintained and noise levels did not rise too high. During one Friday evening service in August 1906, a man named Otto Smith about whom we know nothing further was arrested on charges of disturbing the peace. He had created great commotion by rising to his feet and lashing out at the mission "for their manner of service." In court the next day Smith was found guilty and fined ten dollars. In a "lengthy" lecture, the judge instructed him that even if he didn't agree with what was going on at the mission, the Constitution of the United States guaranteed the Azusa Street worshippers the freedom to worship as they chose, so long as they did not break the law.

During a Sunday service the following month, the policeman stationed at the mission was forced to intervene again. A woman named Mrs. Spangler claimed that the Lord had given her the message and she was going to deliver it one way or another. She must have tried to do so when it was clear to the others that either the timing or the message was wrong. When a local evangelist who was present at this meeting, William Boyd, interfered with the arresting officer, he was also arrested. Boyd was ultimately fined twenty dollars, while Mrs. Spangler got off with a warning from the judge to stop such objectionable conduct. She promised the court that she would, "if the Lord will let me."

The city's action in stationing a police officer next to the mission strongly suggests that the issue of order within the meetings was not always resolved satisfactorily—especially when heated discussions arose during the times of public testimony. Such scrapping over theological positions was a common practice in the Wesleyan holiness movement, and as the mission and its adherents tried to come to terms with new Pentecostal realities, harsh words were sometimes exchanged. Outsiders didn't always understand the limits of such exchanges.

Any analysis of Seymour's sermons reveals the extent to which the pastor attempted to move his people with his preaching. Many of his sermons seem to have focused on the need for his followers to receive the baptism in the Spirit so they might carry the gospel message forward to others. Even if Seymour spoke extensively about the need for conversion or sanctification, he generally finished by encouraging his flock to seek their baptism in the Spirit. If the sermon dealt with baptism in the Spirit, he assured them that they could not get to that experience without first being converted and sanctified. For him, each was a piece of the whole. Seymour was committed to the idea that the work Christ did on the cross of Calvary needed to be applied to every individual. In a message clearly intended to be heard and read by leaders who would take the message to Los Angeles, he exhorted,

> Let us lift up Christ to the world in all His fulness, not only in healing and salvation from sin, but in His power to speak all the languages of the world. We need the triune God to enable us to do this.
>
> We that are the messengers of this precious atonement ought to preach all of it, justification, sanctification, healing, the baptism with the Holy Ghost, and signs following. "How shall we escape if we neglect so great salvation?" God is now confirming His word by granting signs and wonders to follow the preaching of the full gospel in Los Angeles.

Pastor Seymour continued this line of thought in a sermon titled "River of Living Water," based on John 4. He reminded his congregation that when the woman of Samaria received the "living water" from Jesus, she ran off to tell the city what she had found. Seymour went on to exclaim,

> How true it is in this day, when we get the baptism with the Holy Spirit, we have something to tell and it is that the blood of Jesus Christ cleanseth from all sin. The baptism with the Holy Ghost gives us power to testify to a risen, resurrected Saviour. Our affections are in Jesus Christ, the Lamb of God that takes away the sin of the world. How I worship Him today! How I praise Him for the all-cleansing blood.

He concluded,

> Above all, let us honor the blood of Jesus Christ every moment of our lives, and we will be sweet in our souls. We will be able

to talk of this common salvation to everyone that we meet. God will let His anointing rest upon us in telling them of this precious truth. This truth belongs to God. We have no right to tax anyone for the truth, because God has entrusted us with it to tell it. Freely we receive, freely we give. So the Gospel is to be preached freely, and God will bless it and spread it Himself.

In a short piece titled "Counterfeits," Seymour warned his followers about some who had come to the mission, faking tongues and making untrue claims. He singled out the spiritualists, making it clear that when they came they were indwelt by demons which had to be exorcised. He went on to quote from Zechariah 4:6, reminding his followers that the work they were about was not accomplished by "might nor by power but by my Spirit"; he encouraged them to be baptized in the Holy Spirit so that they would be up to the task. Jesus' final instruction to his disciples had been that they "tarry until" they had received the Holy Spirit, and Seymour urged his followers to do likewise. In another short piece titled "Receive Ye the Holy Ghost," he issued an altar call. "Glory! Glory! Hallelujah!, O Worship, get down on your knees and ask the Holy Ghost to come in and you will find Him right at your heart's door, and He will come in. Prove Him now."

While Seymour insisted that his followers should receive the baptism in the Spirit, he was concerned that their quest not focus on "tongues" as such. "Dear one[s] in Christ who are seeking the baptism with the Holy Ghost," he advised, "do not seek for tongues but for the promise of the Father, and pray for the baptism with the Holy Ghost, and God will throw in the tongues according to Acts 2:4." He went on to tell them that these tongues would "come just as freely as the air we breathe. It is nothing worked up, but it comes from the heart. . . . So when the Holy Ghost life comes in, the mouth opens, through the power of the Spirit in the heart. Glory to God!"

Not all of Seymour's sermons exhorted his hearers to receive the baptism in the Spirit. From time to time he used sermons to address a specific problem at the mission. A number of problems

Seymour faced revolved around sex and marriage. Someone had come in, perhaps a spiritualist, preaching "free loveism." Seymour took this head on and condemned it. Others advocated sexual abstinence except for purposes of procreation, even within marriage. Once again, Seymour used Paul's teaching in 1 Corinthians 7 to condemn this. Others argued that divorce and remarriage were permitted. In his sermon "The Marriage Tie," Seymour warned that marriage had been instituted by God and was a holy institution. He argued that while Jesus might have given permission for someone to divorce for cause, he never gave permission for them to remarry while the divorced partner lived. Still others argued that they could ignore their families or even leave or divorce their spouses and go off on their own into some form of ministry. *The Apostolic Faith* ran an unsigned article that may well have been written by Seymour, titled "Bible Teaching on Marriage and Divorce," that reprimanded both men and women for even considering such options.

Pastor Seymour regularly called his flock to live lives of holiness, and keeping the marriage covenant was part of what it meant to live a holy life. At one point he warned them that when people stop living holy lives free from sin, "the Holy Spirit . . . turns them out, and they know when they are turned out of this church. They don't have to go and ask their pastor or their preacher, for they feel within their own soul that the glory has left them—the joy, the peace, the rest and comfort." In spite of this, he always held out hope. If they confessed their sins, God, the Holy Ghost, would "accept them back into the Church."

A second important practical series of teachings concerned money. As part of their worship, people at the Azusa Street Mission gave tithes and offerings. Perhaps most interesting, until 1908 no offerings were ever taken at the Azusa Street Mission. A mailbox on the wall, just inside the door, was the place where people dropped their offerings, though sometimes they simply gave their money to another person. Seymour did not preach on giving so much as he preached on stewardship. One article attributed to him was titled "In Money Matters." In it, he went out of his way to affirm property ownership, but he was also clear that "if the Lord says, take $200 or $500 or $1,000 and distribute here or there, you do it." This had to be done wisely, of course, for no one was to bring children into the world and then leave them half naked. Such actions left the guilty person in a state "worse than an infidel." He warned in his sermon on "Christ's Messages to the Church" that his followers were not to get tangled up in debt, rendering themselves unable to pay their "grocery bills, furniture bills, coal bills, gas bills, and all honest bills. God wants His people to be true and holy and He will work."

One of the reasons Seymour felt so strongly about sanctified living and empowerment through the baptism in the Holy Spirit was that he saw this baptism as a sign that the return of the Lord was close at hand. In his sermon titled "Behold the Bridegroom Cometh," based on Matthew 25:1–13, Seymour encouraged his congregation to live the sanctified life and pursue baptism in the Spirit so they would be prepared for the return of the Lord. Indeed, baptism in the Spirit seemed to guarantee a place in the rapture of the church. Those without it took their chances and might even have to endure the Great Tribulation.

"Behold the Bridegroom cometh!" Seymour warned his congregation.

O the time is very near. All the testimonies of His coming that have been going on for months are a witness that He is coming soon. But when the trumpet sounds, it will be too late to prepare. Those that are not ready at the rapture, will be left to go through the awful tribulation that is coming upon the earth. The wise virgins will be at the marriage supper and spend the time of the great tribulation with the Lord Jesus. They will have glorified bodies. For we which remain unto the coming of the Lord will be changed in the twinkling of an eye.

Many precious souls believe today that in sanctification they have it all, that they have already the baptism with the Holy Ghost or enduement of power; but in that day, they will find they are mistaken. They say, "Away with this third work." What is the difference, dear ones, if it takes 300 works? We want to be ready to meet the bridegroom.

In his sermon "Rebecca: Type of the Bride of Christ," based on Genesis 24, Seymour brought a similar message. In this passage of Scripture, Abraham sends his servant Eliezar to search for a bride for Abraham's son, Isaac. Seymour treated Isaac as a "type" (a pre-figuring) of Christ, Eliezar as a type of the Holy Spirit, and Rebecca as a type of Christ's bride, the Church. As Seymour painted the picture of the interaction of these three figures, he noted that Eliezar was "seeking a bride among His brethren, the sanctified." In fact it is the Eliezar figure upon whom Seymour concentrated. He then announced that the Holy Spirit was standing at the door of the heart of each sanctified Christian asking, "I pray thee is there room in thy heart that I may come in and lodge?" He described the benefits that come when one receives the Holy Spirit, then encouraged the congregation to do nothing that would stop them from receiving their baptism in the Spirit.

Worship around the Altar

As soon as it is announced that the altar is open for seekers for pardon, sanctification, the baptism with the Holy Ghost and healing of the body, the people rise and flock to the altar. There is no urging. What kind of preaching is it that brings them? Why, the simple declaring of the Word of God. There is such power in the preaching of the Word in the Spirit that people are shaken on the benches. Coming to the altar, many fall prostrate under the power of God, and often come out speaking in tongues. Sometimes the power falls on people and they are wrought upon by the Spirit during testimony or preaching and received Bible experiences.

ANONYMOUS

The mission's beliefs were found in a statement published regularly in *The Apostolic Faith* as well as in a tract-like handout, but they were also well summarized by one local news reporter, who used language

that most ordinary Christian folk in Los Angeles could understand.
"There are three phases in the Holy Roller religion," he began.

> One is "justification." This is the man or woman who leads a
> pretty straight life, goes to church on Sundays and Wednesday
> nights, says his prayers as often as needful and what the world
> commonly accepts as a Christian.
> The second phase is "sanctification." This is where the justi-
> fied one has reached the point where he can sin no more.
> From the services last night and the testimony he appears to
> have a mighty hard time getting there, but he must be sanctified
> before he can receive the baptism of the Holy Ghost.
> This baptism is the third degree and when he gets to that
> point he can heal sickness by the laying on of hands, cast out
> devils, talk in the unknown tongues and several other things. To
> get any one of these three the applicant must kneel at the altar
> and "seek."

The Azusa Street Mission taught that all three elements were
essential parts of the Apostolic Faith. Great emphasis was placed
on each one. People were urged to come to the altar and give their
hearts to Christ, to be born anew, then to seek sanctification, and
then to tarry for their baptism in the Spirit. Of course, all of these
things could take place in a single service, as was announced in the
case of one young woman. She came to the meeting "unsaved,"
fell under "deep conviction" during the sermon, and within five
minutes of the time she went to the altar, was "saved." "Before the
evening was over," *The Apostolic Faith* rejoiced, "she was sanctified
and baptized with the Holy Ghost and had the gift of the Chinese
tongue and was singing in Chinese in the Spirit." Most who came,
however, received only one or another of these things in a single
visit to the mission.

Because such a large number of people were converted, sought
and received sanctification, or sought and received baptism in the
Spirit at the Azusa Street Mission, many hours were spent around
the altar and in the various upstairs prayer rooms. This was, per-

haps, the most important time in any service. People could come and enjoy the singing, the testimonies, and the preaching, but if they wanted to encounter God, they were told that they needed to spend time seeking him either at the altar or in the upper room. Altar workers were assigned to meet them at both places. Among these workers were such people as Glenn Cook, Lucy Farrow, Abundio and Rosa de Lopez, and undoubtedly Florence Crawford. Other seasoned workers joined them.

Deliverance and Conversion

Not everyone who came to the mission was ready to receive what God had to offer. Some had to be "emptied" first. For example, spiritualism was a major concern for the people at Azusa Street, in part because some of the experiences present at Apostolic Faith meetings also showed up among the spiritualists. As Joseph Smale later recounted,

> We discovered that the same manifestations as take place in the meeting of spiritualists, were prevailing among us, such as shakings, babblings, uncontrolled emotions. In spiritualist meetings there are those who talk in several languages and write voluminously in the unknown tongue. In the extraordinary spiritual manifestations among religious people in Los Angeles, the peculiarity as witnessed in some was their imitation of animal sounds, as the dog, coyote, cat and fowl.

Frank Bartleman claimed that spiritualists and hypnotists went to the mission "to investigate, and to try their influence." The very fact that such people came to the mission and frequented other early Pentecostal meetings, notably at First New Testament Church and the Eighth and Maple Church, gave ammunition to critics of the fledgling Apostolic Faith movement. The mission was frequently criticized for being a hotbed of spiritualism, free loveism, hypnotism, mesmerism, and the like. As Alma White later accused, "False leaders have taken the advantage of these conditions, and prepared the ground for this, the climax of demon worship."

Charles Parham criticized the mission at this point as well, complaining repeatedly that, "Religious orgies outrivaling scenes in devil or fetish worship, took place in the upper room." His criticism emerged from his visit to the mission in October and November 1906. He had been invited to speak there, but when he claimed, "God is sick at His stomach" (with how the revival was being conducted), he was shown the door. Over the next several years, he wrote a series of ever more scathing attacks against the mission. "The Holy Ghost does nothing that is unnatural or unseemingly," he later wrote, "and any strained exertion of body, mind, or voice is not the work of the Holy Spirit, but of some familiar spirit, or other influence brought to bear upon the subject." Those who imitated the sounds of "the cackling of hens" or the "shrill cry of the panther," he protested, were engaged in activities typical of "spiritistic mediums."

One observer who strongly supported the mission in spite of Parham's criticism charged that "spiritualists seeing so much spirit-power thought it was time for them to move in, so they came and taught." Seymour's commitment to allow anyone to take the floor undoubtedly made such things possible. But this eyewitness—most likely Elizabeth Sisson, a widely recognized holiness and Pentecostal missionary, evangelist, and writer—went on to observe, "When they [the spiritualist teachers] were seated, the meeting ran on as before and God confounded them. It soon became too hot for them and they ran away." Those who stayed, however, ended up undergoing exorcism, renouncing spiritualism, and aligning with the revival. According to one report, "Demons were cast out of many that were oppressed by the devil."

On one occasion, a known "spiritualist medium" came to the meeting allegedly on the verge of suicide. Those in the mission determined that he was "so possessed with demons that he had no rest." As *The Apostolic Faith* described the event, the medium was "instantly delivered of demon power" and then converted, sanctified, and "filled with a different spirit." Clearly the altar workers

This cartoon was published on the Front Cover of *The Burning Bush*, January 24, 1906. Just below the cartoon, the caption containing words loosely based upon 1 Corinthians 12:14–26 read, "THE FOOT CANNOT SAY TO THE HEAD, I HAVE NO NEED OF THEE." The caricatures and stereotypes portrayed in the cartoon are evident, though it is interesting to note that there are no black faces in the crowd.

stood ready to confront such people and engage in what would later be called "spiritual warfare." Deliverance and exorcism became regular features of the mission's ministry.

Not all "deliverance" involved exorcism, however. One man came to the altar with a plug of tobacco in his pocket. After twenty-five years of using the stuff, he had decided it was time to be delivered of it. He reportedly took it out and gave it to one of the altar workers, "and immediately the Lord began to bless his soul, and he got victory over his old enemy."

One of the more colorful people who attended the Azusa Street Mission was a woman named Bridget Welsh. Everyone knew Bridget. She had an extensive criminal record, and she had a powerful testimony that she gave everywhere she went. This former woman of the streets with her piercing blue eyes and her flaming red hair would become a household name in early Pentecostal circles. Born about 1861, she had been placed in the care of a convent in St. Louis by her parents, who hoped that institution would provide the discipline she needed. As a young teenager, she ran away from the convent and worked her way around the country as a "dance hall girl." She married a well-known gambler named Joe D. Nesbit and traveled with him from Montana to Mexico. He introduced her to drugs, and before long they were both addicted to alcohol, morphine, and cocaine. Eventually they separated, and Bridget ended up in San Francisco working as a prostitute in an attempt to earn her drug money. Over the next twenty-five years she moved in and out of asylums and hospitals, and she served time in prison. Her addictions grew and her health declined.

On March 31, 1902, Bridget Welsh was converted while staying in a "rescue home" in San Jose. Following her conversion and sanctification her life was utterly transformed—she began to share the testimony of her conversion wherever she went. In 1906 she traveled to Los Angeles and attended the Azusa Street Mission. There, in her uniquely demonstrative way, she testified of her experience to that time and then proceeded to be baptized in the Spirit. Bridget adopted Romans 8:11 as her lifelong theme: "My mortal body is quickened by His Spirit, and I can witness that I am

These two photographs were published side by side as pre and post-conversion poses, on the cover of the tract that told Bridget Welsh's conversion story. The first photograph shows her in 1901, while the second one shows her in 1917. Such "Before" and "After" comparisons were common fare in many Pentecostal tracts during this period.

never tired," she said. As itinerant printer Ned Caswell put it, Welsh was "a miracle of God's saving grace." In 1912 she was still at the mission, and though her arms were covered with the scars of the needle marks that witnessed to her past life, according to British Anglican pastor Alexander A. Boddy she was now "full of faith and good humor."

Once someone had been converted at the mission, workers

encouraged them to be baptized. Existing records suggest that hundreds of new converts were baptized in mission-related baptismal services. The first of these was held in July 1906. As many as five hundred worshippers sang and shouted as they took the Salt Lake Railroad train to Terminal Island, where Pastors William J. Seymour and Hiram Smith baptized 138 blacks and whites, mostly women, in the waters of the Pacific. Eighty-five more were baptized the same way on September 11, 1906. During the 1907 camp meeting, over a hundred more were baptized, this time in a dammed-up portion of the creek running from the San Gabriel Mountains through Pasadena to the Los Angeles River.

Seeking Sanctification

Sanctification was the next step in the Christian life, according to mission teaching. As with conversion, holiness leaders had taught that one must engage in an intensive time of prayer in order to receive it. Sanctification was supposed to be a "cleansing to make holy," a "crisis" experience, a datable moment of purification. The mission's faith statement claimed that in this event, the believer was cleansed from "inbred Sin" and "inbred Disease." In 1911 this doctrine would be challenged as never before: In that year, Chicago pastor William H. Durham returned to Azusa Street with his theory of sanctification based on the "finished work" that Christ had accomplished on Calvary. At the time of conversion, he maintained, one was sanctified by being placed "in Christ." From that time on, holiness became a life-long quest, in which the believer would mature as he or she grew in grace. Durham's "finished work" position would split the movement (see chapter 7). At the beginning of the revival, though, the Wesleyan position prevailed: entire sanctification came in a moment.

On a warm September evening in 1906, a Los Angeles reporter visited the mission where, following the evening service, "about an even dozen" sought their sanctification. His account, published the next day, told a great deal about the process that many went through in their quest for sanctification:

There were Negro men and women, and some of the white men and a few of the white women looked like they might be members in good standing of some west side church. Several persons of the highest type of intelligence and refinement were kneeling at the rude altar, "seeking."

Most of them prayed silently. But one big black woman, with a voice like a megaphone, continued howling, "O Lo'd, let me git it. O, Lo'd, let me have it."

For about fifteen minutes she kept this up. Then she got it and she got it good and plenty, whatever it was.

She began rocking and writhing and in five minutes she was on the floor apparently in the greatest pain. Her eyes rolled wildly, and if her arms and legs hadn't been fastened on they would have been scattered to the four winds. She jumped to her feet and some of the unregenerate who had looked on with open-mouthed wonder fled from the building in terror. But she didn't intend to do any one any damage. She had received sanctification, and was simply expressing her joy in her own peculiar way. All the brethren and the sistern gathered around her and Amened and Hallelujahed until they were hoarse, evidently as happy as she was.

Several others of the kneelers also received sanctification and were equally pleased over it.

This kind of total abandonment before God that led up to sanctification was often demonstrated at the altar through public displays of tears, groaning, and crying in anguish for past sins, as well as groveling on the floor while in prayer—almost literally in sackcloth and ashes. Or it could also be demonstrated through enthusiastic, festive celebration, with singing, shouting, clapping, leaping, and dancing. One newspaper reporter described this latter mode well,

Sunday night a score of blacks and whites prostrated themselves on the floor in the center of the hall, while the leaders loudly and separately sought in prayer for the visitation of the Holy Ghost.

In a sudden lull a Mexican leaped from among the prostrate forms and jumped up and down and waved his arm. "I've got it; hallelujah!" he shouted.

Two negro women who had been exhorting him fell together in a stage embrace, and then started, "I've been saved in the blood of the crucified one." The Mexican joined in his own tongue.

It was a fair example of how others "get it" every night.

The intensity of the people's prayers, as they sought what was for them the ultimate encounter with God, did not conduce to a silent atmosphere at the mission. The woman who sought "with a voice like a megaphone" was not alone in the way she went about her quest. One can only imagine what it must have been like to have hundreds of people seeking some divine blessing, all at the same time. In its opening salvo on the mission, the *Los Angeles Daily Times* had indicated that the night was "made hideous in the neighborhood by the howling of the worshippers." Several months later the *Times* informed its readers that those who lived close to the mission

> have existed without sleep for so many nights that they are almost convincing themselves that it is great sport to sit on the edge of a bed about 1 A.M. and listen to the terrific howls of some alleged linguist, who spouts away in broken English and a mixture of a dozen other languages, calling residents of Los Angeles to prepare for some great disaster said to be impending.

Days later the *Times* repeated its claim that every evening those who still had breath continued to make the night "hideous with their yells and squeals."

Another newspaper counted "innumerable" complaints lodged against the mission regarding what it called the "noises of insane people." On another occasion it announced that the services held the previous night would be "long remembered" by anyone within "five blocks," since it had been so "emphatically enthusiastic."

Another reporter likened these services to a union meeting, in which "every occupant of the place might be [viewed as] a walking delegate from the excellent control of lung power which is exercised at the most surprising and continued intervals."

Noise was not the only feature of time spent around the altar. What came to be caricatured as "gymnastics" was another. As people crowded around the altar or lay on the floor of the upper room, they jerked and twisted, shook and rolled. One of the most common experiences at the altar was the phenomenon of being "slain in the Spirit." In one *Times* article, the reporter explained that a "buxom dame was overcome with excitement and almost fainted." In a second article, the reporter claimed that "some of them talked at top speed until they became exhausted and fell prone on the floor."

Other actions captivated news reporters even more. One informant reported to the police that worshippers were leaping over chairs and jumping through open windows in their ecstasy. A *Times* reporter investigated and concluded, "It is a queer mixture of rich and poor which congregates in this building, and all are afflicted alike—with some peculiar impulse to perform astonishing gymnastic feats and shout so they may be heard for blocks."

A less sympathetic reporter complained that on another occasion the police had been forced to enter the mission and clean up a potential moral disaster. The reporter alleged that

> several women spent at least a part of the night lying flat on their backs on the dirty floor of the room, each endeavoring to kick her heels higher in the air than the others. As a result the fanatical and almost hysterical females were practically standing on their heads in the midst of a large audience.

The reporter moralized,

> As such exhibitions are not allowed even in the tough resorts in the city, the police were forced to call a halt to this part of the "holy kickers" rites. When the women were forced to desist

they became wildly hysterical and screamed and preached until they sank exhausted and nearly unconscious to the floor.

Perhaps the most caustic account came from a reporter who declared that speaking in tongues was on the decline. What had replaced it, the reporter exclaimed, was "ground and lofty tumbling." The reporter went on to claim that the five months of experience the mission congregation had enjoyed practicing their "grasshopper activities" had led them to a "high state of perfection." Thus, the meetings were now "given over to the Holy jumping, although the members of the sect still claim the gift of the Pentecost."

Such gymnastic activities did unquestionably crop up at the mission. The people who worshipped at the Azusa Street Mission were a group that embraced various forms of emotional expression. African Americans, Caucasian revivalists, Russian and Armenian Molokans, Mexicans and Mexican Americans, and other groups each offered a distinctive type of spirituality. And each of these spiritualities embraced some form of emotional expression that, though accepted as "orderly" by the Azusa Street leadership, stood out as new and strange compared with the more traditional forms found in the city's historic congregations, In the end, however, most of the people who participated in such activities would claim that they had encountered the Living God and that their actions resulted from that central divine encounter they called "baptism in the Spirit."

Baptized in the Spirit

Once believers had been sanctified, they were ready to be baptized in the Spirit. Seekers were encouraged to pursue and embrace an intimate encounter with God in which he bestowed upon them this baptism. The leaders at the mission agreed that baptism in the Spirit would be recognized when someone spoke in tongues, and not a moment before. As a result, at first they embraced *all* who spoke in tongues. As time passed and Pastor Seymour reflected further upon the subject, he decided that speaking in tongues could be accepted as the Bible evidence of a person's baptism in the Spirit only if it were also accompanied by divinely-given love. Without evidence of this "fruit" of the Holy Spirit in the claimant's life, Seymour was not convinced that the tongue had been divinely given.

We are privileged to have a rich stockpile of testimonies from those who were baptized in the Spirit at the Azusa Street Mission. These testimonies bear many similarities, and a quick analysis of a half dozen of them should suffice to help us see where baptism in the Spirit fit into the scheme of things.

Adolph Rosa, an evangelist from the Cape Verde Islands, came to the Azusa Street Mission in September 1906. He stood to testify, but before he could speak he was struck with the question, "What does God think of me?" He became speechless. "I could only weep for some minutes," he later wrote,

> and the power of God came upon me until I dropped to the floor. I was under the power of God for about an hour and a half, and it was there that all pride, and self, and conceit disappeared, and I was really dead to the world, for I had Christ within in His fulness [sic]. I was baptized with the Holy Ghost and spoke in a new tongue.

It is not often that a preacher gets tongue-tied, but Adolph Rosa certainly did. As he stood with this burning question on his mind, he experienced a deep emotional response. He began to weep; then he fell to the floor. This phenomenon of falling, which he described with the common phrase "under the power," was a familiar one at the Azusa Street Mission. But it was neither unique to the mission, nor did it begin there. It had been a frequent feature of many revival meetings at least from the time of John Wesley onward, especially among the revivals along the western American frontier, in the Wesleyan holiness movement, and in much African American worship. It may even find a basis in the apostle's experience described in Revelation 1:10–18: while he was "in the Spirit," he fell "as dead" when confronted by the risen Lord.

For an hour and a half Rosa lay on the floor as he realized his unworthiness before God in a fresh way. He saw himself over against the one who is totally "other," a holy God. This encounter with God forced Rosa to face his own pride, selfishness, and conceit until these had "disappeared." We might call that a decentering moment, a time in which his selfish concerns no longer concerned him. His recognition of the difference between himself and God was crucial to the success of this moment. What had held meaning for him before this moment held no meaning for him after the encounter with God. This sounds like the language one would expect to hear from the newly converted, but Rosa was a seasoned minister.

Rosa made no excuses for himself; he simply became, in his words, "dead to the world." At the same time, he became aware that he had been filled with "Christ...in His fullness." The language of filling and fullness is a language of completion and possession. According to his testimony, Rosa found his character newly permeated by the presence of Christ. His explanation of what had occurred in this encounter was simple: "I was baptized in the Holy Ghost and spoke in a new tongue."

A second testimony comes from William H. Durham, who heard about the Azusa Street revival while serving as pastor of a congregation in Chicago. In February 1907 he traveled to Los Angeles, determined to set aside the time necessary to encounter God at a deeper level. He spent over two weeks attending the Azusa Street meetings and praying for the baptism in the Spirit. In the Tuesday afternoon meeting, February 26, 1907, as he later wrote, "Suddenly, the power of God descended upon me, and I went down under it."

As in Adolf Rosa's case, Durham's encounter began when he went down under the "power of God." He quickly found that an adequate vocabulary eluded him. "It seemed to me that my body had suddenly become porous," he wrote, "and that a current of electricity was being turned on me from all sides." For two hours, he lay on the floor in this condition, feeling utterly "transparent" and noting that a "wonderful glory" had come into his soul. The same thing happened to him two days later, on Thursday, February 28, and he believed that he received "a great spiritual uplift."

The following evening, Friday, March 1, William Durham again attended the mission. He continued his quest for his baptism in the Spirit, and for three hours he was conscious of God's "power," touching him and causing his body to "quake." This power seemed to work over his entire body, beginning with his arms and then moving section by section throughout this body. In his words, "it was strange and wonderful and yet glorious." Finally, at 1 A.M. on Saturday, March 2, Durham received the object of his quest. "He [God] finished the work on my vocal organs," Durham recalled,

> and spoke through me in unknown tongues. I arose, perfectly conscious outwardly and inwardly that I was fully baptized in the Holy Ghost, and the devil can never tempt me to doubt it. First I was conscious that a living Person had come into me, and that He possessed even my physical being, in a literal sense, in so much that He could at His will take hold of my vocal organs, and speak any language He chose through me. Then I had such power on me and in me as I never had before. And last but not least, I had a depth of love and sweetness in my soul that I had never even dreamed of before, and a holy calm possessed me, and a holy joy and peace, that is deep and sweet beyong [sic] any thing I ever experienced before, even in the sanctified life. And O! such victory as He gives me all the time.

Durham's description of his encounter with God, culminating in his baptism in the Spirit and God's speaking through him "in unknown tongues," is remarkably similar to that of Adolph Rosa.

Around October 1, 1906, a man named Arthur B. Shepherd, who was probably a Free Methodist but certainly a man who had been "saved" and "sanctified" according to holiness teaching, returned from a trip to Colorado. His testimony parallels that of many who had been part of the holiness movement. "I had the real anointing on my soul," he wrote, "and could not believe that I did not have the baptism [in the Spirit]." Shepherd went on to insist that "tongues bore no more significance to the baptism than any of the gifts as recorded in 1 Corinthians 12."

Two things troubled him, however. First, he saw that all the New Testament accounts that told of people being baptized in the Spirit (Acts 2:1–4; 10:44–48; 19:1–6), with the exception of the account of the Samaritan pentecost recorded in Acts 8:4–19, mentioned that the recipients of baptism in the Spirit spoke in "new tongues." And even in the debatable passage in Acts 8, something out of the ordinary had occurred that led Simon, the magician, to make an offer to the apostles for the secret to their power.

Second, after reading 1 Corinthians 12—14, Shepherd concluded that he had been wrong about the possible connection between baptism in the Spirit and the evidential character of speaking in tongues. He concluded that these chapters did not condemn the use of tongues. They merely sought to regulate the proper role that speaking in tongues might play, according to what he called "the law of love." These observations on Acts and 1 Corinthians sent Shepherd on a five-month quest for his baptism in the Spirit.

Arthur Shepherd's answer came in the early evening of Sunday, March 3, 1907. He was praying in the upper room of the mission about 6 P.M. when, like William Durham just two nights before, he "fell under the mighty power."

> The Spirit worked my flesh with great vibrations for some time. At last I felt as thougt [sic] I were dying, and I was told I looked like it. Slowly, surely my life seemed to ebb away, until at last unconsciousness took place. How long I lay I do not know, but the first thing I was conscious of was a new life flowing in. Soon my jaws and tongue began to work independently of my volition and the words came, a clear language. All glory be to God. Now I feel a power for witnessing I never had before and an assurance of power in service that shall grow as I remain faithful.

These three accounts share many features. Adolph Rosa, William Durham, and now Arthur Shepherd were all overcome by what they described as the power of God. All fell to the floor. Rosa described a decentering moment that removed his pride, selfishness, and conceit. Shepherd described it as something like dying, the ebbing away of consciousness. While William Durham spoke of quaking, Shepherd experienced "great vibrations." Rosa described his encounter as the time when he received Christ in his fullness. A "living Person" had entered Durham, and Arthur Shepherd was conscious of new life flowing into him. All three men testified that as a result of this new encounter with Christ, the living Person, and the flow of new life, they had begun to speak in tongues.

Mrs. Lucy Leatherman—the wife of a physician, and a former student at the Nyack Bible College—provides us with a fourth testimony. "While seeking for the Baptism with the Holy Ghost in Los Angeles, after Sister Ferrell [sic] laid hands on me," she began,

> I praised and praised God and saw my Savior in the heavens. And as I praised, I came closer and closer and I was so small. By and by I swept into the wound in His side, and He was not only in me but I in Him, and there I found that rest that passeth all understanding, and He said to me, you are in the bosom of the Father. He said I was clothed upon and in the secret place of the Most High. But I said, Father, I want the gift of the Holy Ghost, and the heavens opened and I was overshadowed, and such power came upon me and went through me. He said, Praise Me, and when I did, angels came and ministered unto me. I was passive in His hands working on my vocal cords, and I realized they were loosing me. I began to praise Him in an unknown language.

Lucy Leatherman reported in a matter-of-fact way how her quest for the baptism in the Spirit had led her to encounter Christ in a new and deeper way. Leatherman was seeking her Spirit-baptism when Lucy Farrow laid hands upon her. While she was praising God, she received a vision of her savior, Jesus, in the heavens. In that vision she began to move closer to him. She became so small that she was "swept into the wound in His side." Once again, we are confronted with a type of decentering language. Her focus was not upon herself—it was upon her Savior. She became progressively less interested in herself until the time that "He was not only in me but I in Him." The mutuality, the transcendent yet immanent quality of the encounter, transformed her until she had found a "rest that passeth all understanding." Once she found that "rest," Christ spoke to her, informing her that she was now "clothed upon and in the secret place of the Most High."

Mrs. Leatherman then told the Lord that she wanted the "gift of the Holy Ghost." This language was commonly used by many early Pentecostals to describe baptism in the Spirit. "The heavens opened," she said, "and I was overshadowed, and such power came upon me and went through me." In this encounter, now supported fully by the structure of the vision, Leatherman became a passive participant. She continued to praise Jesus according to his instruction, while angels came and ministered to her and she received something new. Finally, through her "eye of faith," she saw an angel massaging her vocal cords, loosening them, while her vocal praise moved from praise in English to praise in "an unknown language."

We have the testimony of a fifth person, identified only as a Brother Burke from Anaheim. He had heard about the mission, but what he had heard about it was not good—local folks had told "awful stories about this work." But that did not stop Burke from having his own encounter with God. He prayed, telling the Lord to "search my heart and melt me down." What happened next resembles the other testimonies we have reviewed, and yet it is unique. "It seemed to me," he wrote later, that

I grew smaller and smaller till I felt about the size of a grasshopper. I asked the Lord to put the Holy Ghost on me, and it came like the outpouring of water on the crown of my head and it went though my entire body to the very tips of my toes and fingers and my heart seemed to expand ten times larger. Then something rushed through me like I was under a fawcet [sic]. It was the Holy Ghost and the next thing I knew, something began to get hold of my jaw bones and tongue. I said, Lord whether I ever speak in tongues or not, I want the baptism with the Holy Ghost as they had it on the day of

Pentecost. I went home and it seemed a music band of a thousand instruments was set up within me.

Burke's vision has all the earmarks of a new self-perspective, as he prayed that God would search his heart and melt him down. It was his decentering moment. Like the others, he was fully aware of his surroundings as he asked the Lord to "put the Holy Ghost" on him. As he attempted to describe what came next, his language moved to metaphor. The Spirit came upon him, he wrote, "like the outpouring of water on the crown of my head and it went through my entire body to the very tips of my toes and fingers and my heart seemed to expand ten times larger. Then something rushed through me like I was under a fawcet [sic]."

Scripture uses water as an important symbol of the Holy Spirit (Joel 2:28; Eph. 5:18), and Burke's choice of words is consistent with that imagery. His description of the Spirit touching him, enveloping his body—beginning with his head and running through to the tips of his toes and fingers, filling every nook and cranny and causing his heart to expand—shows that he was aware, as were many others, of *physical* phenomena during his intimate divine encounter. This "possession" language describes the moment when Burke found himself overwhelmed by the Holy Spirit.

After this metaphorical description of his baptism in the Spirit comes his statement that "something began to get hold of my jaw bones and tongue." Like Lucy Leatherman, who seemed to see an angel massaging her vocal chords, or William Durham, who felt he had been physically possessed to the extent that God could take control of his vocal cords and speak any language he chose, Burke next felt his jaw bones and his tongue being touched. He had moved from a simple, everyday description to metaphorical language as he struggled to describe God's pouring forth of his Holy Spirit with all its physical accompaniments. And he concluded with the expectation that he would now speak in tongues—a language transcending both everyday speech and metaphor. He would accept the language of tongues, as long as he received the baptism he desired so strongly.

Finally, we have the testimony of George E. Berg. George and Mary Berg had worked as holiness missionaries in India from 1901 to the summer of 1905. Upon their return stateside George Berg became interested in what he was hearing about the Azusa Street Mission. He attended an afternoon meeting on September 15, 1906, where he was baptized in the Spirit. His testimony resembles Brother Burke's to a remarkable degree.

"I was meeting God alone," he wrote,

And the Holy Ghost fell on me like balls of fire, and went through me from the crown of my head to the soles of my feet. The Spirit flooded my whole being and enlarged my heart till I was afraid the vessel might not be able to hold the glory and the power that seemed to rush into me like water poured out. Before I realized it, the Spirit got hold of my tongue as I used it for the glory of God in speaking in an unknown tongue.

The coming of the Spirit upon George Berg was a powerful reality for him. Whereas Brother Burke had described the Spirit's coming in terms of a flood of water that struck the crown of his head and went to his very toes, George Berg used the metaphor of "balls of fire." Berg's encounter was an intimate one, involving his entire body. and he mixed metaphors as he described it, moving from a consuming fire to an overwhelming flood. Brother Burke had said that his heart felt expanded by tenfold; George Berg said that when the Holy Spirit "flooded" his being, his heart enlarged so much that he was afraid it would burst.

Berg's encounter with the Holy Spirit brought a strong sense of the "glory and power" of God that seemed to rush through him like water gushing through a pipe. Brother Burke recounted a similar gushing, as though he were the faucet through which the Holy Spirit rushed. Finally, George Berg moved beyond metaphor to the response of speaking in tongues. The Holy Spirit had, in his words, "got hold of my tongue and used it for the glory of God in speaking in an unknown tongue."

These six testimonies help us understand something of why the people at the Azusa Street Mission danced, and fell, and shouted, and jumped, and spoke in tongues, producing noises and actions that struck outsiders as unseemly. These testimonies of what happened *within* those who often carried on with such abandon tell us more than the actions described by the many voyeuristic outsiders who came to watch them. They speak of a personal quest for a divine encounter that put them in direct touch with the God they worshipped.

As they drew close to God, they became aware of how different they were from him. He was holy; they were not. He was totally "other"; they were but flesh. He was overwhelming; they were overwhelmed. This led them to see their unworthiness, their sinfulness, and their need for personal change. As they continued their quest, they frequently manifested some physical or mental change. Some were "slain in the Spirit," while others shook or jerked or moved their hands and feet without thinking about it. Some had visions. As they focused upon Christ, several were overwhelmed by a sense of well-being or wholeness, in which they felt God's power, God's love, God's peace, God's joy, and God's presence.

When they tried to explain what had happened to them, they began with ordinary words, moved quickly to the word pictures of metaphorical speech ("It was like . . ."), and then, as they struggled to express themselves, came to the end of words altogether. The essence of the encounter included death to self and empowerment by Christ through the Holy Spirit. The one who encountered them, the Holy Spirit, began to speak through them, and they received something they wanted to share with the world. They became passionate, compelling witnesses who were now empowered by the Holy Spirit (Acts 1:8) through this thing they called "baptism in the Spirit."

5

EVANGELIZING A CONTINENT: SPREADING THE REVIVAL

ତ୍ୟୋ

The "gift of tongues" craze, which started some months ago in a tumble down, barn-like building in Azusa st., this city, has caused more than one war among the various religious denominations of the city since its noisy introduction.

From the beginning, the crowds that gathered nightly at Azusa st. were made up of followers of many churches and many sects.

The charm mystery, which worked like wild fire among the frequenters of these motley gatherings, extended its influence to such an extent that other churches were soon feeling the effects.

LOS ANGELES RECORD

THE REVIVAL REACHED out to the rest of the world with a rapidity that is hard to imagine. It was like a fire lit in dry tinder when nobody was looking. It exploded—billowing up and scattering its sparks in every direction. Some of these sparks damaged nearby holiness congregations. Frank Bartleman painted a vivid image of this when he wrote that as a result of the Azusa Street revival, the Pillar of Fire, a Wesleyan holiness church affiliated with Alma White, had "gone up in smoke." The Burning Bush, another holiness congregation, all but disappeared when its pastor, A. G. Garr, left it in July 1906 to serve as an Apostolic Faith missionary in India. When Pastor William Pendleton and ninety percent of his congregation joined the Apostolic Faith Mission, the remainder of his Los Angeles Holiness Church struggled to survive.

The Elysian Heights Nazarene Church sustained significant losses when it expelled those who had accepted the message of

Azusa Street. Second Pentecostal Church of the Nazarene[29] suffered heavy damage when its pastor left with a large percentage of the congregation after they were baptized in the Spirit. The Free Methodist Church in the nearby (northeasterly) suburb of Hermon and the Peniel Mission in the heart of Los Angeles both received heavy blows as their members switched allegiances to the Apostolic Faith. Finally, July 1907 saw the summary firing of Will Trotter, director of the Union Rescue Mission in downtown Los Angeles. Trotter, whose mission had been sponsored in large part by the churches of the Los Angeles Church Federation, had attended the Apostolic Faith camp meeting and been baptized in the Spirit. As Mr. Giles Kellogg, President of the Board of the mission, noted,

> The news of Mr. Trotter's action came to us so suddenly that we have had no opportunity to formulate any plans. We could do no less than drop his name from the list of officers of our mission, as we cannot indorse the step which he has taken. We do not indorse this Apostolic movement and we place no credence in the claim that the members have the 'gift of tongues.'

Some have argued that such things took place because the Azusa Street Mission had a plan to proselytize its neighbors—especially those churches theologically closest to it. Such a charge, however, assumes much more than what these people had in mind. Their motivation was not to destabilize any other church. In fact, the mission stated both clearly and regularly that its intention was not to harm any other church, but to bring about unity. Those who believed that they had been touched by the very finger of God when they were baptized in the Spirit simply wanted to share their testimony and encourage their friends to encounter God in the way that had been so meaningful to them. Some of their friends accepted their testimony and joined them. Others rejected their experience as too radical. And their rejection all too often brought sharp words, hurt feelings, and disappointment to everyone involved.

If some sparks set off fires that damaged some congregations, others caught fire in ways that spread the revival. By year's end, nearly a dozen churches and missions either sprang up or reoriented themselves, identifying with the Azusa Street revival. Frank Bartleman established a new congregation in Los Angeles at the corner of Eighth and Maple. William Pendleton and much of the congregation from the Los Angeles Holiness Church joined him there. Shortly after its opening, Bartleman moved on and Pendleton became the sole pastor of this mission for the next decade. Charles Kent established a small unnamed mission on Fifty-first Street. Franklin Hill, drawing heavily from the Second Pentecostal Church of the Nazarene where he served as pastor, opened the Vernon Mission on Central Avenue between Forty-third and Forty-fourth Streets. Thomas Atteberry, pastor of the People's Church at Sixth and Mateo Street, led many of his congregation into the revival after hearing from Azusa Street evangelists. Arthur Osterberg's Full Gospel Mission became a Pentecostal congregation. The holiness church in Sawtelle, at the western edge of the city, became a Pentecostal congregation known as the Gospel Mission. Charles Parham, who was no longer welcome at the Azusa Street Mission, established another Apostolic Faith Mission in Los Angeles. Joshua Sykes established the Apostolic Church in East Los Angeles. He adopted the tenets of the Azusa Street Mission, with one significant difference. He baptized his converts in the name of Jesus Christ and did not invoke the traditional Trinitarian formula.

At least three "ethnic" or "foreign language" works emerged during this period. Abundio and Rosa de Lopez had been serving as Spanish language missionaries at the Gospel Detective Mission, a mission aimed at Latinos employed by the Southern Pacific Railroad, when they received their baptism in the Spirit. After their baptism they worked at the Azusa Street Mission and continued to hold open air meetings on the historic Mexican plaza known as La Placita. By April 1907 a group of Swedish converts, mostly young people, had opened up a Swedish language Pentecostal Mission at 775 Wall near the corner of East Eighth Street. At the same time a group of Armenians and Russians, who had come to Los Angeles in the Molokan immigration, opened cottage prayer meetings on Victoria Street between West Fourth and Fifth Streets that would quickly develop into an Armenian-language Pentecostal church.

While Joseph Smale at First New Testament Church had not agreed with everything taught or done at the Azusa Street Mission, he had proved a strong ally during the first six months of the revival. In late October 1906 that would all change. First New Testament Church would split over issues of order—that is, issues of how certain gifts were to be manifested in the congregation—and by year's end Smale would drop his support of the revival. When Smale and his First New Testament Church cut their relationship with the Apostolic Faith movement, those who believed he was wrong formed a new congregation, led by Pastor Elmer K. Fisher. This congregation, which soon joined hands with the Azusa Street Mission in perpetuating the revival, ultimately became known as the Upper Room Mission.

Although we cannot lay out the entire story of these churches, a look at four of them should adequately illustrate how the revival spread throughout the city of Los Angeles.

The Eighth and Maple Church

The first of the new "Pentecostal" congregations to emerge after the Azusa Street revival was the Eighth and Maple Mission. For two years Frank Bartleman had attended First New Testament Church. Until the Azusa Street Mission came along, Bartleman was very happy there. When the revival broke at Azusa Street, he quickly found himself with torn loyalties. He hoped that Pastor Smale at First New Testament Church would enter with both feet into the stream of revival flowing from the Azusa Street Mission. But Pastor Smale had not done so. From Bartleman's perspective, Smale was too cautious—Bartleman would come to call him the "Moses" of the movement, able to see it but not to fully enter into it, just as Moses had been with the Promised Land (Num. 20:7–12; Deut. 32:48–52; 34:4–5). William J. Seymour was the "Joshua" of the movement, the man who led his people into the Promised Land of

Frank Bartleman rented this building, the former home of the Pillar of Fire, and began holding meetings in August 1906. It became known as the 8th and Maple Church. Ever the gadabout, Bartleman invited William Pendleton, former pastor of the Los Angeles Holiness Church, to serve with him as the congregation's co-pastor. Within a very short time, Bartleman decided to turn the church over to Pendleton and Bartleman left. He returned on occasion to worship or to preach, but Pastor Pendleton led the congregation for many years. In 1910, the name changed to the Pentecostal Assembly. In 1913 it relocated to 1162 E. 43rd Street, and in 1914 the address was 749 Kohler. In 1916, Frank Ewart apparently became co-pastor. William Pendleton died January 3, 1917 and was succeeded by Frank Ewart.

revival (Josh. 1:1–9). Always outspoken, Bartleman tried to stretch Pastor Smale. He soon found that Smale and the board of First New Testament Church did not want to be stretched as he had hoped. In fact, they sought to muzzle Bartleman.

Bartleman was in a difficult place. He had spent many years in ministry himself. He seems to have been looking for someplace in Los Angeles where he could extend his influence. In the end, he moved from First New Testament Church to Azusa Street. But there, too, he found himself limited in his ability to get things done his way, since Pastor Seymour was clearly the leader already in place. Bartleman finally rented the building at Eighth and Maple where the "Burning Bush" people had previously worshipped, and then he invited a number of friends from First New Testament

Church and acquaintances from the Azusa Street Mission to join him there.

Among those who joined Bartleman were Pastor William Pendleton and his congregation. In May 1906 a teamster named Henry W. McGowan had picked up materials at the lumber yard adjacent to the Azusa Street Mission. While he waited, he ventured into the Azusa Street Mission and became convinced that what he saw there was from God. He later testified in the Los Angeles Holiness Church about the meeting he had attended that day at Azusa Street. He urged Pastor Pendleton and the rest of the congregation not to reject what he had seen but rather to go with him to the mission and see it for themselves. About thirty-five people, including Pastor Pendleton, followed him to the Azusa Street Mission. By June Pastor Pendleton and most of the congregation had received their baptism in the Spirit. When word of their "conversion" got to the leaders of the Holiness Church, Pastor Pendleton was put on trial. We are fortunate to have accounts preserved by both sides in the events that led up to his trial and its resolution. In the end, Pendleton was stripped of his position at the Los Angeles Holiness Church, and the Holiness Church Association, which held the church property, forced his loyal congregation to vacate the premises. With nowhere to go, they joined the saints at the Azusa Street Mission for a time.

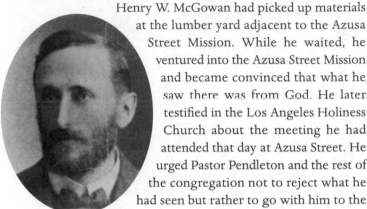

Frank Bartleman in 1906

Frank Bartleman must have met this group within days of their arrival. He invited Pastor Pendleton to serve as co-pastor with him at the Eighth and Maple church. While most of Pendleton's congregation followed him, a few stayed at the Azusa Street Mission for the time being. Local businesswoman Phoebe Sargent, for instance, joined Seymour's staff at first. The young but experienced mission worker Ivey Campbell stayed until late November

William and Sarah Pendleton

1906 when she left Los Angeles and carried the revival to Ohio and Pennsylvania.

As soon as the Eighth and Maple congregation had held its first services, Bartleman, always the itinerant, began to itch for greater challenges. He left the congregation in the capable hands of William Pendleton and moved on. Relationships between the Azusa Street Mission and the Eighth and Maple Church remained warm and cordial. Pastor Pendleton became a regular part of Pastor Seymour's Monday morning leadership meetings, and Seymour reportedly spoke often at the Eighth and Maple facility. Over the next several years, these two congregations would cooperate on a number of levels.

The People's Church

During the summer of 1905 Miss Bell White, a laywoman with a special interest in bringing the gospel to street children, founded a second congregation, the People's Church. She had begun it as a ministry to the children of the poor in her neighborhood in Boyle Heights, an area very near downtown. Soon she had a Sunday school with fifty boys. As her work progressed she raised enough money to build a new facility where these boys could worship and be diverted from life on the streets. An independent minister, Thomas G. Atteberry, gave a substantial contribution to this project before joining her as pastor, and by February 1906 the work had developed into a full-fledged congregation of 125 members. By April a new building was under construction at 598 Mateo Street, and the project received both regular and positive news coverage.

In September 1906 Glenn Cook, Adolph Rosa, and Bridget Welsh visited the People's Church, possibly at the invitation of Pastor Atteberry. There they shared their testimonies of what was taking place at the Azusa Street Mission and how it had changed them. As a result, Pastor Atteberry and others within the People's Church quickly sought and received their baptism in the Holy Spirit as well. Atteberry began a new occasional paper, *Apostolic Truth*, where he wrote on such topics as "The Gift of the Holy Spirit," "Ten Reasons Why I Believe in Divine Healing," "Signs and Miracles," and "Tongues."

For some months Pastor Atteberry was able to tip the scales at

Newspaper Sketch of the People's Church

the People's Church in favor of the revival. He encouraged people to seek their baptism in the Spirit there. He set aside an "upper room" where seekers could tarry, and he brought in Adolph Rosa to help. Pastor Atteberry ran into trouble when a twenty-one-year-old woman named Maude Snyder became interested. Her mother was horrified when Maude went to the church's upper room where Adolph Rosa, sometimes described as a Negro, prayed for people that they might receive their baptism in the Spirit. At another service, Maude's brother-in-law intervened when Maude was slain in the Spirit. He carried her to another room to recover, where he stood at the door threatening bodily harm to "any negro who sought admission." His threat was clearly aimed at Rosa.

Over the next two weeks, with the remainder of the Snyder family working hard to make her see why this revival was nonsense, Maude decided she had merely been a victim of "hypnotism." She left the church. The public coverage given to the case of Maude Snyder did not help either the revival or the People's Church. By November, the press was vilifying Atteberry, charging that he had begun

> to jump with the Holy Rollers, they who "serve the Lord" with rag-time songs and cake-walk accompaniment, and his institutional church at Sixth and Mateo streets has become the lodging-house, meeting-house, and general headquarters of the ludicrous bunch of fanatics.

While Belle White liked Pastor Atteberry and continued to speak highly of him, she did not like the fact that his conversion to the Apostolic Faith had brought ill repute to the People's Church. As a result, she left the People's Church, erected a tent about eight blocks away, and began yet another Sunday school. By mid-November she had another 103 people participating in this new venture. Because Belle White had been the founder of the People's Church and Thomas Atteberry had a mixed reputation with members of the Los Angeles Church Federation, the federation stepped into the situation and raised the stakes. They argued publicly that Belle White should be able to keep the church property and set the tone of the place. Even though Atteberry had been one of the congregation's primary financial contributors, the fact that his name appeared on the title of the church rankled the federation. By early 1907 Atteberry could no longer take the pressure. He signed everything over to Belle White and her congregation, and those who had received their baptism in the Spirit under Attebury's leadership had to find other places to worship.

Abundio and Rosa de Lopez and Latino Outreach

Soy testigo de el poder del Espiritu Santo, en perdon, en sanctifi-cacion, y bautismo en fuego. Acts 1:8; Mark 16:17–18. Doy [sic] gracias a Dios por esta combiesion [sic] y poder. Recibibo de Dios comforme a sus promesas el os giara [sic]. John 16:13–14. Gracias a Dios por la ordenacion de ir a la Calle de Azusa a la Mission Apostolic Faith. Old time religion llo [sic] y mi Ezpoza [sic] el dia, 29th of May, 1906.

ABUNDIO L. LOPEZ

Mexicans of Spanish decent, descendents of Mexico's indigenous peoples, and Mexican Americans joined together at the Azusa Street Mission from the beginning. In fact, when Pastor Seymour had first taken possession of 312 Azusa Street, Arthur Osterberg brought several "Mexican" laborers with him from the construction company where he was employed, to help clean out the building. During the cleanup, one of them had been converted. On the whole, the Latino presence at the mission has been largely overlooked in previous accounts of the Azusa Street story. This may stem, in part, from a lack of sources in English, as well as the fact that many of the Latinos who were in Los Angeles at the time of the revival were not bilingual. In some cases, the silence may arise from prejudice. But the Latino contribution must be given its place in any future study of the Azusa Street revival.

Aldolfo C. Valdez and his family are just one example of a Mexican American family that attended the mission in its early years. The Valdez family were what is known as a *Californios* family—

that is, true Californians, Californians who predated California. Their forebears had come to the region as part of Gaspar de Portolá's expedition in 1769 that resulted in the founding of the Franciscan mission chain that dots both lower and upper California. For his faithfulness, Portolá gave A. C. Valdez's great-great-grandfather a land grant adjacent to the mission in San Buenaventura [Ventura], California. When the revival hit Azusa Street, A. C. Valdez was ten years old. His mother, Suzie Valdez, was ill, and when she went to the mission, she found both salvation and healing. She returned to the mission, bringing her husband and her son, Albert. Their lives were changed completely. Later Suzie Valdez would work with the faith healer Dr. Finis Yoakum, ministering among prostitutes, the drug and alcohol addicted, and the homeless poor alongside the women of Yoakum's Pisgah Home movement. She also evangelized in San Bernardino, about fifty miles east of Los Angeles. A. C. Valdez would go on to become an internationally known Pentecostal evangelist.

Another Latino couple, Abundio de Lopez and his wife Rosa de Lopez, maintained a significant relationship with the Azusa Street Mission. *The Apostolic Faith* published their testimony in October 1906. On May 29 they had come to Azusa Street seeking sanctification, and by June 5 they had also received their baptism in the Spirit. In November, *The Apostolic Faith* told how they worked among other Latino seekers who came to the mission and how, for a short time they had gone to San Diego to spread the message. This couple regularly preached and distributed tracts on *La Placita*.

When the couple arrived at the Azusa Street Mission, Abundio was thirty-six. He had come to California from Guadalajara, Mexico at fifteen to work as a laborer, probably for the Southern Pacific Railroad. Somewhere along the way he became a Christian, and in 1902 he married Rosa in a Spanish-language Presbyterian Church in Los Angeles. For years they lived in railroad housing, first on San Fernando Road where the Gospel Detective Mission backed up to the freight yard tracks, then on South Alameda one block from the Southern Pacific Depot. The Lopezes attended services at the Azusa Street Mission from 1906 through at least 1909. Abundio

Lopez received ordination from Pastor Seymour, leaving no doubt that Seymour saw him as a gifted leader. During this same period, Abundio served as the "missionary" or pastor at the Gospel Detective Mission—an outreach work to the Latinos who worked for the Southern Pacific Railroad. Clearly Lopez's primary leadership was to the Spanish-speaking people of Los Angeles.

The fact that during the late teens Lopez's congregation was officially called an "Apostolic Faith Mission" strongly suggests that he continued to have a close relationship with William Seymour until the latter's death. During the early 1920s, Lopez led the Hispanic outreach for the famous Pentecostal mission Victoria Hall. Through at least the 1940s, Abundio Lopez would continue to serve as a Pentecostal Minister in the Hispanic community, ministering for a time in the Latin American Council of Christian Churches founded by Francisco Olazábal, a dynamic evangelist and church planter popularly known as *El Azteca*.

First New Testament Church and the Upper Room Mission

Where there are in our city and church those gifted with the tongues living beautiful Christ-like lives, there are others, and they are not few, from whom in the exercise of their gift sweetness has gone, love has gone, charity has gone, meekness has gone, reverence for the house of God has gone, respect for church order and Holy Ghost offices within the church has gone, and alas, a sound mind also, proving that a person may have the gift of tongues and know next to nothing of the Holy Ghost. As it was in Corinth, so it is in Los Angeles.

JOSEPH SMALE

The first major church casualty to the Azusa Street revival was First New Testament Church. Pastor Joseph Smale had played an important role by providing advocacy in the early days of the revival. Through the summer months of 1906, however, he began to rethink his position in light of some pastoral problems that emerged in his congregation. While Smale was convinced that some of what was taking place was the work of the Holy Spirit, he was nevertheless concerned about maintaining decency and order within the worship services at First New Testament. He set forth a few guidelines, but by late summer they were being attacked from an unexpected source.

Dr. Henry S. Keyes had been among Smale's closest friends and loyal supporters. As a member of the Board at First Baptist Church, Keyes had supported Smale in his effort to bring revival to Los Angeles. When Smale resigned from First Baptist Church,

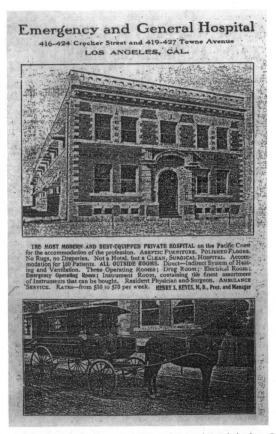

This advertisement for the Los Angeles Emergency and General Hospital, where Dr. Henry Sheridan Keyes served as President and Surgeon-in-Chief, appeared in one of California's medical journals. Dr. Keyes was a graduate of the University of the South, Sewanee Medical College in Tennessee. He went on to do a residency in surgery at the Medical Department in Harvard University. He was licensed to practice medicine in the State of California in 1900, License #4087.

Keyes went with him. Well-known and widely respected in the city, Keyes had completed his M.D. at the University of the South in Sewanee, Tennessee, and post-doctoral work in surgery at Harvard University. In 1900 he moved to Los Angeles and set up practice, opening offices and establishing the Emergency and General Hospital of Los Angeles.

In mid-July 1906 Keyes's sixteen-year-old daughter, Lillian, received her baptism in the Spirit at the Azusa Street Mission and began to speak in tongues (allegedly in Chinese), write in tongues, and prophesy. She could also frequently be found on the floor of the church, "slain in the Spirit." The local press saw her as a perfect candidate for sensational reporting. She was, after all, the daughter of a leader in Los Angeles society, a white girl who worshipped both in the largely African American Azusa Street Mission and at First New Testament Church. The press must have wondered how Keyes would respond to their questions. When the *Times* interviewed him in his hospital office, they found that not only did Keyes condone his daughter's behavior but he, too, claimed to speak and write in tongues. When the reporter pressed him to show them how he did it, Keyes wrote in tongues. He then took the reporter for a walk where he asked Mr. Lucius LeNan, a laborer employed by the Los Angeles Brick Company, to write an interlinear interpretation to his "tongues" message—which LeNan allegedly did. Seeking to verify Keyes's claim that this was actually a language, the *Times* reporter sought out Baba Bharati, described as an "eminent oriental scholar." Bharati, a Bengal Vaisnava missionary who had come to the United States in 1902, was in the process of establishing a Krsna temple in Los Angeles. Bharati declared that it was not a language that he knew. The next day this entire sequence of events was recounted in the *Los Angeles Daily Times*, with the clear implication that Dr. Keyes had gone off into fanaticism.

This story opened up a much larger one that had begun two months earlier when Lillian Keyes had handed Pastor Smale a written prophecy claiming that he had grieved the Holy Spirit. Allegedly this rebuke had arisen because Smale had been too strict with those who wanted more freedom of the Spirit. Smale was

This drawing of Dr. Henry Sheridan Keyes appeared in the *Los Angeles Daily Times*. It accompanied the article in which he was described as writing in tongues.

stunned! He decided that Lillian had crossed a line, and he hoped that his long-time friend would understand. He wrote to Dr. and Mrs. Keyes and suggested that Lillian had "become a victim of fanaticism" and that her transgression might have been caused by an evil spirit, like the case recorded in Acts 16:16–18 of the girl who announced that Paul was a servant of the most High God. Smale advised the Keyes family that what was needed was deliverance from the work of the adversary, the accuser of the brethren in these perilous times.

Dr. Keyes was upset that Pastor Smale would think such a thing about his daughter, who was described to me by Smale's daughter as the "apple of [Keyes's] eye." Before Dr. Keyes could respond, however, Lillian delivered a second judgment—this one warning Pastor Smale "to give up ambition in connection with his church work." Once again Pastor Smale responded to this sixteen-year-old girl by

Sketch by "Examiner" Artist of the Seventeen-Year-Old Girl, Follower of the Rev. Joseph Smale, Who, it Is Claimed, Has Been Given Power to Talk Language Which She Never Studied.

This is a sketch of the seventeen-year-old Lillian Keyes drawn by a newspaper artist in September 1906. In the accompanying caption, she was described as a "follower of the Rev. Joseph Smale, who, it is claimed, has been given power to talk language which she never studied." When she delivered a written "prophecy" that Smale was quenching the Spirit at First New Testament Church, Joseph Smale tried to speak with her father, Dr. Henry Sheridan Keyes about the fact that he did not believe the "prophecy" was genuine. Keyes was angered by the implication that his daughter was operating under the influence of evil spirits and split First New Testament Church. The split became known as the Upper Room Mission. Later, Lillian Keyes became a Presbyterian missionary in China, where she worked with her husband until 1954.

addressing her parents in a letter. He expressed shock at her behavior and implored the Keyeses to pray that she be delivered. When, in a subsequent service, Lillian Keyes stood to her feet and tried to deliver yet another word, Pastor Smale intervened, asking the people to ignore her as he led them in a song. Smale's public censure of Lillian led Dr. Keyes to break off their longtime friendship. Keyes sincerely believed that the Holy Spirit was working through his daughter, and he refused to correct her.

The people of the Azusa Street Mission took sides in this argument, which once again made front page news. Without giving any detail, Frank Bartleman summed it up, "They did not break through at Pastor Smale's Assembly. There was too much reserve there. God had taken them as far as he could." Although Pastor Smale tried to mend the fence with Keyes, the doctor would not allow it. Smale finally explained to his congregation, "I do not condemn all of what purports to be the

Elmer K. Fisher, Pastor of the Upper Room Mission

gift of tongues. Some of my people have it without a doubt and they are good, conscientious Christians, but the devil, as well as God is having a hand in this."

The Upper Room Mission stood at 327 1/2 South Spring Street. Elmer Fisher served as the pastor to this congregation from September 1906 until 1914. It moved to 203 Mercantile Place in 1914, to 406 1/2 North Los Angeles Street in 1915, and ceased to exist in 1918. Elmer Fisher died in the influenza pandemic that swept the world, January 19, 1919.

Dr. Keyes left the church, taking Smale's new associate pastor, Elmer K. Fisher, with him, and together they founded a congregation that would soon become known as the Upper Room Mission. With his ties to Pastor Smale now irreparably broken, Pastor Fisher built a relationship with Pastor Seymour and with Pastor Pendleton, and began attending the Monday morning leaders meetings at Azusa Street. Together they would continue to promote the Apostolic Faith position in Los Angeles.

Pastor Smale remained in Los Angeles, leading First New Testament Church, for several years before starting an independent Baptist congregation that he led until his death in 1926. For several years, Dr. Keyes and his family worshipped at the Upper Room Mission.

Following the Streetcar Lines

If the Azusa Street revival ran quickly through Los Angeles, it also spilled over just as rapidly into several surrounding towns, thanks in large part to the Pacific Electric Railroad. Huntington's railroad made access to these communities an efficient reality. By the time the Azusa Street Mission celebrated its first anniversary, workers related to the mission had established new congregations or converted older congregations in nearby Highland Park, Pasadena, Monrovia, Whittier, Santa Ana, and Long Beach. A brief overview of three of these centers will provide an idea of how the revival spread.

Pasadena and the "Household of God"

I do not care for witnesses. I am a servant of the Lord Jesus who sent me in His name to proclaim His gospel and I have only acted as the laws of the commonwealth and my God give me the right to worship according to my own dictates. God bless the witnesses against me. May they all be saved.

This is not the contest of man versus man, but the battle of God versus the devil. I have the power to disturb the devil. Glory, Hallelujah. I will suffer as Christ has suffered. I am ready to suffer martyrdom as did Christ. Glory be to God.

ANSEL HOWARD POST

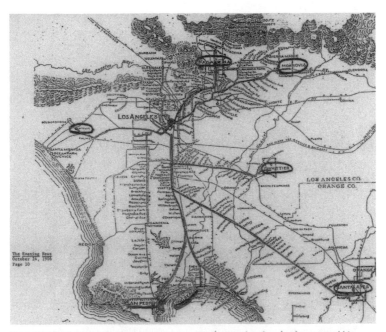

Henry Huntington's Pacific Electric streetcar system in 1906 Los Angeles Area served his needs well. Not only did it connect virtually every household in the city (within four blocks), it also connected many outlying suburbs to the heart of the city. In addition, Huntington had bought up much of the property in what would become a variety of beach towns, and he simply extended the line as needed to make that property available to newly arriving investors. At the end of each one of the main lines served by Pacific Electric, the people of the Azusa Street Mission established new preaching points or full-fledged missions that joined with the Apostolic Faith Mission at Azusa Street to further the goals of the revival.

During the summer of 1906 the Azusa Street Mission expanded its influence beyond the city of Los Angeles. This happened first through Ansel H. Post, who was holding a tent meeting in Pasadena under the auspices of William F. Manley's "Household of God." Pasadena, the crown city of the San Gabriel Valley, lies just twelve miles northeast of downtown Los Angeles. It was easily accessible from downtown by means of the Pacific Electric Railroad. When Post heard of what was taking place at Azusa Street, he decided that he had to see it for himself. Over a period of several days he visited the mission, and on June 25, 1906, Post had a highly demonstrative experience when he received his baptism in

Ansel and Henrietta Post

the Spirit. Many witnesses recalled it in later years. Within a week, others in his tent meeting in Pasadena were also speaking in tongues, shrieking, and groaning well into the night. Neighboring businesses, especially a rooming house next door to the tent, began to lose customers. This put the proprietors up in arms against Post and his meetings. Post was not swayed by their complaints to him, citing the freedom of the Spirit. On July 1 someone on the second floor of the adjacent boarding house threw a bucket of cold water on the worshippers in an attempt to quiet them down. It didn't work.

Finally Mrs. West, the owner of the house, approached the city council asking for relief. The council instructed the chief of police to assign an officer to the meeting. Post was told that he had to close his meetings at 10 P.M. While Post complied with the 10 P.M. curfew, Mrs. West, who wanted the city to close Post down, fumed. She went back to the City Council demanding that they close Post down completely or move him to another location. Post was offered another place, but he refused to leave his prime location, allegedly declaring through a tongue and an interpretation that the Lord had instructed them not to move.

On July 9 Mrs. West circulated a petition among a number of local business owners and took it to the city council. Once again, she demanded that Post and his tent be removed as a public nuisance. The mayor sought counsel from the city attorney and then rescinded Post's permit to hold the tent meeting. Post refused to leave. About 9:15 P.M., July 12, Post was arrested while conducting a meeting. He was arraigned and tried the following day.

Post did not deny the fact that he was holding noisy meetings, but he contended that he was noisy because the Holy Spirit made him noisy. He couldn't help it, he argued. He believed that his right to make noise in worship was covered under the U.S. Constitution and the Bill of Rights as a manifestation of his religious freedom. He viewed the city as doing the devil's work, and announced that he intended to "obey the will of God rather than men." *The Apostolic Faith* published accounts of Post's plight, highlighting his faithfulness to God in the midst of persecution. Post's arguments became the stock in trade of all subsequent Azusa Street defenses when arrests occurred.

In the end, Post was found guilty and given twenty-four hours to re-think his position or face a sentence of fifty days in jail or a fifty dollar fine. The following day Post quietly took down the tent and set up shop in a rented facility two blocks from where he had been holding meetings. Having watched the events of the previous week unfold, Post's new neighbors brought their complaints to the city council immediately. This time the city changed tactics. It went after the landlord, who was forced to close Post down. Post moved two or three more times before opening the Alley Mission. It would ultimately become the source for two Pentecostal congregations in Pasadena, one of them an Assembly of God, the other a Foursquare congregation.

Carrie Judd Montgomery visited Post's Alley Mission in December 1906 and described it as a place of "sweet unity of spirit" with "quiet but powerful manifestations of the Spirit of God." Pastor Post joined Seymour's Monday morning leaders' meetings, and he continued to maintain a close relationship with Pastor Seymour. While he led the Alley Mission he made regular trips to the Azusa Street Mission, where he encouraged Seymour and his congregation "with his messages from the throne and with the unction and divine love with which God fills him." Joining the Assemblies of God in 1914, Post served as a missionary in Egypt until his death in 1931.

The Monrovia Holiness Church

For want of a section of the law under which to prevent meetings, authorities at Monrovia fear that "holy Rollers" gatherings there will result in offering their babies as human sacrifices. Marshal Miller, the chief police officer, is on the alert to prevent the slaughter of the innocents, but is not at all confident that he can successfully combat the determined efforts of the fanatics to carry out the threats which they have openly made. The little foothill town is in a frenzy of excitement, and a conflict between the authorities and the enthusiasts is expected.

THE EVENING NEWS

To the east of Pasadena lies the town of Monrovia. Pastor Owen Adams of Monrovia's Holiness Tabernacle embraced the message of the Azusa Street Mission about the same time that Ansel Post did. By the third week of July, Glenn Cook was traveling regularly from Los Angeles to Monrovia via the same Pacific Electric line that passed through Pasadena. He held evangelistic meetings in the Holiness Tabernacle during the evening, while numbers of the congregation's members availed themselves of daytime excursions to Azusa Street.

Glenn Cook was a dynamic preacher, known for his emotional worship and his provocative style. About July 19 Cook preached a sermon in Monrovia in which he based his remarks on Genesis 22 and the testing of Abraham. He told the people of how Abraham had his faith tested, and he talked about Abraham's willingness to trust God even when God demanded that he sacrifice his only son, Isaac. He encouraged the people to live lives of sacrifice when the Lord called upon them to do so. To strengthen his point, Cook illustrated his sermon with some of the accounts of the early Christian martyrs. They had been called upon to make the ultimate sacrifice, the sacrifice of their lives, and he encouraged the people of the Holiness Tabernacle to stand firm even if such things came their way.

Cook undoubtedly portrayed the early martyrdoms in graphic terms. "The old days when people were burned at the stake were the joyful days of the church," Cook exhorted the congregation. When he called for the people of Monrovia to be willing to give up or sacrifice their children in order to do the will of God, those outside the church heard something else. Cook surely had in mind the troubles that Ansel H. Post had faced just two weeks earlier in nearby Pasadena. Post had played the role of the martyr in Azusa Street's accounts of the incidents in Pasadena while the judge and councilpersons, like the ancient Roman authorities, were clearly cast in the role of persecutors. Post had been persecuted for the sake of righteousness, and people in Monrovia were already critical of the congregation of the Holiness Tabernacle. These were troubled times for the Apostolic Faith movement, times that called for great personal sacrifice in the face of public derision and persecution.

What Cook did not fully appreciate was Monrovia's rumor mill. The church's neighbors passed along the latest gossip regarding the Apostolic Faith folk at the local Holiness Tabernacle. They made it sound as though Cook was asking his followers to sacrifice their children. With services running from 10 A.M. until 2 A.M. the following morning, and the windows wide open because of the summer heat, the neighbors were fed up with Cook. They turned to the city marshal to "put on the lid" because "Morpheus" had "about stopped calling at the houses along the avenue."

As their fears increased, the community prevailed on Marshal Miller either to sit in on their meetings or assign one of his deputies to do so. Apparently Miller had seen similar things in the past. He sat in on several meetings before declaring to the public that they had nothing to fear. "These revivals wear out in time, you know." He viewed these people as possibly "somewhat fanatical" but did not see that they were breaking any law, so he counseled the town to leave them alone. The church continued to serve the city of Monrovia for many years, later becoming part of the Assemblies of God.

Preaching the Apostolic Faith in Whittier

> The News does not pretend to criticize what to the ordinary mind seems rank fanaticism in the exercise of alleged "unknown tongues;" it's none of our concern if blacks and whites join together and shout themselves into insensibility, and none will question the great American privilege of one's worshipping God according to the dictates of his own conscience, but no person has the moral or legal right to indulge in practices which interfere with the peace of a community.
>
> WHITTIER DAILY NEWS

The town of Whittier was established in 1887 by Quakers, about twelve miles south of Los Angeles. By mid-August 1906 folks from the Azusa Street Mission had traveled to this town by another of Huntington's Pacific Electric lines, with their message of baptism in the Spirit. They attempted to establish a Pentecostal presence through a combination of street meetings, cottage prayer meetings, and meetings in a rented hall known as "the barracks." They found a variety of Wesleyan holiness folks in Whittier as well as a range of critics.

A local resident, Mr. W. S. Lemon, invited Azusa Street's evangelists to hold meetings in Whittier. They received free lodging at a home on South Greenleaf Avenue owned by Daniel Scott, and they held meetings at the corner of South Greenleaf Avenue and Hadley Street. The first Apostolic Faith Mission evangelists to arrive in Whittier were a Rev. Taylor and Mr. [Tom] Anderson. In subsequent months the city would be visited by others from the mission, including Henry and Mrs. McLain, Mae Field Mayo, Agnes Jacobsen, Anna Hall, C. E. Nichols, William Millson, and the young African American preacher Henry Prentiss.

The local press supported the Apostolic Faith evangelists' right to hold meetings within reason, shaming any resident who did not embrace religious toleration, but it also warned them not to disturb the sleep of those who needed it in order to earn an honest living. "It's none of our concern," wrote the editor, "if blacks and whites join together and shout themselves into insensibility."

Pastor Seymour held at least one meeting there in mid-September, though he probably held more. The meeting began with a testimony from Anna Hall, who had worked first with Charles Parham in Texas and now with Pastor Seymour in Los Angeles. A number of other testimonies followed. Seymour preached in "the barracks" from Malachi 3, and following his sermon he gave an altar call. A group of workers who had accompanied Seymour to the town helped the various seekers pray for their baptism in the Spirit. That evening one of the seekers, David Griffith, fainted. At first the altar workers thought he had simply fallen "under the power," but when he did not regain consciousness, they became alarmed. They commandeered a horse and buggy and quickly took him to a local physician. It turned out that he suffered from a condition that led to sporadic fainting spells, and he revived on the way to the doctor. Two weeks later a fifty-nine-year-old woman, Mrs. Donisa See, began seeking her baptism. She, too, was soon on the floor, and the group allowed her to remain in a trance-like state with periods of semi-consciousness for two full days. By the time the group realized that something was wrong, she was clearly unconscious. Within days she died of what had been a stroke.

Whittier had been tolerant of the evangelists from Azusa Street at first, but these incidents and the incessant shouting, screaming, and wailing that came from their meetings soon turned many in the town against them. On one occasion, some of the local teenagers created excitement when they filled the feathers of a live chicken with cayenne pepper and threw it into their meeting. While the chicken squawked and flapped, and people scrambled to capture it, the pepper spread through the air, causing great commotion among the worshippers and the premature dismissal of the meeting.

The arrest of Azusa Street evangelists Henry McLain, his wife, Miss Mae Field Mayo, and Agnes Jacobsen in October 1906 on charges of disturbing the peace produced a notorious incident. Complaints had been filed by a neighbor who claimed that he was unable to sleep with all the noise they created. As soon as word reached the Azusa Street Mission regarding the arrest, a group of fifteen more workers boarded the Pacific Electric and made their way to Whittier to take their place.

Using an older form of English akin to that found in the King James Version of the Bible, the local newspaper parodied the case under the title, "The Parable of the Holy Roller." It began,

> And it came to pass in the second year of the reign of the Anti-Push, and in the seventh month, there came into the land a certain tribe, being gifted of many tongues, who took up their abode in the fourth ward.
>
> And they grew and waxed strong until they became a nuisance and the people were alarmed.

Judge Gidley addressed the defendants, inviting them to leave town in return for dropping the charges against them. The women eventually gave in and returned to Los Angeles, but Henry McLain did not. When he announced to the judge that he would not be leaving town, according to the parody he asked the judge,

> "What would'st thou have me to do that I may likewise obtain my freedom?" And after the magistrate had an end of writing he frowned upon this man, and looking over the top of his spectacles (for they had waxed worn), he spake unto him, saying:
>
> "Verily, I say unto you, lest before the cock crows this evening thou hast deposited thirty shekels within the coffers of the treasury, thou shalt tarry within the confines of the bastile for a like number of days."

McLain chose the thirty-day sentence in jail, where he worked on a chain gang with a number of Mexicans, shoveling dirt. Each evening, just after the prisoners had eaten, McLain gathered the men around him and attempted to conduct a Bible study. While he had a captive audience, only a couple of them spoke English. McLain reported that they interpreted his Bible study into Spanish for the others. During these studies McLain would occasionally burst into tongues and the prisoners would begin to cry (one can only wonder why). The Lord, he contended, gave him the "Mexican language." He claimed that on one occasion he opened his Bible to Isaiah 55 to preach and he promptly began to say the words of the chapter in Spanish. "I did not know . . . that I had read it until they told me," he remarked. In Henry McLain's eyes, at least, his time in jail was very fruitful.

On yet another occasion late in the year, the African American preacher Henry Prentiss set up shop on a street corner opposite a white southern temperance advocate named Mr. R. H. Morse who was already holding a meeting. Together, the two speakers attracted a racially mixed crowd of several hundred people. Henry Prentiss began to shout, and Morse responded with some racial barbs aimed at Prentiss. Prentiss only grew louder, eventually dropping to his knees to pray very loudly that Whittier be saved from imminent destruction. The growing crowd began to "jeer" Prentiss and his followers, circling them. As one reporter put it,

> Howls, groans, shouts, cheers and hisses made up a noise which sent belated women shoppers scurrying for home, and sent the small boy's heart up into his throat. Fully a thousand people made up the good-natured mob, which surged first to the temperance orator and then to the kneeling rollers, entirely blocking the street at the junction of Philadelphia street and Greenleaf avenue.

Sensing trouble, City Marshal Robert E. Way intervened. He arrested Prentiss and his aides. Their first trial failed to get a conviction, but before their second trial the case was dismissed.

In each of these cases, as well as in many others, public opinion galvanized against the Apostolic Faith evangelists. Within this context of misunderstanding, the Azusa Street Mission developed a legal defense against those who criticized it. Their defense came straight from the pages of the Bible. From the mission faithful's perspective, their critics were not criticizing them—they were criticizing the God whom they served. They were being unnecessarily persecuted for the cause of Jesus Christ. They were a determined—some might even say, a hardheaded—lot, and they would continue to do what they did in spite of the odds, praying for those who "persecuted" them for the sake of righteousness, while claiming that they were subject to God's direction and not the humanly contrived rules of the civil authorities.

Extending the Revival Across the Nation

The Azusa Street Mission commissioned and credentialed a score of evangelists, and many of them traveled to other parts of the West. Franklin Hill and Abundio and Rosa de Lopez both traveled to San Diego for a period of ministry and church planting. In early November 1906 Florence Crawford was named state director for the Apostolic Faith movement that emanated from Azusa Street. As she traveled to the San Francisco Bay area, Florence Crawford was accompanied by the African American evangelist Ophelia Wiley and evangelists G. W. and May Evans, who would serve in San Jose and Santa Rosa. Also with her were the missionaries Lucy Leatherman; Andrew Johnson, a Swedish immigrant who returned to Sweden where subsequently he served as a pastor; Louise Condit, who went on to Jerusalem; and Mr. and Mrs. Thomas Junk, who intended to serve as missionaries in northern China. Along the way, Crawford held meetings in a variety of holiness churches, made converts to the Apostolic Faith, and established new Apostolic Faith congregations. When she arrived in Oakland she continued preaching at independent missions, the Salvation Army, and the Household of God. She ran a five-week meeting at William F. Manley's Household of God, and it became a center for the Apostolic Faith movement in the area. Next, she traveled to Woodland, California, and then on to Salem, Oregon.

Martin L. Ryan, a holiness pastor from Salem, Oregon, had visited the Azusa Street Mission during the late summer of 1906. He returned to his congregation in Salem, Oregon, and began publishing a paper he called *Apostolic Light* after he was baptized in the Spirit. As soon as he returned home he began begging for the Azusa Street Mission to send workers to help him lead his congregation into the revival. Ophelia Wiley, who had traveled to the Bay Area with Florence Crawford, was sent ahead to Salem. She arrived there and participated in highly publicized meetings that began November 15, 1906. It was the talk of the town by the time Florence Crawford and her

Florence Louise Crawford

daughter, Mildred, arrived one month later. Eventually M. L. Ryan moved on to Spokane, Washington, where he convinced thirty of his followers to join him in ministry in Japan. They left for Japan in May.

Among those who had traveled north with Florence Crawford, the Evanses decided to stay in San Jose where they worked to establish a mission, then they moved on to Woodland where they helped to incorporate the new work in that town. Thomas and Mrs. Junk continued north, settling into a small congregation in Seattle for several months, before continuing on to serve as missionaries in China. Louise Condit, Lucy Leatherman, and Andrew Johnson turned east, traveling through Colorado Springs and Denver to New York. Mrs. Leatherman remained in New York for a time, while Louise Condit went on to serve in Palestine and Andrew Johnson returned to Sweden. By the end of December 1906 Florence Crawford could be found holding meetings in a small church led by the African American pastor John F. Glasco, in Portland, Oregon. She led thirty-eight people into their baptism in the Spirit in the short time she ministered there before returning to California.

On March 19, 1907, leaving her family behind, Florence Crawford once again took to the road, traveling back to Oakland where she set a new church in order. She visited the work in San Francisco, held meetings in Santa Rosa, and then proceeded to San Jose. After spending seven weeks in the Bay Area, Crawford moved again to Portland where, from May 3 through July 12, she established an Apostolic Faith base. When she received word that her ten-year-old daughter, Mildred, had suffered a broken arm, and questions were being raised about the teachings of the Apostolic Faith on divine healing, she traveled back to Highland Park, California, where her husband and children lived. Crawford stayed for the remainder of Azusa Street's camp meeting and worked at the mission until November, before leaving once again. This time she left for good. She left her husband and son, and moved with her daughter to Portland. By January 1908 she had swung the allegiance of the west coast congregations that she had established on behalf of the Azusa Street Mission. They would form the core of a new group—her group, the Apostolic Faith Mission of Portland, Oregon.

By the first anniversary of the Azusa Street revival in April 1907 there were Apostolic Faith congregations throughout Southern California and up the west coast to Seattle. They could be found in Colorado Springs and Denver, Colorado, Lamont, Oklahoma, Indianapolis, Indiana, Minneapolis, Minnesota, Chattanooga, Tennessee, Danville, Virginia, Akron, Alliance, and Cleveland, in a number of smaller towns of western Pennsylvania, New York City, Toronto, Canada, and northern Mexico. We do not have space to tell all of these stories although three or four of them will demonstrate how the revival spread across the nation.

Dunn, North Carolina

From the time the Azusa Street revival began, Frank Bartleman wrote about it. He was a prolific advertiser of what he believed was the beginning of a great "latter day" revival at the mission. One of the periodicals he frequently wrote for was a holiness paper called *The Way of Faith*. Published from Columbia, South Carolina, by J. M. Pike, its wide-ranging circulation crossed a number of denominational lines. Among the readers of this periodical was Gaston Barnabas Cashwell, a minister with the Holiness Church of North Carolina. As Cashwell read coverage of the revival, undoubtedly supplied by Frank Bartleman, he determined to visit the Azusa Street Mission for himself. He excused himself from the annual conference of his denomination, borrowed his train fare to California and headed west. He arrived in Los Angeles in late November and found his way to the mission.

At first Cashwell found it difficult to enter into what was going on at the mission, not because it was too demonstrative for him, but because African Americans played such a large role in the meetings he attended. He had come with his share of racial

Gaston Barnabas Cashwell

prejudice, and he would not set it aside. He visited first on a Sunday, and when the invitation was made for those who were in search of their "Pentecost," he went forward and then made his way upstairs to the mission's upper room. He found it difficult to allow any African American to pray for or with him or to lay hands on him. Back in his hotel room, he struggled with his racial prejudice. He later wrote that he had to undergo a "crucifixion" in which he "had to die, to many things." Among these things were his prejudicial attitudes toward African Americans. In the end, he declared that God had given him "the victory" over his racism. He returned to the mission and invited Pastor Seymour and others to lay hands on him in his quest.

For several days he continued his quest for the baptism in the Spirit in the upper room of the mission, but without results. On Thursday of that week, Cashwell had been praying upstairs. He took a break and entered the meeting that was being conducted on the ground floor. Clara Lum was reading excerpts from letters that told of people receiving their baptism in the Spirit around the country. Suddenly, Cashwell began to "speak in tongues and praise God." Having received his baptism in the Spirit, Cashwell returned to Dunn, North Carolina. On December 31, 1906, he gave his testimony in the local holiness church, encouraging the group to join him in receiving their "Pentecost." Many did.

Invitations were quickly sent to a host of holiness preachers in the region, inviting them to a series of meetings that Cashwell would preach in Dunn. Cashwell rented a large tobacco warehouse, and scores of preachers came. The meetings ran for at least three weeks, and by the time they were over, many pastors of the Free Will Baptist Church and most of the leaders of the Fire-Baptized Holiness Church and some from the Holiness Church of North Carolina had received their baptism in the Spirit. Not all Free Will Baptists were open to his message, but those who were formed the Pentecostal Free Will Baptist Church. The Fire-Baptized Holiness Church, which had been a holiness denomination, now became a Pentecostal one. It would split along racial lines, and a largely African American body, under the leadership of

William E. Fuller, would develop into the Fire-Baptized Holiness Church of God of the Americas. As for the Holiness Church of North Carolina, it would change its name in 1909 to the Pentecostal Holiness Church, and in 1911, joining with most of the white members of the Fire-Baptized Holiness Church, it became known as the International Pentecostal Holiness Church.

Cashwell seems to have left his racial prejudices behind him in Los Angeles, for he continued to minister across racial lines throughout the South for some time thereafter. In January 1908 he was invited to Cleveland, Tennessee, where he ministered at a gathering of ministers of the (holiness) Church of God. During Cashwell's sermon, Ambrose Jessup Tomlinson, leader of the group, fell to the floor and began to speak in tongues. As a result, many of the pastors affiliated with the Church of God (Cleveland, TN), which had existed in one form or another since 1886, received their baptism in the Spirit as well. Subsequent to Cashwell's visit to Cleveland, the Church of God developed a "Pentecostal" theology and joined the now-burgeoning roll of Pentecostal denominations.

Memphis, Tennessee

Word had also reached the African American leaders Charles Price Jones and Charles Harrison Mason, co-founders of the Church of God in Christ. In February 1907 Pastor Mason, accompanied by J. A. Jeter and J. D. Young, traveled from Memphis to Los Angeles to see for themselves what the Azusa Street revival had to offer. Their stay lasted six weeks, and before it was over Mason and J. A. Jeter had spoken in tongues.

At the time of the Azusa Street Mission's founding, the South was becoming a more difficult place for African Americans to live. Whites were increasingly moving to disenfranchise blacks in the region. Loose talk, unsubstantiated rumors, and outright lies led to mistrust between the races. In the first decade of the twentieth century an average of sixty-five black men were lynched each year. On April 14, 1906, the day the Azusa Street Mission began services at 312 Azusa Street, three African American men—Horace B. Duncan,

Charles Harrison Mason

Fred Coker, and Will Allen—were dragged by a mob of seven thousand people to the town square in Springfield, Missouri[30] and lynched. On September 22, 1906, a racial riot swept Atlanta, bringing everything to a stop. Over the next week, whites killed blacks, and blacks responded in kind. Troops had to be called in to quell the riots. Other parts of the South may not have experienced such open violence, but anger and hatred lay just below the surface on both sides of the racial divide. Even Church of God in Christ leader Charles H. Mason was infected by it. According to his own testimony, before he could receive his baptism in the Spirit his attitude over the "world's wrongs" had to change.

> That night the Lord spoke to me that Jesus saw all of this world's wrongs but did not attempt to set it right until God overshadowed Him with the Holy Ghost. And He said that "I was no better than my Lord," and if I wanted Him to baptize

me, I would have to let the people's rights and wrongs all alone and look to Him. And I said yes to God.

"Yes, Lord," became a theme that would run throughout Mason's life and into the hymnody of the Church of God in Christ.

Following his return to Memphis, Mason found that some in his own congregation had already accepted the Azusa Street message, brought to town by Glenn Cook. Over the following four months, Mason and Jones debated the meaning of baptism in the Holy Spirit. The Church of God in Christ was a holiness church that equated the baptism in the Holy Spirit with entire sanctification. David Daniels has shown that Mason viewed the baptism in the Holy Spirit as a normative, empowering experience that came upon those who had previously been sanctified. It also included speaking in tongues.[31] Jones was not swayed by Mason's arguments and did not want to add this new teaching to the Church of God in Christ. Mason did. Sides were drawn up over this issue that would play out in a meeting held later in the summer.

The situation was not helped when Glenn Cook, who had intended to stay in Los Angeles until May, left early and traveled to Memphis at the invitation of L. P. Adams, a white leader who would align with the Church of God in Christ. While in Memphis, Cook preached a sermon heard by a young African American, Mr. F. C. Ford, a servant in the home of Mr. Eldridge E. Wright. Eldridge Wright was the son of General Luke E. Wright, the U.S. Ambassador to Japan. When members of the Wright family heard Ford speaking in tongues in their home, they became frightened. As a result, Eldridge Wright had Ford arrested on an insanity charge. Cook and Adams intervened with Memphis's Chief of Police O'Haver, explaining that Ford was "merely in a highly developed [spiritual] state and not insane." Thanks to that intervention, Ford was released.

In August 1907 the Church of God in Christ held a three-day convention in Jackson, Mississippi, where the discussion reached its peak. In the end Jones prevailed, and Mason left with about half the denomination's membership. Mason had given the name to the denomination, however, so over the next two years Mason and Jones fought each other in court over the use of "Church of God in Christ." In 1909 Mason prevailed and the court granted him the denomination's charter and the use of the name. The Church of God in Christ would now be officially recognized as the name of this newest Pentecostal organization. C. P. Jones renamed his group the Church of Christ, Holiness, the following year.

Indianapolis, Indiana

In no place where this gift of tongues is claimed has any one claimed the gift of interpretation. There has been no building up of the church, no winning to duty, no tenderness of fellow feeling, no sharing of burdens, cares or sorrows of others. Here in our city the most disgraceful disorder has characterized the meetings and the result has been the dividing asunder of the church and God. Confusion has reigned, and self-display and an unseemly mixing of races and sexes. The result is that the evil forces so control the meeting that there is an absence of reverence in the handling of holy things, such hysterical abandon that evil is nourished as in a hothouse, and the name of God is blasphemed.

THE REV. G. D. WOLFE

Glenn Cook left Los Angeles on December 4, 1906, bound for Lamont, Oklahoma. He held a series of cottage prayer meetings there, where he brought a number of people into a dynamic encounter with the Holy Spirit. He then turned northward to Chicago. After spending two days in the Windy City he continued on to Indianapolis, Indiana, arriving January 18.

Glenn Cook began meetings in Indianapolis that weekend at the Union Gospel Tabernacle, located at North Senate and West St. Clair Streets. This corner straddled the line that separated the black and white communities in Indianapolis. On January 21, Cook wrote to the Azusa Street Mission, informing them of his work in Oklahoma and requesting prayer for his new Indianapolis venture. Within ten days, his work in Indianapolis would be on the lips of many in that city, as he sought "to inspire belief in the transmission of the power granted the apostles." Cook continued to minister to this congregation until March, when he returned for a short visit to the Azusa Street Mission. When Cook went back to Indianapolis a month later, the Union Gospel Tabernacle had moved to the Murphy League Hall at North Alabama and East New York Streets.

Even before Cook left for Los Angeles, some of the people had begun to speak in tongues. The *Indianapolis Star* quickly gave them the nickname "Gliggy Bluks." The name was intended to mock the sound of someone's utterance in tongues. During Cook's absence he chose as stand-in Thomas Hezmalhalch, a California preacher previously associated with Dowie's community in Zion, Illinois, who had received his baptism in the Spirit at the Azusa Street Mission in Los Angeles. A teenage girl present in the congregation, Alice Reynolds, would soon marry J. Roswell Flower and become with him a leader in the Assemblies of God. On Easter Sunday, April 17, 1907, however, Alice lay on the floor of the church, speaking in tongues. The next evening Tom Hezmalhalch preached from 1 Peter 2:9, claiming that Pentecostal people "were regarded as 'peculiar people' because others who had not become possessed so as to speak the 'tongues' could not appreciate them."

For the next several months intense news coverage followed the breaking revival in Indianapolis, with reports being published nearly every day. Reporters seemed to look for any angle by which they could embarrass the revival. They complained that Cook and Hezmalhalch were taking advantage of the people, receiving free room and board and substantial offerings, providing entertainment rather than substance, and contributing to the breakup of marriages. In spite of the negative news coverage, or perhaps because of it, by April 21 the revival had built up a congregation of some one hundred and fifty people.

Cook took over the services on his return to Indianapolis, preaching until May 7, when he left for a second set of meetings in Lamont, Oklahoma. During this absence Mr. and Mrs. Reynolds (Alice's parents), Mr. C. J. Quinn, and J. O. Lehman were placed in charge of the meetings (Lehman would soon leave as a missionary for South Africa). Before the end of May, Cook returned to Indianapolis and promptly took charge of the meetings once again.

On the evening of June 2 Pastor William J. Seymour arrived, accompanied by William Henry Cummings, Emma Cummings, and three of their children. They had all participated in the Asberry home prayer meetings in Los Angeles. As Seymour made his way down the aisle, many people greeted him. Glenn Cook "threw both arms about his neck and kissed him," a fact that escaped no one. That act of affection clearly demonstrated to this Indianapolis congregation the interracial freedom and spontaneity that characterized the Azusa Street Mission. When order was restored, Cook turned the service over to Pastor Seymour who, "in a voice that shook the church," led the group in singing "The Comforter Has Come." Three days later the *Indianapolis News* carried a story on the work in Indianapolis. "The 'Gliggy Bluks' are a religious sect in which the color line is not drawn," it reported.

> The members of the sect are supposed to have the gift of 'strange tongues,' and the Negro brother is accorded the same consideration in the meetings of the sect as the white man. Incidentally, a Negro is the 'founder' of the faith.

Over the next several days various people representing the city's police department and the board of public safety visited the group. Undercover detectives were sent to investigate the meetings to determine what, if any, charges could be brought against Cook and Seymour. The newspapers complained about the racial mixing that pervaded the meetings, seemingly without any complaints from the worshippers themselves. "It's de powah ob de Lo'd," Elder Seymour was quoted as saying. Detective William Holtz was not so sure, informing the chief of police that he thought what Seymour was doing might be nothing more than "hypnotic." Charles Tutwiler, a representative from the board of public safety, complained that the racial mores of Indianapolis were being violated in the meeting. To illustrate, he told of a young white girl, who, after "coming out" of one of the alleged trances, walked about the room with a Negro holding his arm about her. He said white women of good appearance attend the meeting and mingle with Negroes freely, holding hands while they call each other "brother" and "sister," and shouting the gibberish.

The following day Joseph Hillery King, the head of the Fire-Baptized Holiness Church, stopped by and preached at Cook's meeting on his way to Alliance, Ohio, where Ivey Campbell had taken the revival.

As the revival grew, local newspapers continued to stir up controversy. Troublemakers began to attend, intent on creating as much disorder as they could. As a result, Glenn Cook asked the police department for protection so the group could continue worshipping unhindered. The police took the opportunity to grill him extensively, even reviewing a recent arrest in Oklahoma, where Cook had been mistaken for a man who had murdered his wife. All the while, the newspapers tattled on what was happening.

On Saturday, two weeks after his arrival, Pastor Seymour joined Glenn Cook in conducting a baptismal service in Full Creek, near the Indiana Avenue Bridge. The service began an hour late when Seymour and Cook came to the river from the nearby home of an unnamed African American. They were each dressed in a black robe. As Cook waded into the water, Seymour began to speak.

Brother Seymour read and discoursed [from the Gospel of Luke]. He read a great deal and discoursed more. Brother Glenn Cook, feet freezing and head baking, stood the picture of patience, while the water continued to swirl. He watched the sun glint on Brother Seymour's gold tooth, but gave no hint of his burning desire that those thick lips should close in solemn conclusion over the glistening ornament. It was long before Brother Seymour's voice dropped to a gutteral "amen! Let's sing numbah twenty-fouh!"

Then the martyr in the water waited for another hymn and a prayer and more talking by Brother Seymour.

Two hundred people stood on the banks while thirteen people were immersed by William J. Seymour—among them Bennett F. Lawrence, who in 1916 would publish the first history of the revival under the title *The Apostolic Faith Restored*. News coverage continued with a blow by blow account of the service, accompanied by a cartoon.

At the conclusion of the baptismal service, the congregation took streetcars back to Murphy Hall, where Pastor Seymour conducted a foot washing service. The women moved to the front of the auditorium while the men gathered at the rear. As they sang "Leaning on the Everlasting Arms" they washed each other's feet, symbolizing their willingness to serve one another. Then they rose and began to hug and kiss one another in a demonstration that the local news simply could not ignore.

White women threw their arms about the dusky necks of negresses and went through performances that would put to shame the most accomplished "park spooning."

Among the men, the conduct was much the same. Negroes

This cartoon making fun of a baptismal service William J. Seymour and Glenn Cook performed in a local creek, appeared in an Indianapolis newspaper. It is interesting to note that the cartoonist notes in his drawing that the congregation was a mixture of races and of ages. While Glenn Cook is pictured as waiting in the water, Pastor Seymour joined him as the two baptized thirteen candidates. The name "Gliggy Bluks" was given to Seymour's congregation in an obvious attempt to ridicule their claim to be able to speak in tongues. This designation was used repeatedly over a several week period.

and whites locked in each other's arms, kissed and patted each other's backs and caressed white faces against black faces and chocolate colored faces and coffee colored faces.

"Smack, smack, smack, smackety, smack"—soft "smacks" in the front part of the room.

"Smawk, smawk, smawk, smawkety, smawk"—big coarse "smawks" in the rear part of the room.

Sister Cripe walked clear down the line of women, kissing all. Negresses were not neglected. Sister Schurmann kissed, everybody kissed.

In the rear part of the room men were clasped in each other's arms. In fond embrace Brother Osborn and Brother Cummings, colored, remained almost a full minute. It was real hugging, no beating around the bush about it. And nearly every other man was going through [a] similar process. And meanwhile among all there were shouts of joy and laughter, And singing—one song right after another.

Following the baptism and foot washing, the group celebrated the Lord's Supper. Later that week, Pastor Seymour left Indianapolis to continue his trip.

Glenn Cook stayed on as pastor of this new Pentecostal congregation. Later that year, Cook could be found leading meetings at the Good News Mission located at 111 North Liberty Street. In November 1908, the following year, the Good News Mission would consolidate with the Apostolic Faith Mission and the two churches would become known as the Christian Assembly.

Akron, Cleveland, and Alliance, Ohio

The new sect has been denounced as a fraud by nearly every local minister, and some people have asked the police to stop the meetings, claiming that the meetings are working harm to the community. Residents in the vicinity of the mission claim they cannot sleep on account of the demonstration by the converts. The police have promised to investigate.

ANONYMOUS NEWS REPORTER

All [mainline] preachers are liars. All newspapers are liars. Preachers and newspapers belong in the same class. Both are disciples of Ananias.[32]

IVEY CAMPBELL

Ivey Campbell was furious when she spit out these charges. Typically soft-spoken except when preaching, she had now been attacked one too many times in the press. She was not about to leave Akron, Ohio, without telling her critics what she thought of them.

Ivey Campbell was a member of the Holiness Church of Los Angeles when she first visited the Azusa Street Mission. She was baptized in the Spirit early in the summer of 1906, and in November she returned to Ohio to share her testimony with friends and family. She had been instrumental in helping to establish the Broadway Mission in East Liverpool, Ohio, before she moved to

Ivey Glenshaw Campbell

Los Angeles, and she wanted to testify to those she had left behind. She arrived in East Liverpool, Ohio, on November 25, 1906. On the evening of Tuesday, November 27, she was asked to conduct the service at the Broadway Mission. She shared her testimony, but most people were skeptical and rejected it. News of her testimony, however, traveled to nearby Chester, Pennsylvania, and to Akron, Ohio. Shortly she began to receive invitations to minister throughout the region.

Claudius A. McKinney, the pastor of the South Street Mission in Akron, invited Miss Campbell to hold a series of meetings at that church. Like many other pastors in the region, McKinney had been praying for revival. Many in the area had heard of what was happening at the Azusa Street Mission. In nearby Alliance, Ohio, a Friends [Quakers] evangelist and head of a Missionary Training School in Alliance, Levi Lupton, had received copies of *The Apostolic Faith* and corresponded with some visitors to the Azusa Street Mission. He had even debated going to Los Angeles to see for himself what was happening at the Azusa Street revival.

Both McKinney and Lupton were pleased with Ivey Campbell's arrival in Ohio. On December 5 she began meetings in McKinney's South Street Mission, and Lupton went there to hear her. Within a month at least forty people had been baptized in the Spirit and were speaking in tongues at the South Street Mission.

Campbell's approach was simple. She told the congregation what she had seen and experienced at the Azusa Street Mission. She told them about their need for salvation, sanctification, and baptism in the Spirit. And she spoke in tongues and interpreted what she had said. Virtually overnight the revival became the talk of the town as crowds began to gather. Pastor McKinney was very excited. He wrote postcards to a long list of pastors and church leaders in Akron, Cleveland, Alliance, and other nearby towns, inviting them to come and see what was taking place at the South Street Mission. Among those who responded were Lupton and J. E. Sawders. Both men soon received their baptism in the Spirit and spoke in tongues.

Lupton was a bit of a maverick within the Society of Friends, and his school in Alliance was independent. In late December Lupton took several of his students to Akron to visit Campbell's meetings. On December 28 Miss Mary L. Corlett [her name also appears as Mamie L. Corlette], a member of First Friends Church in Cleveland who was also a student of Lupton, received her baptism in the Spirit and spoke in tongues.

At the same time J. E. Sawders, an independent holiness evangelist from Akron, had been engaged to lead a revival at First Friends Church in Cleveland in early January 1907. On the evening of January 4, fresh from Ivey Campbell's meetings in Akron, Sawders preached a two-hour sermon there on the baptism in the Spirit. Fifty people went forward at his altar call. A number of them began to speak and sing in tongues. The following day the events at First Friends Church made the front page of the Cleveland papers. The church's minister, Pastor Malone, was genuinely sympathetic to what he saw, though many others were not. As the press sought out the opinions of other ministers, the story took the form of criticism and intrigue. Some pastors ascribed what was taking place to fanaticism and "nervous, implusive [sic] temperament." It didn't help that such revelations came in the Sunday morning newspaper.

That Sunday, January 7, Malone called an executive business meeting following the morning service at First Friends Church, to allow his congregation to express themselves on the recent events. His congregants had three concerns. First, Sawders was not a Friend, and they worried that he was bringing strange doctrine into their church. Second, of those who were speaking in tongues, only Mary Corlett belonged to their congregation. The rest were strangers. Third, they wondered what criteria were being used to determine whether the manifestations that had emerged were divinely given. Malone agreed to a task force to investigate. It would include the clerk of the Ohio Yearly Meeting of Friends, the Rev. Edward R. Mott.

J. E. Sawders met with the task force, which concluded that First Friends Church could not embrace Sawder's teaching. Sawders was allowed to preach one final service without mentioning either his position or the decision of the task force, since it had already been announced. He left Cleveland as soon as the service concluded. In keeping with the findings of the task force, Pastor Malone restored order to his congregation.

On January 10, Charles F. Parham, who had been in Toledo, Ohio, where he had heard about the revival, attended First Friends Church in Cleveland. He stood up in the meeting and declared that the "revival" that J. E. Sawders had brought was nothing more than "monkeyshines." "The real gift of tongues," he contended, "is never accompanied by spasms, jerks, or foolishness of any sort. This Pentecost is never accompanied by rolling on the floor or falling on the back or in spasms. It is a dignified gift and comes to uplift." He went on to charge that it was the devil who "conflicts it with spiritualism, clairvoyance and hypnotism and they enter the flesh and cause these demonstrations." Parham's intervention was ill timed. First Friends Church was no longer willing to listen.

Back in Akron, Ivey Campbell continued to preach her message of the baptism in the Spirit. News reporters described her meetings as resembling the "old-fashioned camp meetings" where people entered into "a cataleptic state for hours"—an obvious reference to people being "slain in the Spirit." People spoke in tongues and tried to converse with strangers in those tongues (though without success). Pastor McKinney cited these manifestations as a clear sign that Jesus Christ was about to return to the earth. The services at the South Street Mission sounded much like those at the Azusa Street Mission.

With all the notoriety fostered by unwanted news coverage, crowds sought out the mission. Neighbors complained about the noise from the mission at all hours of the night, and the mission asked the police department for protection against possible trouble. Still the notoriety of the revival continued to increase. Each day the newspapers seemed to find another minister or rabbi to render a decision on what was happening. It was on January 8 that Ivey Campbell unleashed her fury, condemning them in no uncertain terms and threatening them "with the curses of God for their ridicule." By mid-January, after a five week engagement at the South Street Mission, Ivey Campbell moved on, preaching in Ohio and Pennsylvania as other churches opened up to her.

After receiving his baptism in the Spirit, Levi Lupton determined that his should be an Apostolic Faith school. He informed the Azusa Street Mission that Lupton's Missionary Faith Home had received "the Pentecost" and it had become a Pentecostal "center of power" in the region. Local newspapers in Alliance, Ohio, began to run cartoons ridiculing Lupton.

Lupton had founded First Friends Church in Alliance, Ohio, so people in that town of ten thousand were well aware of who he was. Through the winter months the press investigated and criticized him. Some saw him as nothing more than a huckster, while

You will notice that Levi Lupton is portrayed as though he were speaking in tongues. The words are "Hotentot Palaver." Hotentots, of course, are indigenous people from southern Africa that have at times been known as "bushmen" or "Bantus." Palaver is a term given to strange and enticing speech. This kind of ridicule appeared in many newspapers around the country as newspaper reporters sought to portray early speakers in tongues.

others viewed him as confused. They even accused him of learning phrases in other languages from a Chicago-based firm that offered Berlitz-like language learning on phonograph discs, and passing off what he had learned as the gift of tongues. When the newspaper found out that this claim was untrue, it failed to print a retraction.

By mid-January, just a week after attending the debate at First Friends Church in Cleveland, Edward Mott was invited to preach at First Friends Church in Alliance. He preached for two hours, addressing himself to claims that Levi Lupton was making about speaking in tongues. This began a series of actions by the Friends that finally led to a painful confrontation on February 8 between Lupton and the Friends Quarterly Meeting. On March 9 the Alliance Monthly Meeting of Friends voted to remove Lupton from its rolls.

Throughout the spring the revival begun by Ivey Campbell con-

Many attempts were made to discredit early Pentecostals. In this case, Levi Lupton was accused of learning words or phrases of a foreign language from a Berlitz-like language learning program that made use of recordings, and then putting on a performance that deceived many. While the accusation made front page news, the fact that the company that sold the language program to Lupton investigated the charge and found it to be false did not.

tinued to spread to places like New Castle. Frank Bartleman arrived in Conneaut, Ohio, on April 30, where he began a meeting on May 1 that lasted a number of days. He ministered among the Christian and Missionary Alliance in Cleveland and Youngstown, preached at Pastor McKinney's South Street Mission in Akron, and held five services for the Christian and Missionary Alliance in New Castle. In early June the United Tabernacle of Columbus, Ohio, joined the revival, holding all-night meetings for those seeking baptism in the Spirit.

In June 1907 Levi Lupton opened his grounds for a "Pentecostal Camp Meeting." It began June 13. The lengthy list of ministers and workers who attended this single meeting would become a *Who's*

Who of early Pentecostal leadership. The evangelists E. W. and Mary Vinton, the missionary George Berg, the evangelist and provocateur Frank Bartleman, the evangelist Ivey Campbell, and H. W. Allen all hailed from the Azusa Street Mission. People came from miles around to the meetings, which continued for ten days. By the second day of the camp meeting, seven hundred people had arrived, comprising representatives from twenty-four states. People came from Canada, China, Egypt, South Africa, England, South America, the West Indies, and Australia. While four hundred people, black and white, stayed in tents on Lupton's property, the others were housed in nearby Alliance hotels. The camp went off well, though it was marred on Saturday night, June 22. About midnight, a gang of young men invaded the camp ground, armed with "squirt guns" containing diluted sulphuric acid. The acid burned the clothes off of some people's bodies and caused painful burns on at least a dozen. Lupton was forced to call a physician. To my knowledge, no one was ever arrested for this crime.

In spite of this attack, Lupton claimed the next day that he had received a vision directing them to establish "The Apostolic Faith Association." The group agreed with the idea, and Levi R. Lupton became the self-appointed president, with C. A. McKinney as his vice president. Frank Bartleman and J. H. King were chosen as board members. Alliance was declared the national headquarters of the association, and it was agreed that the organization would publish a paper from Alliance. On June 24, 1907, Levi Lupton, George E. Davis, I. O. Courtney, Frank Bartleman, and Lewis C. Grant traveled to Columbus, Ohio, and incorporated "The Apostolic Faith Association of Alliance." Before the week was out, Levi Lupton took for himself the title "Apostle."

In the end Ivey Campbell, the woman who had brought the Azusa Street revival to Ohio, returned to Los Angeles a broken person. Apparently the criticism she had received at the hands of so many was too much for her. Campbell never recovered, and she died in Los Angeles on June 26, 1918.

6

EVANGELIZING THE WORLD:
AZUSA STREET'S MISSIONARY PROGRAM

ೕೲ

> We rejoice to hear that Pentecost has fallen in Calcutta, India,
> over ten thousand miles away on the other side of the world.
> Praise God. We have letters from China, Germany, Switzerland,
> Norway, Sweden, England, Ireland, Australia, and other coun-
> tries from hungry souls that want their Pentecost. Some of
> these letters are in foreign languages. Missionaries write that
> they are hungry for this outpouring of the Spirit which they
> believe to be the real Pentecost. The world seems ripe for the
> Pentecost in all lands and God is sending it. Amen.
>
> THE APOSTOLIC FAITH

IF PASTOR William J. Seymour and the people of the Azusa
Street Mission wanted to spread the message of salvation, holiness, and spiritual empowerment across North America, they
wanted even more to carry it around the world. They believed
that God was restoring something to the church that had been
missing for centuries. They read ominous significance in the fact
that this was occurring at the beginning of the last century of the
second Christian millennium. This seemed to signal the imminent return of the Lord. Time was running out, and people
needed to be saved!

The very name "latter rain" that they often used to describe
their revival, a term derived from Joel 2:23, suggested just this. The
"early rain," they argued, had fallen on the New Testament church
while the "latter rain" was falling on those touched by this new

revival. These two showers acted like bookends on the church age. The imminent return of the Lord compelled participants in this revival to proclaim to everyone their "full gospel" (a term they had purloined from the Wesleyan holiness movement).

Developing a Practical Theology of "Tongues" for the Mission Field

Charles F. Parham had proposed a clear link between the restoration of the gift of tongues and the Second Coming. He had claimed that through their baptism in the Spirit, those who spoke in tongues were being specially equipped to carry out God's endtime global missionary mandate. The tongues they spoke when they were baptized in the Spirit would point them to the country or countries where they would spend what remained of the current age. There, they would evangelize the people, leading them into a saving knowledge of Jesus Christ. They would instruct them to pursue a crisis experience of sanctification. They would preach that these new converts should trust God for their spiritual and physical needs. They would proclaim the imminent return of the Lord Jesus Christ. And they would encourage these new believers to expect him to baptize them in the Holy Spirit. They would know that it had happened when they, too, spoke in tongues. Through this spiritual encounter, new converts would swell the ranks of the Apostolic Faith, hastening the fulfillment of the Great Commission.

Initially Pastor Seymour had agreed with Parham's position that tongues were actual human languages, given for missionary use. But by mid-1907 he seemed to distance himself from Parham on the issue. Seymour hesitated because, while many believed they could identify the new languages they were speaking, Parham's theory regarding God-given foreign languages had not yet been proven. The tongues spoken at the Azusa Street Mission *might* be genuine foreign languages. God was certainly able to give such a gift. But then again, they might be something else. Only testing on the missionary field would finally answer the question to Seymour's satisfaction. In the end, the bestowal of tongues on the people of the Apostolic Faith might best be explained in another way.

In spite of Seymour's personal concerns, the faithful at Azusa Street continued to speak in tongues in anticipation that much of this new speech could be used in missionary service. Thus many people sought to identify the tongue in which they spoke. None of these people were trained linguists. Most of them, like most Americans, were not even bilingual. They were ordinary folk who spoke and understood only one language—English. Those who spoke a second language were typically recent immigrants who spoke some European tongue like German or Swedish or Spanish. For the most part, such languages were not the languages that the Azusa faithful claimed to be speaking when they spoke in tongues.

The first issue of the mission's newspaper, *The Apostolic Faith*, demonstrates something of the breadth of their linguistic claims.

> The gift of languages is given with the commission, "Go ye into all the world and preach the Gospel to every creature." The Lord has given languages to the unlearned Greek, Latin, Hebrew, French, German, Italian, Chinese, Japanese, Zulu and languages of Africa, Hindu and Bengali and dialects of India, Chippewa and other languages of the Indians, Esquimaux, the deaf mute language and, in fact the Holy Ghost speaks all the languages of the world through His children.

"Chinese" was among the favorite languages "identified" by those who frequented Azusa Street. Azusa's faithful never specified Mandarin or Cantonese or any particular regional Chinese dialect. They had spoken simply "Chinese." Another common claim was to the language—or languages—of India and of Africa. The implications were huge! The problem, of course, was verification. All we have are the testimonies of those who allegedly spoke these languages and the testimonies of those who claimed to hear them speak. These far-from-objective claims have led to significant speculation as well as substantial criticism regarding the nature of the various "languages" that the faithful contended were spoken at the mission.

Samuel J. and Ardella K. Mead, who had spent twenty years as Methodist missionaries in Angola, were often mentioned as helping to identify the languages spoken at the mission—though they were not alone in doing so. To what extent they even knew a foreign language other than Portuguese, the major language of colonial Angola, is not clear. The Meads's descriptions of speaking in tongues were sufficiently vague to raise significant doubts about their ability to identify specific foreign languages. Ardella described her own experience like this: "I have been shown that what I speak is an African dialect." But who showed it to her? Was it God? Was it her husband or another worshipper at the mission? Or was this a personal intuition? And why did she not specify the dialect, since she had spent twenty years in Africa? Obviously we have no answers to such questions, but the fact that they cannot be answered today leaves legitimate room for doubt about the accuracy of what she claimed to have been shown.

Samuel Mead's attitude toward the tongues he heard is even more problematic. While *The Apostolic Faith* clearly named him as identifying various tongues that people spoke at the mission, when he was asked specifically if he believed that these tongues would be used on the foreign field, he hedged his bet with the response, "As for myself I cannot say. My God is able, this I know."

Clearly the faithful affirmed both the theoretical and the theological possibility that these "tongues" were human languages. But without a sound recording or the conclusions of a contemporary linguistics expert, we cannot verify the many claims that were made by the people at the Azusa Street Mission. We can only go by evidence that takes us beyond the simple claim: How did these people fare when they arrived on their specified foreign field? Were they able to do what they believed they were being empowered to do—namely, communicate the "full gospel" in an unlearned language?

Appointing Missionaries

Importantly, the leaders of the Azusa Street revival were people of action. Charles Parham had posited that "tongues" were Holy Spirit–bestowed "foreign languages"—that is, that the "gift of tongues" was a God-given language spoken by a community other than the speaker's own—a language otherwise unknown to the speaker. Yet while he made a few claims that one or another of his followers had spoken a specific language, and one Houston newspaper report claimed that U.S. government linguists had verified such things in a Parham meeting, his own inability to verify his theory or to validate the languages spoken apparently led him to be cautious. As a result he sent out very few, if any, missionaries during this period.

At the Azusa Street Mission, exactly the opposite was true. This is why I have chosen to highlight the Azusa Street Mission as the birthplace of global Pentecostalism. Essentially, when someone spoke in a tongue, the mission followed a simple four-step program. First, they attempted to identify the language. Second, if they felt they had identified it, they sought to establish whether the speaker believed he or she had a received a missionary "call." Third, if the tongues-speaker claimed to have such a call, the mission staff tried to discern whether the call was genuine and whether the person was ready and willing to go. Finally, if the person testified to a readiness to go, and the mission discerned the necessary gifts and call, then they gave the candidate the money to reach the foreign field, and he or she left town within days, if not hours. Alfred G. and Lillian Garr provide a good example of how this process worked.

The Garrs had been at the Azusa Street Mission for only a couple of weeks when they were baptized in the Spirit. Because they had been pastors of a nearby Los Angeles church, however, many people knew and trusted them. After their Spirit-baptism, Alfred announced that he had received the Hindustani language of India, and Lillian announced that she could speak the Chinese language. They promptly offered themselves up as Azusa Street's first missionaries to the foreign field, and within fifteen minutes they had received twelve hundred dollars in cash to send them on their way.[33] They were by no means the only people who experienced this sort of rapid, supportive send-off. The mission extended this generosity time after time in similar ways. Once they had given them the money, the congregation would often accompany the new missionaries to the nearby railroad station, singing and shouting all the way there. Then they would hold a public meeting in the station until the train left. There were those, however, who did not fare so well. The mission subjected the call of George and Daisy Batman to an extended process of discernment, although they finally accepted it and sent the Batmans out. On the other hand, they ultimately rejected the call of T. J. and Annie McIntosh.

The Pentecostal historian Vinson Synan has wittily described this sort of missionary program pioneered at the Azusa Street Mission as the program of the "one way ticket." The mission faithful believed that the Lord would return before their missionaries needed to come back home. If it should become necessary for them to return, however, the mission was equally convinced that their missionaries' ticket home would be covered by relying upon God in faith to meet the need. The faith of the mission was simple and it seemed to have no boundaries.

At first glance such a program might rightly seem foolhardy. Yet the willingness of many Azusa Street participants to respond to their perceived call through such actions, the urgency they felt for the need, the zeal and immediacy with which they responded to it, and the personal sacrifices they were willing to make to see that others heard the full gospel before it was too late, could also be described as selfless and admirable.

Charles Parham did not agree with Seymour's strategy. Quite frankly, he was embarrassed by it. Parham accused Seymour of sending evangelists and missionaries around the world that were ill prepared and ill equipped to carry out such a ministry. And Seymour was indeed doing just that. Many of the missionaries that went out from the Azusa Street Mission had never had any missionary training or even any theological training. They did not know the languages or the customs of the countries to which they believed themselves called. These simple believers took the Bible and their experience at face value and intended to share them with others.

Such a missionary program obviously led to certain problems that subsequent missionary theologies, programs, and strategies have tried to address. To the Azusa Street faithful who were ready to take on the missionary challenge, however, it mattered little what Charles Parham thought. They firmly believed that God would provide for their needs if they were faithful to Jesus' command to "go and make disciples" (Matt. 28:19). With a strong commitment to share their personal stories of God's work in their lives, and the desire to spread the "full gospel," Pastor Seymour and his staff did everything they could to honor those who believed they had received a divine call. They tried to discern the call and to identify and test gifts such as the would-be missionaries' new languages. They blessed the missionaries by issuing credentials, and they provided them with enough money to get them where they believed God had called them. It is difficult, therefore, to know exactly how to tell the story of the Azusa Street Mission's missionary outreach. The number of missionaries who underwent this process and were sent out from Los Angeles during the first three years of the mission's existence is simply staggering.

One group of people that went as missionaries could best be described as itinerant missionary evangelists. Frank Bartleman, Lucy Leatherman, Daniel Awrey, and to a lesser extent A. G. and Lillian Garr would probably best fit this category. The Garrs ministered in India, Ceylon [now Sri Lanka], Hong Kong, Macao, China, and Japan. The others operated more globally.

Frank Bartleman wrote of his travels in more or less serial fashion, to a wide range of holiness and Pentecostal periodicals. Ultimately he collected many of these short travel logs and compiled two books on his travels, *Around the World by Faith, with Six Weeks in the Holy Land*, which covered 1910–1911, and *Two Years Mission Work in Europe Just before the World War: 1912–1914*. During those trips he visited virtually every Pentecostal work in Western and Eastern Europe, the Middle East, and Asia. Lucy Leatherman was equally well traveled. Her ministry included periods of work in Europe, the Middle East, Asia, and ultimately South America. Daniel Awrey spent a half dozen years giving Bible studies in Asia, Africa, and Europe. In short, these people seemed to cover the globe, and all of them shared the stories of their travels and ministries by writing to a growing list of Pentecostal periodicals on the home front.

A second category of Azusa Street missionaries comprised veteran missionaries who, until the revival, had worked for an array of denominations and missionary agencies. These missionaries heard the stories of what God was doing at the Azusa Street Mission and came to Los Angeles to see it for themselves. Upon their arrival at the Azusa Street Mission, they were baptized in the Holy Spirit. They returned to their mission fields to continue serving, this time as Apostolic Faith or Pentecostal missionaries.

Samuel and Ardella Mead had served as Methodist missionaries in the African region of Angola for over twenty years. Because of their ages—he was fifty-seven and she was sixty-three—they had recently retired and had not intended to return to Angola. Once baptized in the Spirit, however, they decided to return for another short stint, this time accompanied by another new Azusa Street missionary couple, Robert and Myrtle Schideler.

Similarly, from 1901 to 1905 George and Mary Berg had served as independent holiness missionaries in India. Because Mary Berg's health had declined precipitously during that term, the couple returned to Southern California. When they started hearing news reports of what was taking place at the Azusa Street Mission, George Berg decided to investigate. He was baptized in the Spirit on his first visit there, on the afternoon of September 15, 1906. In February 1908, the couple returned again to India for a successful second term, this time as Apostolic Faith missionaries.

Paul and Nellie Clark Bettex were another such couple. Nellie Bettex was working in China with the London Missionary Society when Paul Bettex arrived, fresh from the revival at the Azusa Street Mission. Paul had worked as a holiness missionary in South America in the 1890s, but following his visit to Azusa Street he went to Kwang-chan-fu (Canton), China. The couple married in 1910, and for the next year and a half they continued to minister as Apostolic Faith missionaries in Canton and elsewhere in southern China. Their ministry together came to a sudden and unexpected end, however, when on October 11, 1912, Nellie Bettex succumbed to a brain aneurism. Still, Paul continued to work in the region until he was murdered there in 1916.

Several veteran missionaries already serving in China, among them Antoinette Moomau, Hector and Sigrid McLean, and Bernt and Magna Berntsen, also found their way to the Azusa Street Mission. Antoinette Moomau was the first to do so, and the one who would complete the longest tenure (thirty-eight years) in China. She had served as a Presbyterian missionary in Shang-hai, China since 1899. In 1906 she began to hear the stories of the Azusa Street revival from other missionaries. In October 1906 she visited the Azusa Street Mission and was baptized in the Spirit, whereupon she returned to Shang-hai to serve as an independent Apostolic Faith missionary until her death in 1937.

The Azusa Street Mission also produced several long-term missionaries with no previous missionary experience. Ansel H. and Henrietta Post were two such. At the end of 1907, following his baptism in the Spirit, Ansel left his family in Los Angeles and traveled to London, then by way of South Africa to India, Ceylon, and Hong Kong. After accomplishing the bulk of his initial foreign ministry on this first trip to Asia, he returned to Los Angeles in 1909. Then, taking his family with him, Post traveled to Alexandria, Egypt, arriving March 8, 1910. There the Posts served, first as independent missionaries and then, from 1916 until his death on June 23, 1931, as Assemblies of God missionaries.

A large number of those sent out by the Azusa Street Mission were short-term missionaries, intent on communicating the full gospel through their newly given tongue. Most of these folks lasted on the foreign field between six months and a year, especially when their initial expectations were disappointed. While they did not endure for long on the mission field, we should not ignore their contribution. First, their testimonies from the field appeared in many stateside periodicals, motivating others to follow their example. And second, some of them left permanent fruit in the churches they pioneered.

Most African Americans who went to Liberia did so as short-term missionaries. Some, such as Lucy Farrow and Julia Hutchins, returned to the United States after a single term of six to eight months. Several of these missionaries, however, can be counted as "short term" only because they died within weeks of their arrival—either from malaria or its complications. It is among the short-term missionaries that the Apostolic Faith ranks suffered their first deaths on the mission field.

Protestant Complaints against the Apostolic Faith Missionaries

As we come face to face with these idol worshipping, mistaught multitudes drifting towards eternity, how our hearts long that the representatives from Los Angeles now in India would seek to use the gift in winning the perishing from the wrath to come instead of in edifying (?) missionaries who are already saved.

MABEL E. ARCHIBALD

THOSE who went abroad as Apostolic Faith missionaries were probably all well-intentioned. Given their general lack of training and their overall lack of experience, however, we should not be surprised to find a number of concerns raised and a number of criticisms lodged against them. These concerns and criticisms reveal some of the challenges that these new missionaries faced— challenges they might have overcome had they received certain theological, cultural, and linguistic training before they embarked on the missionary enterprise.

Criticism began to emerge first among Protestant missionaries serving in India and China. While some were open to hear the case for speaking in tongues, others clearly thought such claims simply incomprehensible and therefore ignored them. Correspondence sailed back and forth between missionaries in India and China and their mission boards in the United States and England. Mrs. Jesse Penn Lewis, a popular writer in the circles of the Keswick Convention in England, wrote numerous articles on the claims of the Apostolic Faith people, charging repeatedly that this new movement of missionaries was being led by demonic spirits, not by the Holy Spirit.

At the same time, the Presbyterian theologian and longtime supporter of missions Arthur T. Pierson wrote a series of articles on speaking in tongues that appeared in 1907 on both sides of the Atlantic. Pierson based his comments on his exposition of 1 Corinthians 14. As he laid out his case, he argued that too much attention was being given to what he called the "least" of the gifts. It was true, he contended, that the ability to speak in tongues was a gift of the Holy Spirit, but scriptural rules or guidelines governed its use. The gift of tongues was to be used to build up the church. As Pierson surveyed the reports coming in from the mission field, he concluded that wherever tongues appeared, instead of edification, problems had developed. The results were fanaticism, division, and hysteria. Surely this was not what God wanted. While Pierson maintained that a genuine gift of tongues could exist in 1907, he interpreted the fruits of the Apostolic Faith workers as signs that their tongues were nothing more than demonically inspired imitations.

Strong opposition to the claims and practices of Pentecostalism also arose in Germany. In September 1909 a group of Pietist-holiness leaders published a statement that became known as the "Berlin Declaration." In no uncertain terms it declared that the Apostolic Faith movement was "not from on high, but from below." Once again, these critics viewed the Pentecostals' practices as demonically inspired. The Pentecostals in Germany published a response known as the "Mülheim Declaration," but the damage had been done. For the next eighty-five years, the Berlin Declaration cast its shadow over Pentecostal and charismatic claims in Germany.

S. C. Todd, working with the Bible Missionary Society in Macao, took great pains to investigate the work of A. G. and Lillian

Garr, M. L. Ryan, and T. J. and Annie McIntosh. In the end, he produced an open letter and several articles in which he raised serious questions regarding their claims. "At no time has there been any *known* tongue spoken, all has been an *unknown* utterance," he asserted.

Other criticisms were also raised. These went beyond questions related to the claims about the gift of tongues, to the insensitive style of some Apostolic Faith missionaries' presentation. After interviewing people whose lives had been touched by their ministries, S. C. Todd concluded that a "dual movement" was at work in their ministries, "one from heaven, the other from hell." On the negative side, he concluded, Pentecostals did not suffer merely from "wrong doctrines and mistakes"; they had actually been influenced by "a real spirit of evil, personal demons, sweeping down upon God's children, marked as an angel of light—but who comes from the pit."

In June 1909 *The Independent* published an unsigned article, most likely from the pen of S. C. Todd. The author accused A. G. Garr of using abusive rhetoric against those who disagreed with him.

> The visitor entering the hall, caught loud tones of denunciation, and when he retired some fine specimens of anathema followed him into the street, often with a personal application. Garr frankly consigned to the bad place the faithful missionaries of Hongkong [*sic*].

T. J. McIntosh did not fare much better in the article. While the writer conceded that McIntosh was "cast in a gentler mold than the authoritative Garr," he complained that McIntosh's "ignorance is so great that he can read only simple English."

T. J. McIntosh had belonged to the Holiness Church of North Carolina when G. B. Cashwell returned to the South from his visit to the Azusa Street Mission. Cashwell's meetings had a profound effect upon the young and energetic McIntosh, and he had determined to become a missionary to China. In June 1907 he had traveled to the Azusa Street Mission. Azusa's leadership had chosen not to endorse and support him as one of their missionaries. It is possible that they were concerned about his stability. In spite of Seymour's reticence to send him, McIntosh received enough money from people at the mission to travel to China. The McIntoshes arrived in the Portuguese colony of Macao off the coast of Hong Kong on August 7, 1907.

Apostolic Faith Concerns about Missionary Training

The burgeoning Apostolic Faith missionary movement clearly needed to take responsibility for addressing concerns regarding missionary service. As early as June 16, 1908, the subject had been raised at the Sunderland Conference in England, an invitation-only international conference of early Pentecostal leaders convened by Alexander A. Boddy, an Anglican priest. Boddy, who had recently been baptized in the Spirit but would always remain in Anglican orders, openly identified with what was taking place at the Azusa Street Mission. Instead of bowing to early expectations that he would leave the Anglicans, he helped the burgeoning global Apostolic Faith movement by fostering comprehensive theological discussions. Along the way, he gave the movement some of the wisest pastoral advice it would receive during its earliest years. At the Sunderland meetings, someone cited the failures of certain Apostolic Faith missionaries who had gone to Liberia, the Congo, and Japan and asked whether "the call of all the Apostolic Faith Missionaries was of the Spirit." Elizabeth Sisson led the ensuing discussion, arguing that they had all gone to the mission field after a proper period of discernment.

The following year two Azusa Street missionaries also raised questions about what constituted appropriate missionary preparation. The first of these was John G. Lake, a missionary to South Africa who had been baptized in the Spirit at the Azusa Street Mission. In early 1909 Lake wrote to the Upper Room Mission in Los Angeles with what can only be described as a highly emotional plea that the tide of well-meaning missionaries be stemmed until certain preparations had been made. First, Lake complained, too many American missionaries were "rushing" to the foreign field without making advanced preparation. "American missionaries" warned Lake, "should not run over here until they know what they are doing, and under what conditions they can be received." In addition, he argued, the churches that sent the missionaries needed to bear the responsibility for their ongoing support.

Second, Lake warned that the mission field was not the place for those who thought that they had all the answers before they arrived. Unlike Garr—who may have been too authoritarian in the way he proclaimed the Apostolic Faith in India—Lake called for the new missionaries coming to Africa to show more deference. "We have a tremendous native work on our hands," he wrote, "and we heartily welcome REAL MISSIONARIES, but they cannot come to Africa with the thought of a lot of 'brand new American ideas' to teach to the natives." Lake warned that American workers must respect local culture, and too many already on the mission field did not understand that fact.

Four months later Antoinette Moomau, working in Shang-hai, weighed in on the subject of missionary preparation with two equally pointed concerns of her own. One of these related to the level of maturity necessary for a missionary to accomplish anything of value. "More than the baptism of the Spirit is needed to come to a foreign field," she warned.

> It is no place for the rearing of spiritual babes. If the dear ones at home could only feel the powers of darkness for a time here they would understand. Too many, rush off in response to a call which comes from the influence of their own minds.

We do not know who "Nettie" Moomau had in mind when she wrote this, but the story of Lillian Keyes and her friend Edith Gumbrell illustrates her concern. Keyes, who had created so many problems for Joseph Smale at the First New Testament Church in Los Angeles, landed with Gumbrell in Peking [now Beijing] and went on to Pao-ting-fu [now Baoding], China, August 1, 1908. They worked in Pao-ting-fu as independent Apostolic Faith missionaries until May 30, 1911. Upon their arrival, Keyes reported to her family that on three occasions, "the Lord...enabled her to speak the language in conversation with Chinese people." She expressed the hope that eventually she would be able to preach in the Chinese language.

As these young women were confronted with the realities of life in China, however, they found that they had to change. By January 1910 both women had applied to become missionaries affiliated with the North China Mission of the Presbyterian Church in the U.S.A. They received a positive recommendation from Charles A. Killie, Chairman of the Executive Committee, and Lillian Keyes ultimately received an appointment with the Presbyterian Church. As a condition of her acceptance, however, she was required to sign the following pledge:

> I promise not to teach that the gift of tongues is an essential mark of the baptism of the Holy Spirit, and not to urge believers to seek the gift of tongues in preference to other gifts in connection with the baptism of the Holy Spirit, because it is contrary to my belief. I do not believe in urging believers to seek any gifts, only God, believing that the Holy Spirit gives unto us according to His will, and such gifts as he would have us have.

Clearly, she had changed her tune from the one she had sung in Los Angeles.

Lillian Keyes had married by 1916, and she and her husband were subsequently reappointed as missionaries by the Presbyterian Church. She served in Shun-tê-fu [now Shijiazhuang] in the Chi-Li Province until 1954. The maturing process she had undergone on the mission field had not ended up helping the Apostolic Faith. Moomau, who had been a Presbyterian before turning to the Apostolic Faith, may have judged Keyes's work a failure because she had left the Apostolic Faith to become a Presbyterian.

A year later Antoinette Moomau once again wrote to the Upper Room Mission. This time she expressed concern about certain missionary evangelists or itinerant missionaries. Once again, without naming any names she protested that "many of these 'touring missionaries' do not accomplish much. If they have a real message, it is felt and known, but some drift about, and nothing is accomplished."

Given even this brief introduction to Azusa Street's missionaries, we find a number of reasons why their story is so difficult to tell. First, literally scores of people rose to the missionary challenge. Second, most of these missionaries did not stay put once they arrived in their field of choice. They moved about, often spending a week here or a month there, attempting to minister as they went. Third, like the balls on a billiard table, they had received their initial impetus at the Azusa Street Mission when they were baptized in the Spirit, but once they began to move about they passed their energy on to others who also moved about. Finally, their claims and their methods changed over time.

It is time to look at the work that some of these missionaries undertook. Owing to space limitations, my introduction to this aspect of the Azusa Street missionary story will sketch only some of the work accomplished by a few of the missionaries working on two continents: Asia and Africa. I hope to demonstrate their impact on Europe, Latin America, and other parts of Asia in a future study.

Azusa Street Missionaries in India

Pastor Seymour's commitment to send forth missionaries to the ends of the earth meant that within the first year of the mission's existence nearly two dozen missionaries left Azusa Street bound for foreign fields. Over the following two years, these would be joined by as many more. The first to leave were Alfred G. and Lillian Garr. They left Los Angeles in July 1906 and traveled east to complete some personal business. Accompanied by an African American woman, Maria Gardener, who had agreed to serve as a nursemaid to their three-year-old daughter, they sailed to India in January 1907.

Alfred and Lillian Garr

When the Garrs arrived in Calcutta in northeast India, they found that, with the exception of the suitcases they carried, they had lost all of their baggage. Demoralized and without any local contacts, they made no secret of their economic predicament. They took an inexpensive room and prayed that the Lord would open up some opportunity for ministry. The following day a British army officer, Captain Angel Smith, stopped by. He claimed God had told him to give these new missionaries a substantial sum of money. In return, they shared their message with him and prayed. He became the first person they led into the baptism in the Holy Spirit in India.

When they arrived, the Garrs found that copies of *The Apostolic Faith*, first published in September 1906 by the Azusa Street Mission, had arrived in India before them. Members of the missionary community, who had read the reports carried in *The Apostolic Faith*, were anxious to hear what the Garrs had to say about their experience at the Azusa Street Mission. The Garrs were soon invited to attend a missionary convention being held in Carey Baptist Chapel in Lal Bazaar. Otto Stockmeier, a widely known Swiss proponent of the "Overcoming Life" (a non-Wesleyan variant of holiness teaching) as well as the doctrine of divine healing, was one of two speakers at this convention. When the Garrs arrived, Stockmeier gave them the floor to share their account of the Azusa Street revival. The Garrs testified of what they had seen and experienced and then urged the missionaries present to join them by asking the Lord to baptize them in the Holy Spirit.

One of those who supported the Garrs in this endeavor was a Presbyterian named Max Wood Moorhead, Secretary of the Young Men's Christian Association (YMCA) in Ceylon [now Sri Lanka]. Moorhead rented a large house on Creek Row in Calcutta, where the meetings continued even after many of the missionaries had returned to their places of ministry. Over the next two months, a number of people were baptized in the Spirit amid manifestations paralleling those at Azusa Street.

The Garrs had expected the Holy Spirit to enable them, when they arrived in Calcutta, to preach in an indigenous Indian dialect to the local people. They quickly realized that their gift of tongues did not function the way they thought it would. As a result, Garr made the pragmatic decision to abandon Parham's theory, with its promise that missionaries would be able to skip language training school and preach immediately in a foreign language under the direct inspiration of the Holy Spirit. He did not, however, abandon the practice of speaking in tongues. Instead, he turned his attention to the members of the missionary community, among whom he lifted up the merit of speaking in tongues as the evidence of the baptism in the Holy Spirit. The unyielding character of his claim, coupled with the passionate confrontational style so common in the holiness culture out of which he had come, quickly led to debate and criticism within the missionary community. Many missionaries slammed their doors on the Garrs. They in turn "shook the dust from their feet," in scenes reminiscent of the Lord's advice to his followers when they were rejected (Matt. 10:14–15). In spite of their frequent rejection, the Garrs recast themselves primarily as "missionary evangelists" whose task it would be to challenge, encourage, and support existing missionaries in their quest for the baptism in the Spirit. This left them free to move about other parts of Asia, wherever they could gain a hearing.

Meanwhile, since 1905 another revival had been in progress on the western side of India, about one hundred miles southeast of Bombay [now Mumbai]. It was taking place at the Mukti Mission founded by Pandita Ramabai. The Mukti Mission had been established to provide a home and educational opportunities for young Indian widows rescued from the common practice of immolation on the funeral pyres of their deceased husbands. News from the Australian revival of 1903 and the Welsh Revival in 1904–1905 had long provided fodder for discussion at the Mukti Mission. Minnie F. Abrams, a Methodist missionary commissioned by the Woman's Foreign Missionary Society, had joined Ramabai there in 1898.

In 1905 a matron in one of the dormitories, convinced that she saw flames appear over one of the residents, threw a bucket of water on the girl to douse the fire. Ramabai and Abrams came to interpret what the matron had seen as evidence that the girl had been baptized in the Spirit with fire (Luke 3:16). The Mukti Mission quickly became a place of repentance, confession, and revival. Provoked by what she saw, Minnie Abrams described the revival and explained its meaning in a book titled *The Baptism of the Holy Ghost and Fire*. This was published in April 1906, at the time the Azusa Street Mission first opened its doors. Abrams argued that the baptism in the Holy Spirit that so many were experiencing at Mukti brought both purity and power with it—especially the power to evangelize.

While Minnie Abrams did not mention speaking in tongues in this first edition of her book, she did include a section on the restoration of speaking in tongues when the book was republished in December 1906. The fact that news of the Azusa Street revival had arrived in India as early as September 1906 provides one possible explanation for her inclusion of this new section. Another possible motivation is that a number of people had predicted this restoration of tongues before people began to speak in tongues on the scale that they did following the Azusa Street revival. Professor Gary McGee has pointed out that John Ryland, in a rebuke to

William Carey, the first Protestant missionary to India, had said as much as early as 1792.[34] A third possible influence was the indigenous Indians who, by December 1906 when Minnie Abrams published her revised text, were already speaking in tongues. The idea of miraculous tongues was clearly in the Indian air by the time the Garrs arrived.

When Pandita Ramabai heard that the Garrs were holding meetings in Calcutta, she immediately invited them to come to Mukti. Within two weeks, some eight hundred girls had received their baptism in the Spirit and begun speaking in tongues. Over the summer months the Garrs held other meetings in Bombay, India, and later in Colombo, Ceylon.

Azusa Street's impact on India did not, however, only travel in a straight line from Los Angeles. It also arrived, in the person of Thomas Ball Barratt, via New York and Christiania [now Oslo], Norway. Barratt, a Methodist pastor, had received a letter from Mr. A. N. Groves dated January 8, 1908, inviting him to come to India. Groves, who had been sympathetic to the Garrs, was impressed with Barratt's testimony, which he had recently read in a paper from England.

In 1906 T. B. Barratt had been in the United States raising money for a church project he wanted to fund in Christiania. While he was in the U.S. he stayed at the Alliance House in New York City. He was there in November 1906 when Lucy Leatherman arrived from the Azusa Street Mission. Weeks earlier, he had stumbled across a copy of the first issue of *The Apostolic Faith* from Los Angeles and corresponded repeatedly with the staff of the Azusa Street Mission. He was concerned above all to receive his own baptism in the Spirit. Mrs. I. May Throop (once), Glenn Cook (three times), and Clara Lum (once) all responded to his questions with encouragement, advice, and ultimately excitement. When Lucy Leatherman arrived at the Alliance House, Barratt was ready with his questions. She put him in touch with a woman named Maude Williams at a small New York mission. On November 15 at Miss Williams's mission, Barratt asked Lucy Leatherman and an unnamed Norwegian man to lay hands on him. He began to speak in tongues. Then throughout early December, Barratt stayed at the Union Holiness Mission with a group of Azusa Street missionaries bound for Africa, sailing with them at the end of this time for Liverpool. Upon their arrival in Liverpool, the entire group disembarked. Most would board ships to Africa, but Barratt, by prearrangement, returned immediately to Norway.

When Barratt accepted his invitation, Groves published a circular letter inviting a variety of missionaries and friends to come to Coonoor in the Nilgiri Hills, 120 miles southwest of Bangalore in March 1908. That Indian town served as a primary vacation spot for missionaries of all kinds, who took advantage of the city's cooler weather. There, Groves hoped, they would listen "in the spirit of the Beraeans" (Acts 17:11) to Barratt's teachings on baptism in the Spirit. When he arrived in Bombay, Barratt was met by Mr. Max Moorhead, and he stayed in that city to minister for three weeks before continuing on to Coonoor. During Barratt's meetings there, a number of people, including a number of missionaries, were baptized in the Spirit.

Also following the Garrs from the Azusa Street Mission were George and Mary Berg. It is likely that the Bergs and T. B. Barratt were together in Bombay or Coonoor for at least part of the time Barratt was in India. One of the first things George Berg did upon his 1908 return to India after his Spirit-baptism was to meet with a variety of mission leaders and heads of established denominations. Between February and September of that year George Berg traveled over eight thousand miles. He held meetings for Christian leaders from groups as diverse as the Salvation Army, the Church of Scotland (Presbyterian), the Church Mission Society (Anglicans), the Methodist Episcopal Church, and the ancient Malankara Orthodox Syrian Church—for centuries a major factor in Indian Christianity on the southwest coast.

The following year the Bergs settled in Coonoor. There they worked among what George described as the "poor, neglected jungle tribes." In early 1910 the Bergs established their center of activity in Bangalore, from which they would extend their ministry over the next several years. By September 1912 they had established six

Pentecostal stations in southern India and raised up twenty indigenous workers to help them. Berg wrote to readers in the United States, soliciting workers to take over the works he had established in Travancore on the southwest coast of India and in the Nilgiri Hills. That month, the Bergs moved to Kandy, Ceylon, where they finished out their ministry.

Azusa Street Missionaries in China

South China

In early October, while the Garrs were still in India, they received an invitation from several single women missionaries to speak in Hong Kong. They arrived in Hong Kong on October 9, 1907. So taken aback were the Garrs at the horrible conditions under which these women were living that they immediately rented a large home at 4 Ladder Street, invited these women to move in with them, and together established a missionary rest home. Among the women they met were Rosa Pittman and May Law, who had just arrived from Spokane, Washington. Pittman and Law had traveled to Japan with a group of missionaries led by Martin Lawrence Ryan, who had been baptized in the Spirit at the Azusa Street Mission in August 1906. Believing they had received "the language of Hong Kong," they had forged ahead without him. As soon as these women were settled, A. G. Garr began holding meetings at a church sponsored by the American Board of Foreign Missions—an American Congregationalist mission board.

Next, Garr immediately hired a man named Mok Lai Chi to serve as his translator. Mok was born into a Christian (probably Congregational) home, January 10, 1868. He had been trained in English and had taught English in various schools and worked in a number of Christian organizations. For instance, he had served as the secretary to the YMCA in Hong Kong and as a Sunday school superintendent as well as a deacon in a church run by the American Board of Foreign Missions. Garr and Mok became close friends, and as Mok translated for A. G. Garr, he began to listen to the message. Within a month Mok was baptized in the Spirit and had spoken in tongues. He would become a strong Apostolic Faith leader in the Hong Kong area for years to come.

Meanwhile T. J. and Annie McIntosh had been in Macao since August. They soon connected with the Garrs and with Mok Lai Chi in Hong Kong. T. J. McIntosh talked with Garr and Mok about moving to Hong Kong, and he told Mok that the Lord had spoken to him about publishing a paper. He proposed for this periodical the name *Pentecostal Truths*. In the end McIntosh did not publish the paper, so Mok Lai Chi did, publishing the first issue in January 1908. It was a four-page paper, with three pages in Chinese and one in English. McIntosh was unable to sustain his work in Macao. He moved on to Canton where he began to work with a half dozen American women missionaries—financed largely by a recent, well-to-do Cantonese convert. By May 1908, McIntosh and his wife had left for Palestine. They would remain there for several months before returning to the United States. The work in Canton would be carried on by Miss Nellie Clark and a Sister Wynne.

The Garrs continued their work in the Hong Kong area through the beginning of 1908. A smallpox epidemic swept the city in March of that year, killing their nanny, Maria Gardener, and their three year old daughter, Virginia. Devastated, the Garrs moved on to Japan where they ministered for the next several months. While they were in Japan, they connected with M. L. Ryan

Masthead for the first Pentecostal newspaper published in China.

and the remainder of his team. Following a short furlough in the U.S., they returned to Hong Kong on October 4, 1909.

In January 1910 Cora Fritsch and Bertha Milligan, part of M. L. Ryan's group that until then had been working in Japan, traveled by steamer to Hong Kong. They arrived on Tuesday, January 19 and were met by the Garrs, who also housed them. Fritsch and Milligan were soon joined by the Ryans. In addition, T. J. McIntosh, his wife Annie, and their daughter, had returned to the Hong Kong area. The Dixons had arrived from the Upper Room Mission in Los Angeles via Shang-hai. And there were Mrs. Johnson and Nellie Clark, who had also come from Los Angeles with the McIntoshes. Rounding out the contingent were Azusa Street regulars Daniel and Ella Awrey and their children, as well as Rosa Pittman and Anna Deane. In short, a substantial community of Azusa Street and related missionaries had gathered in Hong Kong. They continued to work together for several months, supporting other missionaries and attempting to address the spiritual needs of the Hong Kong Chinese. In February 1910 the Garrs moved on to India, where they spent the rest of the year. From there, they returned to spend a final year of missionary service in Hong Kong before returning at last to the United States in December 1911. Eventually the rest of the group, who had been left in the care of T. J. McIntosh, separated, continuing their ministries in different parts of southern China. T. J. McIntosh was simply not able to hold this ministry together. He once again left the missionary field and returned to the United States.

Northern China

Meanwhile, several Azusa Street missionaries were ministering in northern China. On August 10, 1906, Mr. and Mrs. Thomas Junk traveled from Los Angeles to Oakland, California. The Junks (her name is never given), who were expecting to go to China, must have held some meetings in Oakland for William F. Manley and his Household of God, because the Household of God took them on as missionary candidates and began to give toward their support in

August 1906. Following their stay in Oakland, they continued on to Seattle. There, they led a congregation at 1617 Seventh Avenue. Thomas Junk sent two reports to the Azusa Street Mission from Seattle, the second one dated January 7, 1907. In that report, he informed the mission that some seventy individuals had been "baptized" as a result of their work in Seattle.

Mrs. Junk may have died while the couple was still in Seattle. For a time after *The Apostolic Faith* [Los Angeles, CA] ceased publication in 1908, no correspondence arrived at the mission from Thomas Junk. Consequently it is difficult to trace Junk's movements. Beginning in 1910 and continuing for the next year, however, Junk began to correspond with the Upper Room Mission in Los Angeles as well as the Stone Church in Chicago. Now a widower, he was working alone in Tsao Hsien [now Zaojing] in Shantung Province of northeastern China, where he served for a number of years as an independent Apostolic Faith missionary. He wrote that he was feeling the death of his wife keenly.

Junk's correspondence reveals that like others who went abroad from Azusa Street, he did not arrive in China with the ability to speak the Chinese language. He took that discovery in stride and began to study the language, estimating that it would take him two years to learn it. Meanwhile he had opened up a work in the famine-ravaged region of northern China, and he attempted to become "a Chinaman among Chinese," eating Chinese food, learning the Chinese language, and going to areas that other missionaries had rejected because of the primitive conditions there. Junk viewed himself as a simple preacher who was aided greatly by the healings and exorcisms brought about through his prayers. A brief visit from Bernt Berntsen, another Azusa Street missionary who was working about 130 miles north of his mission, greatly encouraged Junk.

By June 1911 Junk reported crowds of people attending his mission. He held meetings at 6 A.M., 2 P.M., and 7 P.M. daily, and a service each Sunday that ran continuously. He had taken responsibility for forty-three children—thirty-two boys and eleven girls—and had trained several of them to help him in the meetings. Clearly he had some help with his work, for during the spring and summer months he visited fifty-two villages, in which he claimed that only seven had ever had a witness of the gospel.

Junk reported that the wheat supply, the primary staple in that region of China, withered as a result of the weather in 1910 and 1911. Farmers harvested less than half of the normal crop, and as a result, inflation rose to five hundred percent. Those who could not afford to buy food at such inflated prices were starving. In spite of the difficulties, Junk continued to take in the neediest—orphans and those without any immediate family— making them his own "family." As if the famine were not sufficient to dampen his spirits, an epidemic of cholera swept the region, leaving many dead or devastated. The rainy season of fall 1911 added to the desperate situation—the rain fell in torrents, destroying many homes and part of Junk's chapel. In the last two letters we have, Junk complained again of his loneliness and told of his vain attempts to save three baby girls who had been abandoned by their mothers. What ultimately became of Thomas Junk and his work is currently unknown.

Bernt and Magna Berntsen were among several missionaries already in China when the revival began at the Azusa Street Mission. Since 1904 the Berntsens had been serving as independent Norwegian missionaries in Ta-ming-fu [now Tangfeng] in the Chi-Li Province. Bernt Berntsen first heard about the revival when, in December 1906, he came across an early issue of *The Apostolic Faith* from Los Angeles. In early 1907 he traveled to the Centennial Missionary Conference in Shang-hai, hoping to find someone who had experienced this baptism in the Holy Spirit. All he found were people who claimed it was the work of the devil. Convinced there was more to it than these critics said, he returned to his place of ministry. Upon his return he received a letter from someone in Chicago who reported that she had been baptized in the Spirit. Berntsen determined to return to the United States to see the revival for himself.

In August 1907 Bernt Berntsen made the long trip to Seattle. He arrived just in time to find Martin L. Ryan and his team holding meetings there. Berntsen sought for the baptism in the Spirit in those meetings but did not receive it. Next, he traveled to Oakland, California, where he attended the meetings of William F. Manley, again without results. Finally he traveled to the Azusa Street Mission in Los Angeles, where on Sunday, September 15, 1907, he was baptized in the Spirit. When the leaders at the mission heard his testimony, they prayed that he would become "marvelously anointed" as he returned to China to continue his work, and they began supporting him financially.

Berntsen returned to Seattle, where he was joined by eleven other workers who traveled with him to China. Most of them were anxious to join him in order to find out whether they had a call to full-time ministry in China. By the end of 1907 he was once again in Ta-ming-fu. Once he arrived, he wrote to the Azusa Street Mission that in the coming months he planned to focus his attention on working along "the railroad line south of Peking." He hoped he would find a home to house a number of orphans in this famine-racked region. He went on to encourage other potential independent workers who were "filled with the Holy Ghost and fire" to come and stay with him. Berntsen would help these candidates discern, while engaged in service, whether they had a genuine call sufficient to sustain them in long-term missionary service in China.

Berntsen settled in Chêng-ting-fu [now Zhengding], about one hundred miles southwest of Peking. It would become his primary mission station. His sons, ages eleven and eight, and his wife were soon baptized in the Spirit. He rented a store building where he held meetings, morning and evening, drawing good-sized crowds especially from among the poor. Discovering that people were selling their children for a few dollars in order to have something to eat, Berntsen urged his American readers to sell their "idols" and give the proceeds for the work in China.

In January 1910 Berntsen described his work as a "rescue mission." While he had led a number of the poorest people in the region to the Lord, none of them had yet been baptized in the Spirit. By March 1910 he reported that he was caring for thirty orphaned children and a number of "halt, blind, dumb, cripples and other outcasts." In 1912 the Berntsens established a Chinese language newspaper, the *Popular Gospel Truth*, and they continued to work in Cheng-Ting Fu through at least 1916.

Like Bernt Berntsen, Antoinette Moomau had already served in the mission field when she encountered the Apostolic Faith movement. Born December 1, 1872, in Davis City, Iowa, she had attended and graduated from the Northfield School for Girls in Northfield, Massachusetts, as well as the Moody Bible Institute in Chicago. In 1899, following her time at Moody, she had gone to Su-chau-fu [now Suzhou], China, a city about eighty miles west of Shang-hai. There she served for the next six years as a Presbyterian missionary. Before she left on her first furlough, she heard about the revival in Los Angeles and decided to investigate it. In October 1906 she arrived in Los Angeles and stopped by the Azusa Street Mission, not knowing what to expect.

Shortly after the service began Moomau became convinced she was missing something. When the altar call was given, she went forward. At first she struggled over the mission's teaching on sanctification. She did not believe in the Wesleyan holiness theory of a "crisis" experience of sanctification, but rather in the "suppression theory" of sanctification. This was the more classical position on sanctification taught by D. L. Moody and held by most Reformed churches, that believers are continuously sanctified as they live an overcoming life. Their ultimate perfection awaits the return of the Lord. As she spent time in Azusa Street's "upper room," however, she claimed to experience a new dying to self. In the end, she was baptized in the Spirit and spoke in tongues.

When "Nettic" Moomau returned to China, she did so as an independent Apostolic Faith missionary to the port city of Shang-hai. Aided at first by a woman named Leola Phillips, Moomau worked effectively among Chinese women, and before long she had established an Apostolic Faith Mission in Shanghai. By August 3, 1909, six had received the baptism in the Spirit under her ministry.

While Thomas Junk and the Berntsens worked with the lower classes in northern China, Moomau gained access—perhaps through her prior Presbyterian mission service—to the higher

This photograph dates from about 1910 and is clear evidence of the success that accompanied the work of Antoinette Moomau. She is seated in the center of the photograph. The woman in front of the door is Mrs. E. B. Lawler. The boy standing fourth from the left corner is Harland Lawler and the girl on the far right back row with large ribbons in her hair is Beatrice Lawler. The Lawlers were originally part of the group led by M. L. Ryan. During this period they were supported by the Upper Room Mission in Los Angeles.

classes of Chinese society. She was soon ministering to various leaders in the fields of education and government. In December 1909 she reported that the door for the gospel had been opened in the home of the Chinese Ambassador to Belgium. By the 1920s she would count among her converts Mrs. K. T. Soong. Mrs. Soong's daughter, Madam Sun, was the wife of the first president of China, Sun Yat Sen; her eldest son was the minister of finance in Sun Yat Sen's administration.

On January 1, 1910, another group of Apostolic Faith missionaries from Los Angeles joined Antoinette Moomau and Leola Phillips. These new arrivals included Bertha Pinkham Dixon and her husband, and Hector and Sigrid McLean. The McLeans moved into the third floor of the three-story building that housed the mis-

While this photograph dates from 1928, it shows the continuing success of Miss Moomau's work in Shanghai. The woman to Miss Moomau's left is the first woman baptized in the Spirit in the region, now a co-worker. The woman's father is just behind her. He was the first man to be baptized in the Spirit, and in 1928, he was the leading pastor in the area. The women to the right of Miss Moomau were members and donors who had built the mission. Mrs. K. T. Soong, the mother-in-law of Sun Yet Sen is seated to her immediate right.

sion on the ground floor and Misses Moomau and Phillips on the second floor. The Dixons left the following day for Hong Kong.

Throughout 1910 Antoinette Moomau's work continued to mature and thrive, until she needed to move to a larger place in order to continue it. October brought a setback, however, as Leola Phillips contracted smallpox and died. With no close support at that time, Nettie Moomau endured a difficult period. She remained in Shang-hai until February 1911, when she took a furlough to the U.S., leaving the mission in the charge of Thomas Harwood and his wife, sister Lawler and her children, Beatrice and Harland. Following her furlough she returned to Shang-hai, where she continued to work until her unexpected death on March 25, 1937.

Western China

Hector and Sigrid McLean, like Nettie Moomau, were veteran missionaries. Sigrid [Bengtson] McLean, one of eleven siblings, was

This photograph of Hector and Sigrid [Bengsten] McLean dates from 1907, shortly after the birth of their daughter, Karlin.

born in Vermland, Sweden, July 14, 1869. Her father had served as a member of the Swedish Parliament for a number of years. Deeply touched when she read a book by Mrs. Howard Taylor, *From the Far East*, and having attended a meeting in Karlstad, Sweden where Hudson Taylor, the founder of the China Inland Mission (CIM) preached, she answered the call to serve as a missionary in China. In 1900 she attended the CIM Training Home in London. On the day she was to set sail for China, that country's brutal Boxer Rebellion began. As a result, her trip was cancelled. She traveled to Minnesota to visit relatives and then spent time in a CIM home in Toronto, Canada. There she met Hector McLean, who was approved for missionary work with the CIM but serving at the time as a supply pastor for a Presbyterian congregation.

Once order had been restored in China, Sigrid Bengsten traveled to northern China where she began her work. Hector completed his language training, and after two years in China, the couple was married December 5, 1905, in Chung-king-fu [now Chongqing] in the Szechwan Province of western China. They proceeded to Tali-fu [now Dali] where they began their work together. In 1909 they took a furlough, visiting Sweden, England, Canada, and the United States—ending with a two-week stay at Dr. Finis Yoakum's Pisgah Home near Los Angeles. From there they were taken to the Azusa Street Mission, where they were baptized in the Spirit.

The China Inland Mission refused to accept missionaries who claimed such an experience. As a result, the McLeans went out again as independent missionaries, arriving at Shang-hai on January 1, 1910. There they began their "Pentecostal" period of work with Antoinette Moomau, before moving out on their own into Chefoo [alternate Chi-fu, now Yantai] on the northern China coast. Over the next year they developed a relationship with the newly formed Pentecostal Missionary Union (PMU) out of England.

After they had completed their work with the PMU, and four missionary families from Britain had been established in north China, the McLeans moved back to the field they had served in their China Inland Mission days—Yun-nan Province in the extreme south-west part of China. They set up an Apostolic Faith mission in the city of Yun-nan-fu [now Kunming]. Using Yun-nan-fu as their initial mission station, they fanned out, first northward to Ly-küen [now Dayan] in the mountains, 7,857 feet above sea level, then southwest to Shun-ning-fu [now Fengqing or Fengshan], 5,800 feet up. That would become their new center of activity and would remain so for the next sixteen years. They retired in 1927 to Toronto, Canada.

Azusa Street Missionaries in Africa

Liberia

By far the largest number of the first-time missionaries who went out in 1906 from the Azusa Street Mission went to Africa.

These included Lucy Farrow, Julia and Willis Hutchins, Leila Mc-
Kinney, Samuel and Ardella Mead, Robert and Myrtle K. Shideler,
and George and Daisy Batman and their three young children—
Bessie, aged five, Robert, aged three, and an infant whose name we
do not know; thirteen people in all. The adults continued to correspond with the Azusa Street Mission after their departure from Los
Angeles, and all of them arrived in New York City about December 1, 1906, where Lucy Leatherman met and aided them.

Upon her arrival in New York City, Lucy Leatherman had also
continued to correspond with the Azusa Street Mission. While no
letter exists to document that Pastor Seymour and Lucy Leatherman planned a missionary sending strategy that treated these
African missionaries as a single group, several facts point to such a
strategy: First, the thirteen left Los Angeles at different times,
between August and November. Second, they all traveled by different routes and yet arrived in New York about the same day. Third,
they all stayed at or near the same boarding house. And finally, they
all traveled together as far as England on the same ship. Taken
together, this set of facts seems too striking to be mere coinci
dence. Planning had to be involved.

Lucy Leatherman, with her many long-established personal
contacts in the Christian Alliance [later the Christian and Missionary Alliance] in the New York area, seems the obvious candidate
for the role of coordinator for this African missionary venture. She
provided these missionaries with help in housing and in meeting
facilities as they arrived in the city. Several—perhaps all of them—
stayed at the Alliance House at 250 West Forty-fourth Street. They
all worshiped together at the Union Holiness Mission at 351 West
Fortieth Street, a small African American congregation led by
Elder Sturdevant (formerly of Los Angeles). At least one of them,
George Batman, was invited to speak in the Alliance Gospel Taber
nacle in New York City. And all of them sailed to Liverpool,
England aboard the steamer *SS Campania* on December 8, 1906.

When the group sailed on December 8, they were joined by
three new African American converts headed for Liberia. Mr. F. M.
Cook was baptized in the Spirit when Lucy Farrow and George

Batman laid hands on him and prayed. He was accompanied by his wife (unnamed) and a woman identified only as Mrs. Lee. By January 1907 all twelve African Americans were ministering in or around Monrovia, Liberia.

It is not completely clear why all of these new converts chose to go to Liberia. The reason may be simply that Julia Hutchins talked them into it. They may have believed that she had an inside track through her earlier holiness church contacts in the area. On the other hand, Liberia was unique among African countries. Neighboring Sierra Leone had been carved out by the British government as a place where former slaves could be repatriated from Britain to Africa. Liberia had been similarly carved out by the United States in 1822, with the help of the American Colonization Society. During the nineteenth century several thousand African Americans, most of them former slaves, had availed themselves of the American Colonization Society's help to return them to Africa. What we do not know is how much, if at all, these African American Azusa Street missionaries had been influenced by the various "back to Africa" discussions taking place within the African American community in the United States and the Caribbean at the time.

Upon their arrival in Liberia the Hutchinses and their niece, Leila McKinney, moved to Mt. Coffee, a small village about twelve miles northeast of Monrovia. Lucy Farrow stayed in Monrovia at first but then moved on to nearby Johnsonville, about ten miles east of the city. The Batmans, the Cooks, and Mrs. Lee may have moved on to Johnsonville as well. In any case, they stayed in contact with Lucy Farrow.

Lucy Farrow wrote back to the Azusa Street Mission that she had been able to communicate with the natives in the Kru language. The people in Los Angeles as well as Charles Parham believed that her tongue had been a genuine language. Whatever the case, she seems to have had a small but effective ministry among the Kru people, including a local king, in or near Johnsonville. Upon her return to the United States in mid-1907, Farrow claimed that twenty members of the Kru tribe had "received their Pentecost" while others had been "saved, sanctified, and healed," under her ministry. On two occasions, she claimed, the Lord had given her "the gift of the Kru language" and permitted her "to preach two sermons to the people in their own tongue." She bore witness to the fact that the "heathen" in Liberia had been baptized in the Spirit when they "spoke in English and some in other tongues."

Julia Hutchins wrote to the Azusa Street Mission on March 26, 1907, informing them that she had conducted a ten day meeting in a Monrovia school. On the tenth day, two had spoken in tongues. Since then, ten had been sanctified and three more had spoken in tongues. One entire household had been baptized in the Holy Spirit, and the man who headed it was "called . . . to the ministry." He was scheduled to be baptized in water on March 30. Many "natives," she reported, were coming to the meetings and "being saved and sanctified and filled with the Holy Ghost." Many were also being healed.

The story of the Batmans, the Cooks, and Mrs. Lee, on the other hand, was a tragic one. Within weeks of their arrival, the entire Batman family, Mrs. Cook, and Mrs. Lee all contracted either malaria or black water fever and died. *The Apostolic Faith* [Los Angeles, CA] never published an account of their deaths, though they did acknowledge that some folks had been "martyred." Perhaps it was not necessary to publish a full announcement. The Pentecostal movement—from Los Angeles to Portland to Sunderland, England— quickly became aware of the tragedy, no doubt by word of mouth. It was the focus of a discussion among an international gathering of Pentecostal leaders in Sunderland, England in early 1908.

The holiness press, on the other hand, especially *The Free Methodist*, published from Chicago, and *The Pentecost*, published by the Holiness Church in Southern California, carried the story as evidence that God had not called these missionaries to Africa. They had succumbed unnecessarily, these papers announced, because they had believed in the "delusion" of a revived Pentecost taught by Pastor Seymour at the Azusa Street Mission. As if that were not enough, *The Pentecost* charged that Mrs. Julia Hutchins had kidnapped a little girl from her parents in Krutown, Monrovia. While one secular Los Angeles newspaper covered the fact that Mrs. Hutchins returned to the United States with a girl from Liberia, there was not a hint of any irregularity in it. The girl was merely viewed as a spectacle. She had not yet developed any socially acceptable or "civilized" table manners.

Such negative reports served the purposes of certain Wesleyan holiness leaders, providing them with ammunition to slow the erosion in their membership as people moved into the Apostolic Faith movement. The only Pentecostal leader to make a public statement regarding the tragedy in Liberia was Charles F. Parham. He waited until 1912, and even then he used generalized (though humiliating) language. "Seymour, drunken with power and swollen to bursting," he began,

> sent forth a hundred or more of this kind of workers to fill the earth with the worst prostitution of Christianity I ever witnessed; in shame we have had to hang our heads, as fanatics and fools have returned from foreign fields in disgrace and shame, with only a monkey chattering; bringing a just criticism and condemnation from the Christian press and public.

The rise in the level of negative rhetoric in holiness publications did little to deter the subsequent recruitment of Pentecostal missionaries willing to serve in Africa. One example is the family of Frank L. Cummings, a man influenced by Azusa Street who became ordained in the Church of God in Christ. Charles H. Mason, one of the two founders of the Church of God in Christ, visited the Azusa Street Mission in March 1907. While he was there, he was baptized in the Spirit. On May 2, Pastor William J. Seymour left Los Angeles on a several-month trip to Houston, Texas, and Memphis, Tennessee. Shortly after Seymour's departure, the Cummings family decided that they would go as missionaries to Liberia as well.

On or about May 15, 1907, Frank L. Cummings received ordination to "the gospel ministry" in the Church of God in Christ from C. H. Mason and E. R. Driver. While Mason had surely returned to

Memphis by this time, E. R. Driver would soon open up the first congregation of the Church of God in Christ west of the Rockies, and he may have performed the ordination at the Azusa Street Mission. Two days later the Cummings family was noisily escorted by roughly one hundred people from the Azusa Street Mission down East First Street and across the Los Angeles River to the Salt Lake Railroad depot. There, the faithful held a spontaneous service, singing, praying, exhorting, shouting, and crying. As one reporter put it, "the special antics, rehearsed for the occasion at the Azusa st. mission, were enjoyed by every one at the depot, from the boot-black to the depot cat." The Cummings family boarded the train bound for Chattanooga, Tennessee.

Somewhere along the way, the Cummingses connected up with Pastor Seymour. It may have been in Houston, or in Chattanooga, or even in Memphis, Tennessee. On the evening of June 2, 1907, however, the Cummings family and Pastor Seymour arrived at a meeting conducted by Glenn Cook in Murphy Hall in Indianapolis. The Cummings family was clearly raising funds for their projected September 1907 missionary trip to Monrovia, Liberia, by steamer from New York City.

Yet another missionary venture began early the next year. Following their baptism in the Spirit at the Azusa Street Mission in 1906, Edward and Molly McCauley and their family had established an Apostolic Faith Mission in nearby Long Beach, California. In his zeal to spread the full gospel, McCauley had had several brushes with the law in Long Beach. He was arrested in February and again in June of 1907 for disturbing the peace. In spite of his notoriety, McCauley, an African American, had become the successful pastor of a racially integrated congregation, half white and half black. On May 7, 1907, he baptized fifty new converts in the Pacific Ocean off Terminal Island. But within months, for whatever reason, the McCauleys and their associate Rosa Harmon left Long Beach, arriving in Monrovia, Liberia, on November 15, 1907. Upon his arrival in Monrovia, McCauley wrote to the mayor of Long Beach, Mr. F. H. Downs, informing him that he had left the city to become "a missionary to the black race who occupy this republic," and he expected to remain in Liberia "indefinitely." McCauley rented a hall in Monrovia, and on December 1, 1907 he began to hold meetings there.

On December 23, 1908, another Pentecostal, John Reid, disembarked at Monrovia's harbor while his ship offloaded some cargo before proceeding on to Cape Palmas. The Methodists had warned Reid against McCauley, but he took the time to investigate the missionary for himself. Reid found McCauley at home where a painted sign read, "Apostolic Faith Mission." Reid was impressed by what he saw and heard there. McCauley reported that several had received healing in his meetings, a large number had been converted and immersed, and he had 145 people on his church roll. From Reid's perspective, McCauley was doing a fine work. "He is independent of the Mission Boards, yet seems very dependent on God," Reid wrote. "He is just as straight a Pentecostal man as is to be found." As Reid landed on the southeastern end of Liberia, he appealed to Alexander Boddy to send literature to McCauley in Monrovia, so that his work might continue. Another six months went by before we hear anything more of McCauley's Apostolic Faith Mission. By June 16, 1909, McCauley had baptized 154 converts. Many had been sanctified, and they were busy with the construction of a church building with twelve hundred square feet of space.

In September 1913 the Azusa Street missionary evangelist Daniel Awrey left his young family in Los Angeles while he traveled to Liberia. He wrote back that on the night of October 9, 1913, he had preached "to a large congregation in the Apostolic Faith Church" in Monrovia—most likely McCauley's mission. The next day Awrey continued his travels. Unfortunately, he soon contracted a case of malaria and died on December 2, 1913, before he could complete his trip.

Sadly, the foundational work of Mrs. Hutchins, Lucy Farrow, and the Batman family, the Cooks, Lee, McKinney and the McCauleys have disappeared completely from all official histories of missions in Liberia. McCauley's mission was the first permanent Pentecostal congregation on the continent of Africa, and it may ultimately prove to be the source of the Pentecostal theology and experience that produced Prophet William Wade Harris and his

Daniel and Ella Awrey with their children about 1910

millions-strong Harrist Church of the Ivory Coast (Côte d'Ivoire). It was African Americans, not whites, who established this congregation. Their missionary activities push the documented beginnings of Pentecostalism in Liberia back two full years from the date reported in every Pentecostal mission history of Liberia to date.

In each of these cases, the missionaries to Liberia were African-Americans; their stories open a chapter on African Americans' role in the early worldwide spread of the Pentecostal message. These missionaries raised to new heights the vision for missions within the Pentecostal tradition, at the same time modeling a trust in God to meet all their needs as they sought to fulfill the Great Commission.

Angola

Also sailing with these African American missionaries as far as Liverpool, England—were two families named the Meads and the

Shidelers. At Liverpool, these families boarded a ship bound for Angola. The Meads returned to the United States within a year, apparently without any fruit for their efforts. We have no further information on the Schidelers after their arrival in Benguela, Angola.

South Africa

South Africa was another popular destination for Azusa Street missionaries. The first to express an intention to go to South Africa was Thomas Hezmalhalch. Born October 5, 1847 to English parents in Paterson, New Jersey, where his father operated a munitions foundry, young Hezmalhalch made shells for use by the Union troops during the Civil War. Following the war he journeyed to England, where he met and married Charlotte Bass, a native of Leeds. The couple began their family in Leeds but moved to South-

This photograph shows Thomas Hezmalhalch and John G. Lake shortly after they established the Apostolic Faith Mission of South Africa. Hezmalhalch was the first President and John G. Lake was his successor.

ern California in 1884. In "Verdugo," an area that would later become part of Glendale, Hezmalhalch purchased property and became the secretary to the local land improvement association.

From the time they moved to California, the Hezmalhalches were active in local holiness church life. In 1895 "Brother Tom," as they called him, became the pastor of First Holiness Church in Pasadena. He served on a committee charged with producing a hymn book for the Holiness Church of Southern California. He often sang as a soloist, and he produced a number of hymns, some of which were ultimately published in *The Apostolic Faith* [Los Angeles, CA].

In the summer of 1906 Tom Hezmalhalch was baptized in the Spirit at the Azusa Street Mission. By November he had traveled to Denver, where he had shared his testimony with a brand new Pentecostal congregation led by George Frederick Fink. Finally he proceeded to Indianapolis, where he led an Apostolic Faith congregation in early 1907. On Monday, May 6, clothed in a new suit and "armed" with a new set of teeth, Brother Tom left Indianapolis and proceeded to Zion, Illinois. There he held a series of meetings at The Haven, a former hospice that became a center of Pentecostal activity in later 1906.

A second partner in the mission to South Africa was John Graham Lake. He was born March 18, 1870, in Ontario, Canada. In 1891 he was ordained by the Methodist Church, but had chosen a lucrative business career. In 1898, however, Lake visited the faith healer John Alexander Dowie in Zion, Illinois. His wife had been suffering from tuberculosis, and through Dowie's prayers, she was healed. Lake quickly joined Dowie's Catholic Apostolic Church, where he became an elder. In 1907 he traveled to Los Angeles to participate in the Azusa Street meetings.

A third man, Jacob O. Lehman, had left his home in Monrovia, California, in 1901 with his wife Lily, and traveled to the Transvaal in South Africa, where the couple worked for a time as missionaries. They had established a work among the miners near Johannesburg, preaching most evenings and weekends. During those years Lehman had committed himself to learning the Zulu language. In

1906 the Lehmans returned to southern California, where they heard of the Azusa Street Mission. They went to see the mission for themselves and were quickly baptized in the Spirit. In May 1907 Lehman was living in Indianapolis, fully anticipating his return as an Apostolic Faith missionary, and he attended the mission where Glenn Cook and Thomas Hezmalhalch were ministering.

All three of these men decided to stay in the area of Chicago and Indianapolis until the spring of 1908. In February they took part in a missionary convention in Indianapolis and announced that they would go to Johannesburg, South Africa, as missionaries. On April 1, 1908, Tom and Charlotte Hezmalhalch, John G. and Jenny Lake and their children, and Jacob and Lily Lehman boarded a train bound for St. John's, Newfoundland. They had purchased their tickets to South Africa, but most of them had little or no money left over. They were joined by Ida Sackett and the Schneiderman family, converted Jews who intended to minister in London. Together they traveled to Liverpool, England, on April 3, 1908, sailing third class on the *Empress of Ireland*. After a short stay in Liverpool, the group (minus the Schneidermans) proceeded on to South Africa, arriving in Cape Town, South Africa, on May 14.

While the Lehmans had ministered for several years in South Africa and knew what to expect, Hezmalhalch and Lake were very surprised to find Cape Town to be so civilized. They had expected to find a barbarian land. They held a few services in that city but continued their trip to Johannesburg, arriving about May 23. On May 30, Lake wrote that they had been "drawn out toward the native work." As a result, they conducted their first service on May 25, 1908, in a native "tabernacle" owned by the Congregational American Mission, in Doornfontein, South Africa. Roughly five hundred people attended. Lake's letter describing the service shows why the Pentecostal worship style was so well accepted in Africa. "As the service proceeded," he began,

> The Spirit of God fell upon the house in prayer. The natives recognized it just as quickly as we did, and without suggestion fell on their knees to pray as all natives here do, being exceedingly

devout. They didn't wait for one another to pray. Out of the five hundred present, two hundred and fifty broke out in prayer aloud at one time. The [Congregational] missionaries who were with us, as observers, of the starchy churchy order, were amazed and astounded because we did not stop the noise.... They prayed continuously for three-quarters of an hour. They wept tears, confessed their sins, took off their idolatrous charms, etc., and when the service was over 'they of the circumcision' were astonished.

Before long news began to circulate not only among the African natives, but also among members of the white community. Lake's connection with John Alexander Dowie undoubtedly paved the way for the almost immediate expansion of this Apostolic Faith team's work. Dowie had established a number of "Zion" churches in southern Africa through the efforts of his elders Daniel Bryant and Pieter Louis le Roux. Lake, in particular, was able to portray the Apostolic Faith as a logical extension of the message then being proclaimed by the Zionists. The Zion people believed in salvation, sanctification, divine healing, and the imminent return of the Lord. They were also restorationists (see chapter 3), and once they heard the message of Lake and his team, many of the Zionists received the baptism in the Spirit and joined the Apostolic Faith movement. One feature of Zionist practice carried over into the Apostolic Faith movement in South Africa, making that movement unique among Pentecostal groups. This was the practice of baptism by triple immersion, once each in the name of the Father, and of the Son, and of the Holy Spirit.

The initial result was that many of the white Zionists began to attend the meetings held by Lake in the native congregation. And because of the imbalance of power between the races in South Africa even at that time, the whites began to squeeze the blacks out. At that point, just weeks after their arrival in South Africa, P. L. le Roux offered his church to Lake and Hezmalhalch. This Breë Street building—a former Presbyterian Church that le Roux had bought out and filled with a Zion congregation—quickly became the "Central Tabernacle" of the Apostolic Faith Mission in South Africa.

On November 18, 1908, the group began to publish a paper that they initially titled *God's Latter Rain*. In their introductory article, they made clear the tie between this South African group and the Azusa Street Mission.

> Who are we? And what do we teach and practice? We are known as the Apostolic Faith Movement of Johannesburg, S.A., which is included in the great world-wide Holy Ghost Revival which has taken its impetus from the work of Azusa Street Mission, Los Angeles, California, where the Holy Ghost has been poured out on the believers during the past 18 months, and which has already spread throughout the entire world.

When the group decided to create a formal association, Thomas Hezmalhalch became its first president, John G. Lake its first vice president, and Jacob O. Lehman its first treasurer. All three of them seasoned preachers, each had also received his "Pentecost" at the Azusa Street Mission. They immediately began the work of proclaiming the full gospel, latter rain, apostolic faith message to the people of South Africa.

In 1908, one other Azusa Street couple, Henry M. and Anna E. Turney, joined this South African Apostolic Faith work. Henry M. Turney had been a traveling evangelist for the holiness Burning Bush organization. While preaching in Alaska during the summer of 1906, Turney received news of the revival in Los Angeles. Right away he decided to go to the Azusa Street Mission where, on his first visit, he was baptized in the Spirit. That fall, he traveled north with the Florence Crawford party. When she went on to Salem, Oregon, he stayed in San Jose, where he continued to hold meetings at the Florence Mission for a short time. The Turneys then sailed to Honolulu for a year of ministry. In March 1907 the Turneys wrote from Honolulu, informing the faithful at Azusa Street that a young Salvation Army captain in Honolulu had received his Pentecost and was anxious to join forces with the Apostolic Faith movement.

By May or June, however, the Turneys had left Honolulu to pursue a call as missionaries in South Africa. On their way they stopped in England, where they were joined by a woman named Hannah James. The trio then proceeded to Pretoria, South Africa, and for a time they became part of the Apostolic Faith Mission. In fact, on May 27, 1909, H. M. Turney was elected to replace J. O. Lehman as treasurer of the association, while he continued to serve as a pastor in Pretoria.

On February 14, 1910, however, Turney wrote a letter to the executive council, "informing the severing of his connections with the Apostolic Faith Mission," and returning not only his own credentials, but those of his wife and of Hannah James. The Executive Council met on February 25 and accepted his resignation. We do not know what prompted Turney, though it is likely related to a rift that developed when he came under the influence of two men, George Bowie and Archibald Cooper, who were not happy with Lake. In fact, Tom Hezmalhalch was influenced by these men, too, and by the end of the year Hezmalhalch had returned to Southern California, leaving Lake as the head of the Apostolic Faith Mission. Turney gave Archibald Cooper charge over his congregation in Pretoria, and it became the first congregation of a new denomination, the Full Gospel Church.

In 1911 Turney moved on to Doornkop, where he pioneered a new work among the natives. For a time it operated as an independent group, but when the General Council of the Assemblies of God formed in the United States, the Turneys received credentials—although his work never became part of that organization's missionary program. Turney's death in 1921 led to a crisis of sorts when both the Apostolic Faith Mission and the Full Gospel Church sought to gain control of Turney's work. Anna Turney resisted, and Turney's work went on to become the first congregation of the Assemblies of God of South Africa.

While the South African Apostolic Faith churches were surprisingly interracial during the earliest years of Lake, Hezmalhalch, and the other Azusa Street missionaries, during the teens they became racially segregated. White leaders "found it expedient not to jeopardize their position with the government of the day."[35] The churches had already begun to be caught up in the national movement toward apartheid. Yet in the 1980s the Azusa Street myth once again would play a role among the so-called "black," "colored," and "Indian" South African Pentecostals, providing them with a voice to speak out against apartheid. "We trace our history back to the Azusa Street Revival in Los Angeles, in 1906," wrote one representative of this group.

> In the Azusa Street Revival we find the legitimacy to continue our witness as Pentecostals. It was here that God called to himself a prophetic movement in an oppressive society that belied the dignity of black people. It was here that God called to himself humble people to be his witnesses in a hostile world. It was here that powerless people were baptized in the Holy Spirit and endued with power to preach the good news of Jesus Christ, with "signs following."
>
> It is in this tradition that we come bearing a Relevant Pentecostal Witness.[36]

These early Azusa Street missionaries to South Africa have bequeathed one further gift on postcolonial Africa. When Europeans began to withdraw from direct rule in Africa, many people thought it would be the end of Christianity in the region. Instead, especially since the 1960s, the region has seen enormous church growth, largely out of Pentecostal works and the rapidly growing African Independent Churches. True, many in the Apostolic Faith movement do not view these churches as being truly "Pentecostal" in the classical sense—and some wonder whether they are fully "Christian." Yet scores, if not hundreds, of denominations self-designated "Zion," "Apostolic," or "Apostolic Faith"—marked by uniquely African theologies and practices—trace their roots directly to the earlier work of these Apostolic Faith missionaries.

7

THE FIRE BEGINS TO COOL

Azusa Mission is still giving forth the same truth, and the Lord is pouring out His Spirit upon His sons and daughters, and they are witnessing in burning testimonies that Jesus' Blood does cleanse from all sin and He does sanctify and baptize with the Holy Ghost and speak in tongues.

We look for a great outpouring of God's Spirit in saving and healing power and power that fills with the Holy Ghost and fire in the year 1908. May all Christ's people be stirred up over this salvation and sink down in deeper humility at the feet of Jesus.

THE APOSTOLIC FAITH

The Azusa Street revival was nearly two years old when the new year broke in 1908. Much had changed since William J. Seymour had come to town. A number of Pentecostal congregations had been pioneered in various parts of Los Angeles. More of them had been established in the city's suburbs such as Pasadena, Monrovia, Whittier, and Long Beach. Evangelists and missionaries had made their way across the nation and around the world. In some ways, the revival had already become a global phenomenon.

Secular Perspectives on the Revival

Things were clearly changing in Los Angeles. For one thing, the "circus" had packed up and moved on. The news media that had found so much time to cover the emergence of the revival at the Azusa Street Mission in 1906, and had ridiculed the expansion of the revival into other local congregations throughout the latter half of 1906 and much of 1907, had finally lost interest in the subject. People who spoke in tongues were no longer news, unless they created a public disturbance or could be caricatured as a public nuisance. The Azusa Street Mission simply dropped from sight in local news coverage, though a few of the more controversial figures appeared from time to time.

Throughout the summer months of 1908, for instance, an Apostolic Faith or "holy rollers" camp meeting conducted worship on the grounds of the Arroyo Seco once again, between Avenues Fifty-eight and Sixty in Highland Park. The Los Angeles papers had carried many reports on the previous summer's camp meeting, but in 1908 they remained silent.

Each evening throughout the summer, street preachers from the nearby camp proclaimed their messages at the corner of Pasadena [now Figueroa] Avenue and Avenue Sixty-four. That they held these meetings just one block from the property owned by Dr. Finis Yoakum may suggest that Yoakum and his followers at the nearby Pisgah Home were involved. Then again, the preachers' chosen site was also the corner where the streetcar stopped, disgorging the Los Angeles passengers who were headed for the camp meeting. Thus, these street meetings may have been the work of any entrepreneurial preacher, even from downtown Los Angeles.

News of "great things" had come to George B. Studd about the 1908 camp meeting. It had produced "much unity of spirit and power" and led to "many baptisms." On the other hand, many of the residents of Highland Park were just as frustrated over the "noisy character" of the meetings as they had been the previous year. In the end nothing came of their complaints. The camp meeting that had run all summer, with large crowds in attendance, quietly drew to a close in September. Only the *Highland Park Herald*, a tiny weekly, took any note of the meetings. The meetings were simply conducted too close to its offices to be ignored. Even then, its reports were generally no longer than a sentence or two.

The Rev. J. W. Sykes emerged in the news again that summer. He had gotten into trouble. In March 1907 he had been serving as the pastor of the "Apostolic Church" in East Los Angeles, where he had practiced baptism "in the name of Jesus Christ." Since that time, he had teamed up with an African American preacher, Elder H. A. Garrison, and an African American woman, Mrs. Mary Taylor, to hold meetings at 2815 West Tenth Street. Throughout the month of July, the police had been called on repeatedly to protect these "holy rollers" when they were threatened by local residents. The press, with its typical objectivity, identified the sole purpose of their meetings as rendering "the night hideous by their delirious ravings after they have been worked up to a state of frenzy that borders on the insane." Finally a group of sleep-deprived residents filed a complaint against the racially integrated congregation led by this trio. On July 25, 1908, Garrison, Sykes, and Mrs. Taylor each went before Justice Rose, where they were charged with disturbing the peace. The trial was set for August 3. The date, however, came and went with no trial. It seems that the court had erred when it notified the witnesses of the trial date. No witnesses appeared, and the case was dismissed.

Another, more sensational case involved a group of "holy rollers," probably from the nearby Azusa Street Mission, who had begun conducting nightly street meetings at the corner of Marchessault and Juan Streets in Chinatown. The Chinese had put up with the nightly intrusion for about two weeks. On the evening of September 6, 1908, the "rollers" began their meeting as usual. Just after dark a group of Chinese, each armed with a heaping basket of rotten eggs, attacked the street meeting with considerable vigor, pelting the worshippers in a pungent attempt to drive them off.

The next day, the *Los Angeles Herald* announced that

Yells of police, help, murder, fire and screams of freight [*sic*] from men and women filled the air. A riot alarm was sent to the Chinese sub-station, but when the police arrived the Chinese had disappeared as suddenly as they came, and all that was left was a band of much bedraggled men and women, hurriedly slouching along the streets with one hand to their noses and the other mopping thin streams of what had been eggs from their clothing and faces.

Still, no news reports specifically mentioned the Azusa Street Mission. On the whole, the city had moved on, and while many would look askance at participants in the Apostolic Faith movement for years to come, at least it seemed as though the city had finally decided to tolerate the group.

The Apostolic Faith's Perspectives on the Revival

If coverage by the secular press declined in 1908, so also did the accounts that originated from the mission itself. The mission published two or possibly three official issues of *The Apostolic Faith* that year. The first issue came out in January. It contained the traditional reports from abroad as well as several sermon excerpts, but it contained only one short article that gave any real information on the status of things at the mission. Even then, the language that described what went on at the mission was vague. Souls continued to be "sanctified, baptized and saved," the article reported. The mission had celebrated a "blessed day" on Christmas and a "Watch Night" service on New Year's Eve. The writer of the column, probably Clara Lum, compared the mission's plain, humble "old beams and whitewashed walls" to the "barn at Bethlehem" where Christ had been born nearly two millennia earlier. The conclusion: "The Spirit falls on humble hearts and in humble missions and churches."

This article reminded readers that the meetings had continued uninterrupted since April 1906 and the Lord had always provided for every need that the workers encountered. "The devil," on the other hand, was doing everything in his power "to keep the saints from entering into the greater fullness of Christ." The mission had lost some people during 1907, the writer reported, because "they thought the teaching on divorce was too straight." Their loss would not change the mission's position, however, because God wanted to use "a clean people and pure doctrine as a channel for this Pentecostal power." The article closed with an exhortation for the paper's readers to rely completely on the blood of Jesus Christ—for only by doing so would they become "Overcomers."

The second 1908 issue of *The Apostolic Faith* came out in May. It gave virtually no new information on the state of the continuing revival. Surprisingly, it also made no mention of the mission's second anniversary, celebrated April 5–12. This omission suggests that work on the issue had been completed or nearly completed by the time of the anniversary meeting. The May issue did, however, carry a couple of small but interesting notes.

In a single paragraph near the end of the first page, titled "What Hath God Wrought," the writer gave a rather generic report on the status of the whole revival.

> Many are rejoicing with joy unspeakable for the great blessings that God is pouring out in this latter rain. Many saved, sanctified, healed of disease and baptized with the Holy Ghost and fire. Many happy families filled with the Spirit and working for Jesus.

In a short paragraph on the second page, *The Apostolic Faith* reported that Lucy Farrow had been praying with people in the cottage at the rear of the Azusa Street property since her return from Africa, and "quite a number have received a greater filling of the Spirit and some have been healed and baptized with the Spirit."

The paper also rejoiced over the successful purchase, at last, of the Azusa Street property. "When the place was about to be sold so that the Mission would have to move, the saints agreed to purchase it with three years time to pay the $15,000, expecting the Lord to send the money all in before that time, and He has done it, and answered our prayers in a wonderful way."

A third 1908 issue of *The Apostolic Faith* came out that June, although some have questioned its authenticity as a product of the Azusa Street Mission. First, it lacked the standard masthead on the title page—replacing it with the words of Acts 2:16–18. Just below this quotation, in the only extant copy we have, appear the handwritten words, "Vol 2 #14, Los Angeles, Cal, June 1908, Subscription Free." The problem is that we do not know who wrote these words, when the words were written, or whether the original paper carried these words. The format of the paper was essentially the same as it had been in all previous issues of *The Apostolic Faith*, a fact that speaks in its favor. At the top left-hand corner of the second page, a small note identifies it as *The Apostolic Faith* and gives the address, "Apostolic Faith Mission, 312 Azusa Street, Los Angeles, Cal." This paper is likely a genuine issue of *The Apostolic Faith*, but if it is, it must also be acknowledged as an irregular one.

In this issue, editor Clara Lum recalled that many people had responded to the needs of the famine victims in China and India, and assured givers that the mission had forwarded their money to the missionaries in those countries. Still, this issue contains no news originating from Los Angeles more recently than eighteen months before its stated publication date. This suggests once again that something was affecting the quality of production on *The Apostolic Faith*. Clara Lum seemed to be too preoccupied with other things to write up a report on the status of the revival in Los Angeles. She had taken the easy road and simply published excerpts from letters that told of the revival's continuing worldwide impact. We might ask whether the fires of the revival, now two years old, had begun to die down. We might also wonder what personal issues Lum might have been facing at the time.

When subscribers retrieved the July and August 1908 issue of *The Apostolic Faith*, Volume II, No. 15, from their mailboxes, they discovered a surprise. The original masthead was back, but it listed a new city of origin—no longer "Los Angeles, Cal.," but now "Portland, Ore." In the top left-hand corner of the second page, a brief note announced, "We have moved the paper which the Lord laid on us to begin at Los Angeles to Portland, Oregon, which will now be its headquarters." A second note followed, suggesting that offerings of money and stamps be sent to the APOSTOLIC FAITH, PORTLAND, ORE. Perhaps more significantly, the publishers gave no reason for the change.

The lead article, "The Promised Latter Rain," retold the story of the beginnings of "Pentecost" in Los Angeles two years earlier. This was clearly intended to show continuity of the paper's present issue with its past issues. The issue continued with testimonies of the spread of the revival around the world. It even carried the words and thoughts of Pastor Seymour, although this time without identifying him as the speaker. Page three carried news of "How Pentecost Came to Portland, Ore."

These changes have prompted several questions: Was there trouble in Los Angeles? What was the state of the revival as it continued through 1908? Had something happened at the mission that led to Clara Lum's apparently abrupt departure? Why was no reason given for this change? Historians have debated these questions for years with very little satisfaction. Some have argued that Clara Lum left for personal reasons. Others, that racism had reared its ugly head. Still others have claimed that Seymour had compromised on theological issues, necessitating a break to preserve purity in the revival. A few have contended that the revival was in serious decline. Most of the assessments to date, however, have been naïve. They have failed to understand the complexity of the situation. What we have needed is a careful assessment of all the available data.

Individual Perspectives on the Revival

We are fortunate to have access to two diaries and several pieces of correspondence that can give us some insight into this period. Each of these sources gives us only limited information, but taken together, they provide a reasonably clear picture of the whole. The first of the diaries was kept by George B. Studd, who had worked for many years at the Peniel Mission. On September 29, 1907, Studd broke with Peniel and began attending the Azusa Street Mission—he had become convinced that the Lord was working in the Azusa Street revival and he wanted to be baptized in the Holy Spirit. The second diary was kept by Ned Caswell, a holiness layman who worked as a job printer. While Caswell seems never to have received the baptism in the Spirit as it was taught at the Azusa Street Mission, he was still very sympathetic to the claims and the work of Apostolic Faith people.

Both diaries reveal the wide diversity present in Los Angeles holiness and Pentecostal church life during 1908. If George Studd had not been both well-to-do and frugal, and had Ned Caswell not worked at a job that allowed him considerable flexibility, we might wonder how they sustained themselves. Both men spent hours and hours in church services, often during the day and through half the night, and they did so virtually every day of the week. Caswell's diary, which covers a slightly later period than does Studd's diary, is in some ways more helpful. He had a broader perspective on the results of the Azusa Street revival because he traveled up and down the west coast from Los Angeles to Seattle, visiting an array of holiness and Pentecostal missions and taking note of what he saw. He often recorded more background from the secular context than did Studd.

George Studd's entry for January 19, 1908, reads, "First Sunday I have spent in Los Angeles since I resigned from Peniel (Sept. 29th)—Cecil and I attended Azusa St. all day—good meetings." The "Cecil" here was Studd's longtime friend, Cecil Henry Polhill, another well-heeled English layman. Polhill, like Studd, had been born into the landed gentry of England, February 23, 1860. He had grown up on a large estate in Bedford, England. His father had served as a member of the British Parliament. Cecil and George had both attended Eton, an elite school for boys that stands just below Windsor Castle. There, they played on one of the country's greatest cricket teams, earning them fame throughout England even before they went up to Cambridge University. At Cambridge, the two young men continued to play cricket as they pursued their degrees.

After his conversion in 1884, Cecil Polhill became one of the famous "Cambridge Seven," a group of young Cambridge students and graduates who committed their lives to missionary service in China.[37] In early 1885 Polhill left for China, where he married Eleanor Agnes. Together they had three sons and a daughter. They returned to England only in 1900, when it became clear that a serious illness he had contracted while in China would require an extended period of recuperation. Upon Polhill's return to England, doctors convinced him that because of his health, he could no longer reasonably continue as a missionary in China.

Three years later, in 1903, Polhill inherited his father's home. The following year his wife and his youngest son died. In 1905 he was asked by the China Inland Mission to go to China and see what he could do to help them gain access to Tibet. It was to be a one-year assignment. Polhill thought it might do him some good, so he agreed to go. When he completed this assignment, he returned from China to England by way of Los Angeles—and there he met up with his old friend, George Studd. Having attended the Azusa Street Mission and become excited about what was happening there, Studd couldn't wait to bring Polhill to the mission.

On Friday, January 24, the two spent an afternoon with a Mrs. H. G. Clark, who was on her way back to Japan, where she was serving as a missionary. That evening Mrs. Clark joined Cecil Polhill and George Studd at the Azusa Street Mission. On Sunday, January 26, Polhill and Studd returned to Azusa Street for the entire day. The following Saturday, February 1, they attended the "noon" meeting at the mission. The next day they were back again.

Sunday, February 2, 1908, was a day to remember for Studd—he punctuated his journal entry for that day with exclamation points: "What a Sunday at Azusa! Dispute as to taking collections. How the Devil tried to get in! How the Lord defeated him. Is. 59:19.[38] Cecil gave £1500 to clear mortgage on Azusa."[39] The next day Cecil Polhill was baptized in the Spirit, and on Wednesday, February 5, he left for Chicago on the Salt Lake City Railroad, bound ultimately for England.

The dispute over whether to take an offering at the Azusa Street Mission was apparently very divisive, at least in the sense that some people were openly offended by the thought of taking a formal offering of any kind. The mission had never done that before; they had always trusted God and the faithfulness of the people to meet their financial needs. Rachel Sizelove, one of the organizers of the 1907 camp meeting, was there that morning. She would later complain,

How well I remember the first time the flesh began to get in the way of the Holy Ghost, and how the burden came upon the saints that morning when Brother Seymore [sic] stood before the audience and spoke of raising money to buy the Azusa

Street Mission. The Holy Ghost was grieved. You could feel it all over the audience, when they began to ask for money, and the Holy Ghost power began to leave, and instead of the Holy Ghost heavenly choir, they brought in a piano.

For Sizelove, more was at stake than the taking of an offering. She mentioned the arrival of a piano, although not identifying a date, and she seems to have connected the piano with a decline in manifestations of the "heavenly choir." Her complaint about the intrusion of a piano does not surprise: for many years, Sizelove had been a Free Methodist evangelist, and the Free Methodists at the time had been non-instrumental—that is, they did not include musical instruments in their churches. When she connected the advent of the piano with the taking of an offering, she was really identifying changes at the mission that she did not agree with. The mission had never done it that way before, and this shift in established ways disturbed Sizelove.

Klaas Brower was more incensed by the incident than was Sizelove. She blamed the problem on the flesh; he blamed it on the devil. From Brower's perspective, "the devil" had sent from China the seven thousand dollars needed to finish paying for the building and grounds. And someone other than Pastor Seymour, undoubtedly George Studd, had received the money from Polhill with the instructions that the mission incorporate. "They incorporated," grumbled Brower, "and elected trustees and became a denomination as all denominations before them."

Brower's complaint that the mission had incorporated was shared by others. It smacked of organization. And some of the Azusa Street faithful, such as Frank Bartleman, wanted nothing to do with formal organization. At the same time, Brower mistakenly linked the mission's incorporation to Polhill's gift. The mission had been incorporated nearly a year earlier, on March 9, 1907, and an announcement had appeared in *The Apostolic Faith* that same month.

The lot and buildings at 312 Azusa Street have been purchased by the Apostolic Faith Mission. Five Holy Ghost men have been elected as trustees, who hold the property. . . . The property was purchased for $15,000 and $4,000 has already been paid down on it. Any friends wishing to have a share in buying this Mission for the Lord may send offerings to Bro. Reuben Clark, who is secretary of the board of trustees. Address 312 Azusa St., Los Angeles.

It is difficult to know just how deeply feelings ran among the majority of the people at the mission. The depth of the feelings later expressed by Sizelove and Brower did not seem to worry George Studd beyond that one day. On February 16, two weeks after Polhill left Los Angeles on February 5, George Studd attended the mission and wrote, "Very good meetings all day—greatly blessed, myself, at morn. service." Since he was actively praying that the Lord would baptize him in the Spirit, he added, ". . . wonderfully near thro' afternoon in Upper Room. Meeting packed to the doors at night."

Studd returned the following Sunday for the entire day, and he attended Azusa Street every evening that week. A Brother Bowland gave an exhortation on that Sunday evening that led to another clash, but what it was over and how far it may have gone beyond the normal debates that took place in many of the mission's services is not stated. It seems to have left no lasting damage. Studd once again reported "good meeting" on Friday morning, February 28. He noted that there were "a number of seekers and good altar service" at another "good" service that evening. The following Sunday, March 1, he mentioned that the morning service in which a Brother Tingle spoke under the power of the Spirit, and the Word was given by Brother [Elmer] Fisher, was "good."

Day after day, Studd attended the meetings at the mission. Most of his entries do not mention the quality of the services, but he would not likely have continued to attend them if they were not "good." One minor exception, Saturday evening, March 21, has Studd recording that the meeting had not been very good—but two weeks later, on Sunday, April 5, he again judged, "Splendid service at Azusa in the morning."

Another observer, J. H. Sparks, gave equally unrestrained praise of the evening service that same day. "Sunday evening found the house packed from door to door and such a volume of praise as went up to the shining courts; it seemed the angels and archangels must have rejoiced together with us." Two days later, on Tuesday, April 7, Sparks once again wrote his reflections on the service,

> Tuesday evening, (the seventh) Bro. Seymour spoke from the fourth of Luke, first nineteen verses, with demonstration of the Spirit and power, the saints drinking in the Word with shouts of praise and victory. It was truly blessed, especially to see such an unusually large number of young people and little children fully saved and baptized with the Holy Ghost and Fire, witnessing to God's saving and healing power.

On Thursday, April 9, the second anniversary of the outpouring at the Asberry home, George Studd offered an equally effusive assessment: "Good all day meeting at Azusa. God gave me great liberty in my testimony in afternoon—splendid meeting at night—many good solid strong testimonies." The following Sunday, April 12, Studd remarked, "Good service at Azusa at 11 A.M. W. J. Seymour in charge."

On Thursday that same week two African Americans, Azusa Street trustee Richard Asberry and William Seymour's friend from Houston, Joseph A. Warren, accompanied George B. Studd to the Security Savings Bank, which held the deed for the mission. Studd paid off the deed with Polhill's gift. That evening Studd met with the mission's board of trustees, and before retiring for the night he wrote a letter to Cecil Polhill, undoubtedly to inform him of the day's activities. Pastor Seymour and Edward S. Lee led the Easter service the following Sunday, April 19, and on April 26 Studd was excited over the "splendid testimonies, especially to healing" that he heard there.

According to George Studd, Pastor Seymour "spoke well" when he preached the Sunday morning service on May 3, and Studd had a "good time" tarrying in the upper room of the Azusa Street Mission. The following Sunday, May 10, Studd wrote, "Splendid meeting at Azusa in morning—The Lord helped me to sing 'I Am So

Happy in Jesus.' In aft[ernoon], testimony meeting was good, but Seymour seemed to throw away his message (if he had one) by throwing it open for everyone to talk—and some did, too." His remark about the role of the people suggests that the service differed little from some of those reported throughout 1906 and 1907. The people often moved the service along with their sometimes controversial remarks and activities.

On Sunday, May 17, Studd wrote, "Morning at Azusa St. very good—Mrs. Kellaway spoke splendidly with great power and unction. Seymour spoke very funnily of his wedding and wife." Lucy Farrow, who was returning to Houston to live with her son, gave her "farewell" at the Wednesday evening meeting, May 20. Once again, Studd described that service as a "good" one. The next evening was "not very good," but the following two Sunday morning services at the mission, May 24 and May 31, Studd described as "good."

George Studd's numerous entries between February 2 and May 31, and Sparks's for the anniversary meetings in early April, show nothing out of the ordinary happening at the mission during this period. Some kind of clash may have erupted over the idea of taking an offering on February 2, but the revival seems not to have missed a beat. We do find Studd observing that on May 10, Seymour was inadequately prepared to preach the Sunday afternoon meeting, and that several people had taken advantage of the situation. If this observation is accurate, then that might have been a time for mission faithful to air grievances or engage in marginal activity. Still, the reports portray a revival continuing to thrive—with people being saved, sanctified, and baptized in the Holy Spirit. Attendance continued stable. Seymour was still providing plenty of open space for people to testify, exhort, and preach. And virtually every service Studd attended, he evaluated on a range from "good" to "splendid." What is more, the mission had now freed itself from debt.

In 1959, over fifty years later, a participant in the Azusa Street revival named Fred Anderson was asked whether any problems had developed at the mission in 1908. He responded, "In the Spring of the month of May something went wrong. God only knows, but nearly all the people, colored and white, left Bro. Seymour and started up an upper room [read: Upper Room Mission] on So. Spring St." Historians have often taken this statement at face value without exploring its veracity, but George Studd's diary simply does not bear out this portrait of a mass exodus in the spring of 1908.

As the summer months began, George Studd continued to record his observations on the status of the revival. His entry for Sunday, June 7, reported a "good morning meeting at Azusa"—then, to underscore his point, "Very good." He reported an "excellent" morning service on June 14, a "pretty good" service the following week, and on June 28, a "good meeting at Azusa," in which a Brother Stewart from Phoenix, Arizona had preached from John 15. That morning, Pastor Seymour had even preached a second sermon.

On Sunday morning, July 12, George Studd attended the service, marking it afterward as "pretty good." That week he wrote a pamphlet titled "My Convictions," in which he described his year-long journey at the Azusa Street Mission. "I can only say," he reported, "that after being in the closest touch with these dear people and the work of this Pentecostal movement for a full year, my convictions are stronger and deeper than ever; and it is a joy to me to give this testimony. . . . Surely, this is the mighty work of God." He finished his tract on Saturday, July 18. By Wednesday, July 22, the first run had been printed, and he was distributing the finished product.

Studd missed the services the following day, attending the Upper Room Mission instead, but he noted that he had heard that Azusa Street's services had been "good."

At this point the diary of Ned Caswell comes into play. Having attended the meeting that George Studd missed, Caswell observed, "Seymour is in better form." The following Sunday, July 26, George Studd attended a "pretty good" morning service at the Azusa Street Mission once again.

On the first Sunday of August, George Studd spent his first full day at the Upper Room Mission. Ned Caswell attended the afternoon service of the Azusa Street Mission. He dubbed it "pretty good," although he was frustrated that Edward S. Lee had preached the sermon, while all the time Seymour had his Bible out and open, seemingly prepared to preach. Caswell had obviously gone to the mission expecting to hear from Pastor Seymour. In the end, he decided that Lee had simply been "out of order."

The next Sunday, Caswell once again attended Azusa Street's morning service. "Seymour preached with considerable power on Isa. 26," he jotted, and "Mrs. S[eymour?] spoke fluently." Finally, Caswell didn't see Seymour at the Azusa Street Mission when he attended the Sunday afternoon meeting, August 16. The meeting was "tame," he decreed, and marked by "considerable ranting and silliness."

Because George Studd had left the Azusa Street Mission at the end of July, and because of Ned Caswell's work that often took him out of town, neither man provided further diary entries for 1908. Nor do we currently know of any other eyewitness descriptions of the Azusa Street meetings for that year. George Studd recorded one final entry regarding a service at the Azusa Street Mission in 1908. Referring to the service at the Upper Room Mission, he remarked, "Good meeting at night—Small attendance." What was the reason for the small attendance? The answer was simple, "Many had gone for special meeting to Azusa Street."

What, then, can we say of the progress of the Azusa Street revival during 1908? We have virtually nothing from the secular press. We have generally positive statements from the few issues of *The Apostolic Faith* published from Los Angeles. We have a couple of articles and at least one letter for that period. We also have a number of diary entries, most of which come from the pen of George B. Studd, with a few from Ned Caswell.

Studd's observations may be the most important for our understanding of the revival in 1908, for three reasons. First, he was a recognized Christian leader who came to embrace the revival at the Azusa Street Mission. Second, his diary entries, as well as the observations he made in his tract "My Convictions," show that he was not taken in by everything that was said or done in the name of revival. He was able to distinguish between what was good and what was not. He judged what he found at the Azusa Street Mission as late as mid-July as on the whole "good." Third, Studd and Caswell both attended—and "graded"—many Azusa Street meetings. Studd's observations for 1908 carry weight not only because he was an eyewitness, but also because he recorded his impressions of events as they happened. Unlike Fred Anderson, who wrote fifty years later, or Rachel Sizelove, who published her thoughts thirty years later, neither Studd nor Caswell relied on long-term memory. They spoke of contemporary events, using descriptions such as "not so good," "pretty good," "good," "excellent," and "splendid."

In light of such comments, it is difficult to imagine what Fred Anderson may have had in mind when he claimed black and white members had made a mass exodus from the Azusa Street Mission in May 1908. For that matter, we see no evidence of such an exodus at any time in 1908. We could say that in one sense, many of the people who frequented these meetings were fickle. The lines that separated the Azusa Street Mission from the Upper Room Mission were extremely permeable. People flowed freely back and forth between these two churches, their movements depending on who they wanted to see or hear, what they were expecting to happen, and what they were seeking.

The Rev. Elmer K. Fisher was doing an excellent job at the Upper Room Mission. As far as we know, he continued to have a very good relationship with William J. Seymour, even preaching at the Azusa Street Mission as late as Sunday morning, March 1. Fisher's congregation at the Upper Room Mission was flourishing, and George Studd worshipped at the Upper Room Mission during those months about as often as he did at the Azusa Street Mission. Still, one could find Studd attending the early morning Eucharist at St. Paul's Episcopal Church. He might be found at the mission at Fifty-third and Central, or at another independent mission of one kind or another. Sometimes he worshipped in nearby Pasadena. In each case he rendered his judgment on the services, but he never mentions any exodus from the Azusa Street Mission or any sudden influx of people at the Upper Room Mission during this period.

Even though we have established that the revival at the Azusa Street Mission continued to function in a vital way throughout much if not all of 1908, we are still confronted by a few unanswered questions. First, almost from the beginning of the revival itself, a continuous exodus of *leaders* seems to have flowed out from the

Azusa Street Mission. What can we say that might account for that outflow? Second, *The Apostolic Faith* ceased to be published from the Azusa Street Mission in Los Angeles some time in mid-1908 and reemerged as a publication of the Apostolic Faith movement in Portland, Oregon later that summer. How can we account for that? Was the transition a smooth one, or was it difficult? Third, George Studd casually mentioned that William J. Seymour had joked about his recent marriage and his new wife, Jennie Evans Moore. How, if at all, did that marriage affect the mission's ministry?

Finding Places for Leaders to Serve

George Studd had been a Christian leader in the Los Angeles area since he had arrived from England sometime in the 1880s. His anonymous philanthropy had made possible the building of the Peniel Mission in downtown Los Angeles, leaving it debt free. He served as an able Bible teacher, an accomplished preacher, and a one-time editor of that mission's paper, *The Peniel Herald*. He gave regularly to a variety of missionary enterprises. He clearly wanted to play an active role in whatever congregation he attended.

In late July, 1908, George Studd wrote to friends in Britain, claiming that the Azusa Street Mission was now "entirely controlled (humanly speaking) by the coloured people, though white people still attend there." It is difficult to know exactly how to read this note. Some have argued that it is simply a racist remark. I do not believe it should simply be dismissed out of hand as such. Nor should we see it necessarily as a denigration of the Azusa Street Mission—this would be inconsistent with his praise of meetings at the mission throughout much of 1908. George Studd had never been troubled by worshipping in a racially integrated congregation, and he had never before shown himself in any way to be racially prejudiced. I think Studd's remark emerges from his desire to find a place to enter into some form of ministry—and that it merits further exploration.

I take George Studd's note as a factual observation about how the Azusa Street Mission functioned in 1908. I have contended throughout this book that the mission was first and foremost an

African American congregation in which many Latinos, whites, and Asians participated. From Studd's perspective, the mission was unequivocally in the hands of African American leadership. William J. Seymour served as the pastor. Edward S. Lee preached frequently. Richard Asberry and James Alexander served as board members. And Jennie Evans Moore, now Mrs. Seymour, played a frequent role in the mission's music ministry. All of them were African Americans.

Some Latinos played a public role at the beginning. Abundio Lopez, for example, was an altar worker, street preacher, and local pastor. A number of Caucasians had contributed substantially to the early success of the mission, but many of them had moved on, even by 1907. Clearly, however, no one questioned who played the primary and permanent roles in the mission: it was African Americans.

Almost from the time George Studd began to worship with the "saints" at the Azusa Street Mission, he had also worshipped with other Apostolic Faith folks. By August 1908, however, he had reached a personal decision. He would move to the Upper Room Mission. His reason was simple: he had been offered an opportunity to minister by "taking the noon meetings and giving the Bible lessons" there. He made the move on August 4.

This should hardly come as a surprise. I do not think Seymour believed he was building what we have come to know as a "megachurch." What he had in mind was, rather, a coalition of congregations, all working together, all operating under the banner of the "Apostolic Faith." He knew the needs of the city. He realized that the revival had to expand, and he welcomed the founding of other churches. With the number of missions preaching the Apostolic Faith at an all time high, people were able to choose where they wanted to attend. By 1908 the crowds that had previously contributed to the Azusa Street Mission's reputation as the only place to encounter God in a vital "Apostolic" manner *may* have begun to thin, although there is no compelling evidence to support that claim. Still, new leaders were emerging. New leadership roles were opening up at other missions. And those who had been called and equipped to make such contributions should not be criticized for looking for opportunities to engage in ministry.

George Studd must have realized early on that the Azusa Street Mission would provide no permanent role for him, except as an ordinary member. In his association with Elmer Kirk Fisher at the Upper Room Mission, Studd clearly found a new level of fulfillment in ministry that he could not find at Azusa Street. At the Upper Room Mission, he would be called upon to preach and to teach on a regular basis. And from June 1909 the Upper Room Mission would begin issuing its own paper, *The Upper Room*. George Studd would serve as its co-editor, alongside Pastor Fisher.

George Studd was not alone in wanting to stretch his wings. For example, many of the original staff members pictured in the famous photograph of August 1906 left shortly thereafter. Not everyone who left, however, acted with Studd's transparency and integrity.

In September, 1906, Florence Crawford led a group of workers to Northern California, Oregon, and Washington. Of these, the Evanses and the Junks would not return. Glenn Cook was essentially gone by December 1906. While Florence Crawford returned in January 1907, she left again soon thereafter. Seymour had named her the state director of the Pacific Coast Apostolic Faith movement. She would help other missions enter this movement that was led by Pastor Seymour.

In July 1907, while Pastor Seymour was on an extended trip East, Florence Crawford was summoned back to Los Angeles. Her daughter, Mildred, had broken her arm, and the authorities were demanding that she receive medical attention. Crawford returned home to oversee the situation. She took the opportunity to attend the 1907 camp meeting then in progress. Will Trotter, a longtime friend with whom she had worked during her years of rescue work, had just been fired from his position as director of the Union Rescue Mission in Los Angeles because he announced at the camp meeting that he had spoken in tongues and would now identify with the Apostolic Faith movement. Crawford and Trotter undoubtedly shared notes and spoke of the future. By the end of the summer, Crawford and her daughter, Mildred, and Trotter and his family had all moved to Portland. While Crawford would later claim that the formal break with Seymour did not take place until nearly 1908, by September 1907 it was essentially complete.

Crawford's justification for creating the break was that she had heard rumors that Seymour had compromised his teaching on sanctification—that he no longer taught the Wesleyan position that entire sanctification was a second work of grace, after conversion. She even claimed that she had returned to Los Angeles to remedy the situation at the time she was summoned to care for her daughter, but that her intervention had been futile. Richard Crayne, following the lead of Amos Morgan, has suggested that Glenn Cook may have been the reason for the rumor.[40] Joseph Hillery King, head of the Fire-Baptized Holiness Church, claimed that Glenn Cook had changed his position on sanctification by early 1907. If Glenn Cook was the actual reason for Crawford's break with Seymour, then the break was not well founded. First, Cook had moved on to Indianapolis long before Florence Crawford arrived in Los Angeles, so she didn't confront him. Second, no evidence exists to suggest that William J. Seymour ever fluctuated from the traditional holiness position on sanctification. He always preached sanctification as a second, definite work of grace.

Whatever her reasons, by December 1907 at the latest Florence Crawford had taken the initiative and broken her relationship with Pastor Seymour. She quickly formed an independent work in Portland, Oregon. She kept the same name Seymour used—the Apostolic Faith Movement—a decision likely to create confusion among those who knew, from reading The Apostolic Faith [Los Angeles, CA] that this was the legal name of the Azusa Street Mission. But Crawford undoubtedly took that into consideration. She next contacted the Apostolic Faith missions she had helped to bring into the movement along the Pacific coast while serving as state director for Pastor Seymour. Most, if not all, of these missions followed her lead. By taking this action, Crawford struck a critical blow at Seymour's undisputed leadership of the movement along the Pacific coast.

Strangely, neither Florence Crawford nor the churches that went with her seem to have questioned the ethics of her move—or theirs. Why did they so readily side with her? First, they may have changed allegiances out of personal loyalty to Crawford. She had played a personal role in their entry into the Apostolic Faith movement, while Seymour had not. Second, and more important, she may have convinced them to follow her based on the rumor (perhaps originated by her; certainly repeated by her on many occasions) that Seymour had waffled on the doctrine of sanctification. By making this serious charge, which suggested that Seymour was a compromiser, Crawford was claiming that Seymour had failed both God and the Apostolic Faith movement. Since she had kept the faith and unmasked his compromise for all to see, people would conclude that the true center of the revival had moved a thousand miles north to Portland, with her.

What the cases of Studd and Crawford seem to demonstrate is that those who were capable of providing leadership in a growing revival were looking for ways to do so. When they provided leadership outside of Los Angeles, the situation was relatively unproblematic. People such as Glenn Cook, Thomas Hezmalhalch, and others could go elsewhere and start and lead new congregations without interfering with the work at Azusa Street. In Los Angeles, it was trickier. Frank Bartleman, William Pendleton, and Elmer Fisher all succeeded because they maintained a relationship with Pastor Seymour. George Studd would surely say that he did the same. The only one of the early west coast leaders that actually ruptured her relationship with Pastor Seymour in the first year or so of the revival was Florence Crawford. She seems to have thought that she could, in essence, lead a coup d'état that would effectively unseat William J. Seymour, relocate the center of the revival in Portland, and lead that revival into the future.

The Transfer of The Apostolic Faith Newspaper

With Florence Crawford now firmly ensconced in Portland, Clara Lum's transfer of *The Apostolic Faith* newspaper from Los Angeles to Portland during the summer of 1908 obviously played into Crawford's struggle for further control of the Apostolic Faith movement. Though Lum did not transfer the paper at the time of the actual break, she did nonetheless transfer it at a critical time.

Based on an interview he conducted with the Seymours, G. W. Shumway reported in his 1914 thesis that "the woman who was in charge of the publication of The Apostolic Faith [i.e., Clara Lum] became dissatisfied" and "took 'French leave' from Azusa Street, leaving that mission without a paper, which she began publishing for the 'saints' in a northern city." From Seymour's perspective, Clara Lum had violated her trust. She had simply walked away from her job, taking The Apostolic Faith newspaper with her to Portland. Her action meant that the publication would no longer be the voice of Azusa Street.

This is a formidable charge, and historians have wrestled with its meaning. Three facts are beyond dispute. First, The Apostolic Faith's base of publication changed from Los Angeles to Portland in mid-1908. Second, Clara Lum transferred the paper. Third, Florence Crawford and her new Apostolic Faith organization were the obvious beneficiaries of this move. Crawford had nothing to gain by not accepting the paper. But these facts raise at least three questions. First, do we have any evidence that Seymour's charge that Clara Lum left suddenly was correct? Second, did Clara Lum "steal" the paper, or was it hers to take? And third, what reasons did Clara Lum have for leaving Los Angeles with the paper?

What Evidence Supports Seymour's Claim?

Without going into all the details surrounding this event and the subsequent debate, I would like to note that this is a particularly difficult question to answer. Some of the arguments that support Seymour's claim are based on a 1926 tract published by J. C. Vanzandt, "Speaking in Tongues." Vanzandt had attended a number of Crawford's earliest Portland meetings. His tract betrays a strong bias against "Mother" Crawford and her work. In addition, some of his points are based on an issue of The Apostolic Faith that he says Seymour published from Los Angeles in October-November 1908. Historians have not yet located a copy of this publication. This does not mean it did not exist, but it does mean we need to assess Vanzandt's claims carefully.

What we do know is that the May 1908 issue of *The Apostolic Faith* contained the following brief note: "For the next issues of this paper address The Apostolic Faith Campmeeting, Portland, Ore." This note is important for understanding Clara Lum's side of the story. First, Lum clearly intended to attend the Apostolic Faith camp meeting in Portland in 1908. For Clara Lum to attend a camp meeting in some other city would not have been unusual. Other people from the Azusa Street Mission did it, and there is no reason that Lum should not have done so as well. This particular camp meeting may have been problematic for Seymour because Florence Crawford sponsored it, and she had clearly moved to limit Seymour's role in the Apostolic Faith movement along the Pacific coast by setting up a competing organization and taking from Seymour—in the very name of Azusa Street—most of the churches that had fed the Apostolic Faith movement.

Second, Clara Lum clearly intended to meet her publishing deadline, even though she would be doing so from Portland. While the June 1908 issue of *The Apostolic Faith* was an irregularly produced issue without the official masthead, a fact that might be explained by Lum's absence at the time of production, that issue still maintained that it was a publication of the Azusa Street Mission in Los Angeles. Thus, Lum carried through on her promise to see that the next issue was published from the camp meeting in Portland.

Third, and clearly the most provocative point, Lum promised to publish *multiple* "issues" of *The Apostolic Faith* from Portland. She clearly intended to stay in Portland for a period of several months. One would think that as the official secretary at the Azusa Street Mission, publishing the official organ of the Azusa Street Mission, Lum would have needed some form of authorization from the mission to make such a move. At the very least, she should have had an understanding with Pastor Seymour that this would be only a short-term arrangement.

It is here that Vanzandt raises his most forceful point, and he does so by citing William J. Seymour from the issue of *The Apostolic Faith* that historians have not yet located. Seymour, he claims, wrote that Lum had taken the paper "after being warned by the elders not to do so." If this claim is in fact true, it would support the accusation against Lum that Shumway attributed to Seymour in his 1914 thesis. And Seymour's documented actions over the subsequent year seem to give this claim further credibility. In particular, we find that Pastor Seymour traveled to Portland in the latter half of 1908 to try to regain control of the paper. This strongly suggests that Lum had moved the paper to Portland without any agreement or permission from Seymour to do so, especially on a permanent basis.

In 1958 Raymond R. Crawford, the son of Florence Crawford, gave a different reason for Lum's leaving Los Angeles. Clara Lum might have used the camp meeting as her initial cover for going to Portland, but she had actually come to Portland "to work" with Florence Crawford. If Raymond Crawford's reflections half a century later do indicate Lum's real motive for leaving Los Angeles, then Seymour's charges have merit and Lum's actions provide a clear rationale for Seymour's subsequent actions.

Like most of his holiness and Pentecostal contemporaries, and in keeping with the Pauline teaching in 1 Corinthians 6:1–8, Seymour did not believe that Christians should sue one another. Over the subsequent year, the Azusa Street Mission's pastor attempted to find a legal way, without resorting to a lawsuit, to return *The Apostolic Faith* to the mission and to prevent Clara Lum from using a virtually identical—thus purposefully confusing—masthead while publishing the paper from Portland.

The following year, and on behalf of the Azusa Street Mission, Jennie Evans Seymour, Malinda Mitchell, and Edward W. Doak traveled to Portland. On October 11, 1909, they filed articles of incorporation that legally established the Apostolic Faith Mission in Portland, Oregon, as an "auxiliary" body to "the Apostolic Faith Mission of Los Angeles, California." Florence Crawford had not moved to incorporate her work as yet. Seymour's articles of incorporation made two important points. First, they established that the name "Apostolic Faith Mission," even in Portland, Oregon, belonged legally to the Azusa Street Mission in Los Angeles, not to

Florence Crawford. Second, they stated that it was the board of elders in Los Angeles who authorized the establishment of this "auxiliary" body in Oregon, and that same board was responsible for the publication of the mission's official organ, *The Apostolic Faith.*

Seymour's attempt to take back *The Apostolic Faith* in this way, however, proved fruitless. Florence Crawford and Clara Lum refused to give it back. After Florence Crawford intervened, the postal authorities refused to accept these articles of incorporation as proof that *The Apostolic Faith* now being issued from Portland belonged legally to the Azusa Street Mission. Crawford led a congregation and was known in Portland. Seymour was unknown. Seymour's representatives returned to Los Angeles deeply disappointed. Their action would seem inconceivable unless William J. Seymour firmly believed that his claim was based in fact. This, then, leads us to the second question: Did Clara Lum "steal" the paper, or was it hers to take?

Who Owned the Paper?

The question of who "owned" the paper—and therefore, who had the right to publish it—is an equally important one. Most historians agree that Clara Lum probably played the primary role in editing the Azusa Street newspaper. William J. Seymour may have made editorial contributions from time to time, and clearly excerpts from some of his sermons appeared in its pages. But the responsibility for reducing them to the printed page probably rested with Clara Lum, whose stenographic skills made these excerpts possible.

We do not know whose idea it was to publish the paper. Clara Lum came to the Azusa Street Mission with considerable expertise as an editor with the *Missionary World*, a publication of the World's Faith Missionary Association. On the other hand, Seymour had studied with Charles F. Parham in Houston, Texas, and possessed copies of Parham's newspaper, *The Apostolic Faith.* He may have wanted to have a paper of his own. Parham had published his paper first from Melrose, Kansas, and then from Houston, Texas, before Seymour had arrived in Los Angeles. When the Azusa Street Mission began publishing *The Apostolic Faith*, Seymour still viewed his work as in some way an extension of Parham's work. He kept the same name for his newspaper as Parham had used in Houston, but from the very first issue he made it clear that this paper originated in Los Angeles. Parham was not troubled by this development until well after the very painful break between the two men in November 1906.

It seems likely that while the idea of a newspaper had been in Seymour's mind, it was the appearance of Clara Lum that made his dream a reality—although she would later write that the Lord had laid it on her heart to publish the paper. Glenn Cook may have played a supporting role as well, because his employment with a local newspaper would have given him knowledge of the local printers. Regardless of whose "idea" it was, through the efforts of Seymour, and particularly of Clara Lum, *The Apostolic Faith* would become the voice of the revival that had begun in Los Angeles. It would also become the first major international voice for what was happening in the revival as it spread across the nation and around the world. But who owned the paper?

From the beginning *The Apostolic Faith* was identified as coming from the Azusa Street Mission in Los Angeles. As an intentional offering of humility, Seymour and Lum never published the name of the editor. The December 1906 issue explains this decision:

> The writers and workers in the office live by faith outside of what comes for the paper, and we publish no names of editors. All work for the honor and glory of God. This we believe will be a real protection to the paper to keep it pure, for unless one is filled with the love of God, they do not covet to work without honor or money.

This statement leaves little doubt that both William J. Seymour and the readers of *The Apostolic Faith* [Los Angeles, CA] viewed it as the mission's official newspaper, and not the property of any single individual. Obviously, once Clara Lum had moved to Portland, she did not agree.

From June 1907 until the following June, when the newspaper ceased publishing from Los Angeles, readers were told repeatedly that they could help defray the cost of publishing *The Apostolic Faith* by one of two means: They could send United States postage stamps, affixed to the rolls mailed when each issue appeared. Or they could send money orders made payable to the "Apostolic Faith, 312 Azusa Street, Los Angeles, Cal." If *The Apostolic Faith* newspaper were privately or separately owned, but the money was made payable to the Apostolic Faith at the 312 Azusa Street—the address of the Apostolic Faith Mission—then the instruction was unnecessarily confusing. If it were actually a ministry of the mission, then the repeated instruction makes sense and its removal to Oregon bears further investigation.

Why Did Clara Lum Leave Azusa Street?

Studd's diary may provide answers to both the matter of Lum's departure and another question about the health of the revival at the Azusa Street Mission in 1908. In his entry for Sunday morning, May 17, he mentions that William J. Seymour had spoken of his wedding and his wife "funnily" that morning—I take this to mean that he did so in a "humorous" rather than a "strange" manner. William J. Seymour and Jennie Evans Moore had been married in a private ceremony the previous Wednesday, May 13, 1908. Edward S. Lee had performed the ceremony, and his wife, Mattie Lee, and their long time friend, Richard Asberry, were both witnesses to the wedding. The announcement that morning may have surprised some.

Jennie Evans Moore had been the first person to speak and sing in tongues at the Asberry home, and she had been a member of Seymour's ministry team from the very beginning of the mission. She had become a trusted partner in the mission's ministry, leading out in singing; often singing in tongues, testifying, or exhorting; helping to oversee things; and in 1907 traveling to Minneapolis where she held some meetings. Following their wedding, the cou-

This is likely the wedding photograph of William J. Seymour
and Jennie Evans [Moore] Seymour. They were married May 13, 1908.

ple made their home in a small second-floor apartment over the
mission—probably so that they could be near the work.

A number of scholars have asked how—if at all—Seymour's
marriage affected the congregation or the revival. If George
Studd's diary is any indication, Seymour's marriage may have had
no general impact. Studd mentions only Seymour's funny comments regarding his marriage and his new wife, giving no hint that
it caused any problem. Throughout the month of June and all of
July, Studd continued to give good marks to the health of the meetings being conducted at the Azusa Street Mission. The question of
what, if any, role Seymour's marriage may have played in the transfer of the paper, however, is a provocative one for several reasons.

William J. Seymour believed and taught that God had given
marriage to the human race as a "divine institution." He had written in September 1907 that those who forbade marriage were guilty

of introducing "the doctrine of devils (1 Tim. 4:1, 3)." An earlier, unsigned article, published in *The Apostolic Faith* in January 1907 and most likely written or preached by Seymour, insisted it was "no sin to marry." "Many precious souls are in great bondage and need the precious Word to unloose them," the writer pointed out. "If we are governed by His Word, there will be peace, joy, and happiness in our homes, and they will be heaven on earth."

Why, among "Spirit-filled" Christians, would the mission make this effort to explain the legitimate status of marriage between a man and a woman? Serious challenges had been raised to marriage in the mission's social and religious context. Some members of the spiritualist community had come into the Azusa Street Mission and argued both for "spiritual" marriages and "freeloveism." Some within the holiness movement had insisted that they had received new "light" on the subject and that truly sanctified or "Spirit-filled" Christians should abstain from sexual relations within the bonds of marriage. Others argued that sexual relations within a marriage, other than for purposes of procreation, were simply expressions of fleshly lust that needed to be held in check. Some argued that a person who remarried following a divorce, especially before becoming a Christian, should neither bear stigma nor make restitution. Others argued that given the imminent return of the Lord, it was best to live the Christian life single and celibate. "Sanctified" people, they insisted, should not be moved by fleshly acts—and marriage was such an act.

When it came to issues of marriage and sexuality, Seymour had his hands full! He consistently explained that the Bible supported marriage; that sexual relations between married Christians were not solely for purposes of procreation; that they were a normal part of what it meant to be married, and were therefore not sinful. He affirmed the legitimacy of the single celibate state, but he did not do so at the expense of marriage. Only on the issue of divorce and remarriage did he have a change of mind. In the beginning, he allowed those who had been divorced and remarried to engage in ministry. "But after searching the Scriptures," he announced, "we found it was wrong." He therefore came to take the stricter stand.

While Shumway never reported what point of dissatisfaction

led to Clara Lum's departure from the Azusa Street Mission, it may very well have been Seymour's marriage in May 1908. The unmarried Lum might have shared Florence Crawford's convictions that the single was to be preferred to the married state. She might have agreed with Crawford that the Lord was returning soon, and marriage interfered illegitimately with the church's end-times tasks. Or she might have viewed sexual purity or separation within marriage as a more sanctified condition—and thus have thought that Seymour had compromised his sanctification. Lum may have objected to Seymour's marriage on any of these grounds. But another, more pragmatic objection has been suggested.

In his book *Bishop C. H. Mason and the Roots of the Church of God in Christ*, the late Bishop Ithiel Clemmons reports a conversation he had with Bishop Charles H. Mason in 1948. He claimed that Mason had told him Clara Lum had fallen in love with Pastor Seymour and had sought a proposal of marriage from him. Seymour had come to Mason for his advice. Mason had cautioned him against marrying a white woman, given the state of race relations in the United States at the height of the Jim Crow era. As a result, Seymour, who wanted to marry, had chosen Jennie Evans Moore. Although the integrity of Bishop Clemmons is not in question, it seems unlikely that we will ever be able to substantiate this claim, because all the affected parties are dead. But if this is true, then Clara Lum might have left Los Angeles, taking the newspaper with her, out of personal dissatisfaction with Seymour's choice to marry Jennie Evans Moore. Love lost might also have led her to use the newspaper to further the work of Seymour's primary competitor, "Mother" Florence Crawford.

What this discussion reveals is that while on the surface, the revival continued in an uninterrupted fashion at the mission through at least July or August 1908, as early as May or June several factors entered the life of the mission that would ultimately contribute to the end of the revival. Three of these were Seymour's marriage to Jennie Evans Moore, Clara Lum's departure from the Azusa Street Mission staff, and the consequent removal of the "official organ" of both the mission and the revival—*The Apostolic Faith*.

The Fire Cools

While attendance at the Azusa Street Mission remained healthy throughout most of 1908, by the beginning of 1909 it had entered a steady decline. Ned Caswell took note: after stints in Portland (between September and December) and Oakland and San Francisco (mid-January through February), he returned to the Azusa Street Mission on Sunday morning, March 7. He wrote in his diary, "Seymour is fatter. Crowd was smaller, but still good." The following Sunday, March 14, he remarked, "Today was fine and sunny. At Azusa St. there was a small crowd, Seymour and wife leading, and not much doing."

Frank Bartleman and his family had also been away, in the East, for most of 1908. After returning to Pasadena on February 26, 1909 and taking two weeks' rest, Bartleman attended the mission—the same service attended by Ned Caswell on March 14. "I visited old Azusa Mission," remembered Bartleman, "where the Lord met me in great power." Later in the day, he attended services at Pendleton's Eighth and Maple Mission, and in the evening he attended Fisher's Upper Room Mission.

Bartleman gives no indication of the attendance or spirit at other mission services in March and April. About this time, he received a letter from Honolulu, apparently inviting him to come and hold meetings. He said his farewells at both the Azusa Street Mission and the Upper Room Mission, four blocks away, but at neither place did he receive the responses he wanted. Some tried to dissuade him; others warned him of disaster if he went. Never one to submit himself to another person's suggestions, Bartleman took his family to Oakland, dropped them off at Carrie Judd Montgomery's Home of Peace, and on May 15, 1909, sailed for Honolulu. He spent six weeks there before returning to California. Over the following six weeks he held meetings and battled health problems before returning to Los Angeles with his family in mid-September. When he returned to the Azusa Street Mission, he wrote,

> Azusa had lost out greatly since we left. 'How the mighty have fallen' came to me most forcibly. But the Spirit came upon three

of us mightily in prayer one evening there. He assured us He
was going to bring the power back to Azusa Mission again as at
the beginning.

Such a judgment looks very bad on the surface, but it must be
understood within Bartleman's reading of the larger context: "The
work had gotten into a bad condition generally at the time we
returned to Los Angeles. The missions had fought each other
almost to a standstill. Little love remained."

Ned Caswell would probably have agreed. On Sunday, October
3, he observed, "This afternoon I was at Azusa St; the crowd was
fair and the meeting tame, as the 'inner circle' retired to have a private meeting of their own. I saw Owen Lee[41] and his wife, just
down from Portland, where there seems to be considerable friction. I saw Seymour this week also." Caswell's observation that
there was an "inner circle" suggests that he was disappointed by a
sense of cliquishness that may have entered the place. It may have
involved the board of trustees, but he was more probably referring
to the original participants in Seymour's prayer meetings at the
Asberry home. The following Sunday, October 10, Caswell
attended the Azusa Street Mission once again. He didn't stay long.
He just noted, "Only a few old-timers and not much stirring." He
made no further entries on the mission for another year, but the
verdict was the same. From his perspective, the revival had effectively ended.

Virtually every night in the last quarter of 1909, Frank Bartleman continued to attend the Eighth and Maple Mission and the
Azusa Street Mission. Invariably, he had something to say there,
either by way of testimony or of sermon. And inevitably Bartleman complained about what he termed "a spirit of dictatorship" in
the mission leadership. Services were "programmed" "from start
to finish," he growled. There was no longer any room for the Holy
Spirit to break in.

AFTERWORD:
SUMMING UP THREE POWERFUL YEARS

෨ඏ

In recent years I have heard preachers speak lightly of the Azusa
Street meeting, saying they had just as good meetings under
their ministry. The old-timers can only feel sorry for such and
pity them. In this meeting you not only was baptized in the
Holy Ghost, but also lived in such a heavenly atmosphere of love
that you never can forget it, and all else seems so empty and
void. Even as I write these pages the memory of that meeting
comes floating back, my eyes begin to swim with tears, and such
a longing and yearning seizes me for a return of such a condition. I can feel that sacred fire still burning and have the conviction that God will again visit his people in a like manner before
the present dispensation ends.

If God's people would only come together and forget about
doctrines and leaders whose vision is blurred by building
churches and collecting tithes, having only one objective, and
that to be filled with all the fulness of God, I know God would
answer prayer. Doctrines and teaching have their proper place in
the gospel plan but that overpowering, drawing power of the
love of God must come first, and our present lukewarm condition is caused by a lack of this love that "nothing can offend."

GLENN A. COOK

In this book, I have tried to portray the essence of the Azusa Street
Mission and the revival that emerged and continued there from
April 1906 through early 1909. We have looked at the man who
stood at the center of the revival, Pastor William J. Seymour, and
the personal experiences and beliefs he brought to bear on the mission and its revival. We have sketched something of the context of
1906 Los Angeles in which the revival sprang forth. We have covered some of the important features of the revival itself.

The revival came to an African American congregation whose pastor had a vision for multiracial and multiethnic worship, which led them to salvation, sanctification, and baptism in the Holy Spirit. The revival did not stop there, but moved beyond the walls of the mission to the surrounding neighborhoods, across the nation, and around the world. While the mission was a congregation of ordinary people, they were people who were hungry for God. They would satisfy that hunger whatever it cost them, even if it meant crossing the lines of ordinary behavior. They were willing, if necessary, to violate social strictures—especially on the mixing of the races. For roughly three years, in the teeth of a howling secular and religious press, the people of the Azusa Street Mission demonstrated that they could cross these social lines, and bear great fruit as they did so.

The vision and the leadership style that William J. Seymour brought to his congregation enabled the revival to burst forth and extend into full bloom. People's responses as they encountered God mirrored those recorded in Scripture. So did the consequences when they did what God asked them to do. They may not seem to have accomplished much in those early years, but the results stand before us today in the millions of people worldwide affected by the movement. The Pentecostal/charismatic movement that sprang forth from this humble congregation is truly *global* in scope.

Like some people within the movement's early years—and some of its self-identified heirs and successors—many of us today have found it difficult to accept the lessons Azusa Street's people want to teach us. In a nation of Manifest Destiny, soon to wield the "big stick" foreign policy of President Teddy Roosevelt, the Azusa Street faithful tried to show us what it looked like to live according to Zechariah's prophecy, "'Not by might, nor by power, but by my Spirit,' saith the Lord of hosts" (6:4). In a world ruled by graspers, they tried to show us that leadership was about empowering others, not about taking power away or about using power to get one's own way. In a world that valued and divided people according to color, they tried to show us that we can attain racial harmony, intimacy, and inclusiveness when we remember that we are all one in the Spirit of God. Neither skin color nor differences in age, gender, class, culture, or level of education should separate anyone within the body of Christ. They tried to show us that genuine, persistent hunger and thirst for God are ultimately rewarded by life-changing, spiritually empowering encounters with the living God. They tried to show us that their sacrifice on behalf of others was worth the price they paid.

Since they were ordinary people, some of them lived with failure. And their failures also provide important lessons for us today. They show us that the Spirit of God can be supplanted in our affairs when we rely on our own might and power. They show us that pride, arrogance, and selfishness lead to actions unbecoming of us as children of God. They show us that if we allow the social expectations of the world to govern our lives, we will not bear the life-giving Word of reconciliation. They show us that if we allow our own desires to replace the desires of God, we can be set aside and fail to live up to our calling. They show us that when we fail to pay the necessary price, we don't get the results we have hoped for.

The story of the mission did not end with the story of this three-year revival. The Azusa Street Mission did not close down in 1909. Pastor Seymour would continue to serve as its pastor until his death from a heart attack on September 28, 1922. His wife, Jennie Evans Seymour, would succeed him as pastor and lead the dwindling congregation until her death in 1936, although the original building was demolished in the first week of July, 1931.

The Seymours found the years following the revival extremely difficult to endure. By 1911 at least eleven Pentecostal congregations operated in Los Angeles, the largest of which was the Upper Room Mission. It was thriving, while the Azusa Street Mission had reverted to a small, largely African American congregation with a few Caucasians in attendance.

Chicago pastor and evangelist William H. Durham claimed that when he arrived in Los Angeles on February 12, 1911, he found the Pentecostal work in the city in total disarray. From his perspective, all of the movement's leaders in the city had proved incompetent. All who had been touched by the revival had lost confidence in what God had done with them during those earlier years. Durham decided, on his own, to fix the situation.

One of the "problems" that Durham diagnosed was the fact that these congregations still believed in sanctification as a second, definite work of grace. He did not believe in this doctrine, and he moved quickly to change their minds. He first approached the Upper Room Mission's Pastor Elmer Fisher with a proposal. Durham would preach his "finished work" theory of sanctification (that God sanctified the believer at conversion by placing them "in Christ," then the believer matured in holiness as they grew in grace), and Fisher could watch as his congregation grew. Fisher refused, and Durham was furious. As a result, Durham next moved to the Azusa Street Mission, where he claimed that he found "about a dozen colored brethren." Seymour had left on an extended trip. During Seymour's absence, the local leadership (most likely Edward S. Lee) invited William Durham to preach a series of services. Durham had been baptized in the Spirit there in 1907, and people remembered his vibrant testimony.

Durham began preaching there on February 14, 1911, continuing for two and a half months. A compelling speaker and first-rate apologist, Durham's forceful, eloquent preaching won many people over. Within days, the Azusa Street Mission had again become a force to be reckoned with in the city. The place was packed as many of the city's "disillusioned" returned. Frank Bartleman wrote that on February 25, just eleven days after Durham began preaching there, all the seats were filled and five hundred people had to be turned away. Those who held seats refused to move lest they lose them, he claimed, and overnight, the "bottom" simply "dropped out of the Upper Room" Mission.

William J. Seymour returned to Los Angeles in April, fully expecting to continue as the pastor of the mission. What he found was a man in place who had decided that he would be the new pastor of the mission. Even before Seymour's return, Durham began preparing his followers to stand with him when Seymour returned "to get possession of the work." When Seymour finally did return, he sat for several days and watched and listened.

Deciding that what Durham was preaching was not what the mission taught, Seymour confronted the other man—and Durham made his play to take over the mission. On Sunday evening, April 30, Durham asked for a show of hands from those who supported the continuation of the "revival" under his leadership. The response was overwhelmingly in favor of Durham. Seymour sat quietly, and the next day he gathered his duly elected board together. They made a decision and padlocked the door. When Durham returned for services on May 2, he was surprised and angered to find himself locked out.

Durham claimed that Seymour had done him in by going to the "men of his own color," and enlisting them to "stand with him." Durham's version makes it sound as though Seymour simply played a "race" card when, in fact, he had reached a conclusion and made a decision that was in keeping with the mission's statement of faith and consistent with the constitution of the mission. Durham left, taking the crowd with him. The following Sunday, May 7, Durham opened the Full Gospel Assembly on the corner of Seventh and Los Angeles Streets to a crowd of several hundred. He drew most of his congregation from the Upper Room Mission, though a few came from Azusa Street. He railed at Seymour, Fisher, and others who did not see things his way.

When William Durham died of tuberculosis the following year, on July 9, 1912 (at the age of 39), he left as his legacy a movement divided over the issue of sanctification. The Upper Room Mission went out of business, and Elmer K. Fisher retired from the ministry, while Seymour continued to lead a dwindling flock.

Two years later, on April 15, 1913, the momentous Apostolic Faith World Wide Camp Meeting began. Like the previous camp meetings of 1907 and 1908, the 1913 meeting, which ran through to the end of May, met in the Arroyo Seco between Los Angeles and Pasadena. Robert J. Scott, who had served as the organizing chair for the 1907 camp meeting, served in this role once again. People came from around the world to take part in it. The local press estimated that two thousand attended the opening service. William J. Seymour received no special invitation, nor was he seated on the platform. Those leading the movement around the country and in Canada now received pride of place.

During that camp meeting a second major theological controversy developed—this one over the appropriate formula to be used in Christian baptism. Some contended that the appropriate "apostolic" baptismal mode was baptism by immersion "in the name of Jesus Christ," following the model of Acts 2:38. Others wanted to retain the traditional Trinitarian formula spelled out by Jesus in Matthew 28:19. Many had themselves re-baptized in a nearby creek using the "apostolic" formula. Among those who adopted this "apostolic" position were Pastor Pendleton, the Eighth and Maple congregation, and George Studd of the Upper Room Mission. This discussion and the resulting actions unleashed a debate that led to further schism, permanently dividing the movement in 1916. Seymour rejected baptism "in the name of Jesus only" and maintained his commitment to the traditional Trinitarian understanding

The bold attempts by Charles F. Parham in 1906, by Florence L. Crawford in 1908, and by William H. Durham in 1911 to take control of the Apostolic Faith movement, and the doctrinal challenge raised by the "apostolic" revelation that arose during the 1913 camp meeting, hurt William J. Seymour deeply. Parham, Crawford, Durham, and those who promoted baptism in "Jesus' Name" at the 1913 camp meeting were all white folks. When many of the white ministers in the predominantly black Church of God in Christ left that denomination in April 1914 and formed the Assemblies of God, not even the racially progressive Seymour was willing to trust many of his white Pentecostal brothers and sisters. It is easy to understand why.

The following year, 1915, Seymour compiled *The Doctrines and Discipline of the Azusa Street Apostolic Faith Mission*. In an "Apostolic Address" contained in his *Doctrines and Discipline*, Pastor Seymour explained how he had been invited to come to Los Angeles. As he and his friends had sought God, a revival had begun and quickly spread around the world. Very soon divisions had arisen, he observed, and the Holy Spirit had been grieved. Seymour placed much of the blame for these divisions on his "white brethren," although he acknowledged that some African Americans had participated in them as well—most notably when a number of them had adopted the "apostolic" position.

Seymour's solution for the interim was as simple as it was pragmatic. From the time that the *Doctrines and Discipline* was adopted, no white person would be allowed to serve in a leadership role in the Apostolic Faith Mission until the racial climate changed. He felt badly about that decision, noting that it wasn't what God wanted, but he was just as convinced that Christ wanted to see love, not prejudice and discrimination, demonstrated between his children. He laid out his reasons in broad strokes that bear repeating in full.

> We find according to God's word to be one in the Holy Spirit, not in the flesh; but in the Holy Spirit, for we are one body. 1 Cor. 12:12–14. If some of our white brethren have prejudices and discrimination (Gal. 2:11–20), we can't do it, because God calls us to follow the Bible. Matt. 17:8; Matt. 24. We must love all men as Christ commands. (Heb. 12:14). Now because we don't take them for directors it is not for discrimination, but for peace. To keep down race war in the Churches and friction, so they can have greater liberty and freedom in the Holy Spirit. We are sorry for this, but it is the best now and in later years for the work. We hope every one that reads these lines may realize it is for the best; not for the worse. Some of our white brethren and sisters have never left us in all the division; they have stuck to us. We love our white brethrens [*sic*] and sisters and welcome them. Jesus Christ takes in all people in his Salvation. Christ is all and for all. He is neither black nor white man, nor Chinaman, nor Hindoo, nor Japanese, but God. God is Spirit because without his spirit we cannot be saved. St. John 3:3–5; Rom. 8:9.

The ensuing years were difficult for Pastor Seymour, but he kept at his work. His death in 1922 went largely unnoticed—not even meriting mention in the local press. His widow tried to fill the vacuum left by his death, but the congregation continued to dwin-

dle. At last no one remained except the few friends who had originally met at the Asberry home on North Bonnie Brae Street, and
perhaps a half dozen others.

In the middle of 1930, a man named Ruthford D. Griffith, aged
78, began to attend the mission with his wife. He claimed that he
had been a missionary in Africa, and that he had pastored several
African American congregations. Before long, he offered his services to Jennie Seymour. In exchange for some preaching, she provided the couple with temporary housing adjacent to her
apartment upstairs in the mission. Before long, Griffith had
decided that he could replace her as the pastor. He began by
recruiting people who would vote for him. He argued that the mission was in violation of its *Doctrines and Discipline*, since this document stated that the congregation's leader should be a man. Once
he had these two things lined up, he moved on to intimidate not
only Jennie Seymour, but also her faithful following, including the
elected board of trustees. He forced the smaller Seymour party to
worship upstairs, while he took the main sanctuary as his own. He
announced that he was the new bishop of the mission and proceeded to take control.

In January 1931, the situation exploded into an argument that
reduced both parties to throwing hymnals at one another. Police
were called; the mission was padlocked. While Jennie Seymour
sought justice, Ruthford Griffith sought control. The disagreement
finally ended up in various courts, with Griffith suing the mission and
the mission suing Griffith. The matter remained in the courts for
another year and a half. While a lower court found in favor of Griffith, a higher court ultimately reversed the ruling, and in June 1932 it
found in favor of Mrs. Seymour. By then the building had been
demolished, and the group moved back to the Asberry home on
North Bonnie Brae Street, where the revival and the mission had
been born 26 years before. Jennie Evans Seymour died on July 2, 1936.

In spite of this sordid ending to an otherwise brilliant story, the
seed sown at the Azusa Street Mission had been planted around the
world, and it has continued to grow. Today the movement that
erupted from that humble mission is both enormous and vital. It

has much to offer to the historic churches, and if the movement would once again take a humble stance, it might find that it also has much that it could learn from those churches about what it means to be truly "Apostolic" and "Pentecostal."

The centennial of the Azusa Street Mission and revival has now arrived, and still there are lessons to be learned. The term "revival," for instance, is still very much with us. It may conjure up bygone sights and sounds that we value deeply—the preaching, praying, singing, shouting, tears, sawdust, and testimonies that also characterized the Azusa Street Mission. If we simply reflect upon revival, we may easily slip into nostalgia, remembering former glories. Or we may become hopeful about what God still has in store for us. For Pentecostals to be part of a revivalist tradition, a tradition given birth in the midst of revival, is for us to continue to value revival. But it is also possible to value revival more than it should be valued.

In recent years we have heard people describe the ways that God is moving among certain people and churches, reviving them as only God can. We rejoice with such reports, and we pray for a continuous outpouring of the Holy Spirit among all churches around the world. Revival is a wonderful thing! In revival, God reaches down from heaven, stretches forth his hand, and touches us with his finger, with wondrous results. These results both overwhelm and excite us: People who were spiritually dead receive new life. Those who have questioned whether God is among them suddenly find themselves quickened with the assurance that God is very much alive and working through them. Those who were confused suddenly discover new direction for their lives. People who were ill or otherwise incomplete are suddenly healed. Those who thought that they had nothing to say or that they were powerless to say it suddenly find themselves with a message to proclaim and a Spirit-given boldness to do so.

With revival comes the awesome power of God that quickens entire communities. When we speak of revival, we often speak about the purifying fire of the Lord that accompanies it. This fire burns away non-essentials—attitudes, worries, even sin. The revival at the Azusa Street Mission fell upon those who took personal holiness seriously. We may not all agree about how our sanctification is accomplished through Jesus Christ, but there's no debating that holiness is critical to a truly transformed life! When relativism seems to be winning the day, Pentecostals must once again reevaluate their commitment to matters of personal holiness.

As I have reflected upon revival, however, I have come to appreciate another side of it too. On the one hand it brings life. It brings cleansing. It brings power for daily living as well as ministry. It brings a sense of direction. It enables us to overcome. We often revel in the changes it brings to our lives; changes so dramatic that they may even bring us a sense of euphoria or well-being. We treasure those experiences in which God meets us—in which we are very sure that we stand, sit, or even lie down in his presence. Such moments are pure delight, and they lift us up, edify us, and bring us strength, just as they were intended to do.

But as a church historian, I have also come to realize that revival is not the normal state of affairs, nor is it intended to be so. Those of us who appreciate the role that revival plays often miss this. At the core of the term "revival" is the Latin root *viv*—"life." That is what revival does: it brings life into life-less situations or people. And the prefix *re* indicates something being done *again*. We can see how this prefix works in words such as "reawaken" or "reassess": Someone who was once awake has fallen asleep. She is now reawakened. Something that was assessed in the past must now be reviewed. In short, to "revive" is to renew or to give life again. What had once been alive has lost its zest for life. In revival, it is resurrected, renewed, given life again.

We may also think of this in medical terms: Those who faint need to be revived. Someone needs to minister to them and meet their needs. A whiff of smelling salts is often all it takes to bring someone back to consciousness. But smelling salts are strong medicine, with a potent, even uncomfortable smell. Breathing smelling salts is a great deal like breathing ammonia. When we inhale its fumes, it touches us deeply. It causes us discomfort. We suddenly become aware of this sensation and we begin to move, to revive—

in large part, to get away from this sensation! We administer such medicine to bring about change, a new state of consciousness. We do it to revive the person who has slipped into a state of unconsciousness. Once the patient has been revived, though, we stop giving the medicine that brought about the desired effect. The patient, now conscious, is no longer in need of revival. He or she can go about the business of being that person without the continuing aid of smelling salts. Imagine a roomful of people convinced that they need to keep on inhaling smelling salts in order to keep on living.

Within Pentecostal circles, however, our rhetoric—that is, the way we speak about revival—may lead us to think that the normal Christian life must be lived in a constant state of revival. To live with this understanding is to miss an important point about the nature of the Christian walk. Certainly, the Christian life is to be lived to its fullest capacity and in the power of the Holy Spirit is clear. Jesus said, "I have come to give life and to give it more abundantly" (John 10:10). But that is not the same as living in a constant state of revival.

Revivals come and go. Most revivals seem to have a life expectancy of about three years. That is exactly how long the Azusa Street revival lasted before the situation began to disintegrate. A revival may extend longer than that, but it is extremely difficult for people to enter fully into such highly charged forms of spiritual encounter for any extended period of time without losing their focus. Just as a high voltage electrical current can shock someone, so too can such a "high voltage" encounter with God. We can only live with it for so long. Moses, for instance, was not allowed to see God, for no one is able to do so and live (Exod. 33:20). Even the brush of God's fingertip is sufficient to overwhelm us. After a while, it can even kill us.

I place a high premium on both the short-term and the long-term *effects* of revival. Revival results in decisions being made, lives being changed, and new priorities being set. It energizes and inspires for the tasks ahead. But long-term *exposure* to revival is a dangerous thing. We need to be careful about what it is for which we ask. Revival is a two-edged sword. It can build up and it can tear down. It can give and take life at the same time. What happens when people are so infused with the revival experience that they live as though it were normative? Two examples from history should suffice to make my point.

The first example comes from western New York where the great revivalist Charles G. Finney lived and worked. This region was so frequently the scene of revival fires that it became known as the "burned-over district." But if you visit the region today, you will see very little evidence that this region was more visited by revival than any other. When you study the region, you will find that at the very time it was so deeply enthralled with Christian revival, it spawned Mormonism, New Thought, Christian Science, Jehovah's Witnesses, Spiritualism, and the perversion of "free love" communities such as Oneida, New York. The spiritual impulses that accompany revival are not always spiritually discerned as they should be.

The second example comes from the "great Welsh revival" of 1904. In that revival, as many as eighty-five percent of the people of Wales became converted, causing churches worldwide to take notice. Convicted of their sins, led to repentance, and transformed at the deepest levels, the thousands caught up in the Welsh revival were hailed as the forerunners and models for the revival many in Los Angeles were expecting just before the Azusa Street Revival broke. The Welsh revival was also a major subject of conversation before the Pentecostal revival fell in India. Stories abound about the changes these people underwent. In some Welsh mining operations, it was said, the mules that carried the coal to the surface could no longer do so: The foul language of the miners who drove them was so transformed that the mules no longer understood their drivers' commands.

If we look at Wales today, however, we see a very different picture. Only 8.6 percent of the population attends church with any regularity today. It is said that only 2 percent attend anything resembling an evangelical church. What happened to turn this area with a history of intense revivalism into a genuine mission field in less than a century?

In New York, people seem to have sought one new spiritual experience after another, always yearning for higher highs than they had previously experienced. In Wales, those transformed through the revival failed to disciple their children into the ongoing life of the church in any meaningful manner. Ultimately they wound up with less than they had before.

Revival is important to the ongoing life of the church—the story of the Azusa Street Mission shows just how important. It has changed the face of twenty-first-century Christianity worldwide. From time to time the church needs a new infusion of life. That infusion, that revival, is intended to put us back on track. It packs a powerful punch! The forces that threaten the church today, and the responding cries for revival, point to the need for a new infusion of life. But each of us must think about what exactly we are asking for. If we are looking only for a sense of euphoria, some feeling that we want to reproduce, some new experience to erase the boredom of everyday life, we will ultimately be disappointed. We may even end up worse off than we were before we got our wish.

If, however, we are interested only in the God who sends the revival; if we allow his finger to brush us; if we are committed to living lives of holiness, and we are willing to give ourselves away to others in a way that is possible only through the power of the Holy Spirit—then the result will be worth every minute we spend seeking and embracing revival.

The writer to the Hebrews affirmed what we all know—that "Jesus Christ [is] the same yesterday, and today, and forever" (Heb. 13:8). Once we have been revived, the task Jesus has called us to remains the same. We are to take up our cross daily and follow him (Luke 9:23–24). We are to "Go . . . into all the world, and preach the gospel to every creature" (Mark 16:15). Racism has no legitimate place in our lives. And like Jesus, we are to reach out to those around us in the power the Holy Spirit gives us in times of need (Luke 4:18–19). This path may not always seem exciting; it may not make us dance, cause us to shiver and shake, knock us on the floor, or make us babble incoherently. But ultimately we must give an account of whether we were faithful to just *this* path.

NOTES

ༀ

1. The use of the term "mission" to describe a local congregation is relatively uncommon outside the holiness and Pentecostal movements. Among the more radical elements of the holiness movement in the late nineteenth century, the term frequently described works that were independent of denominational control—typically small, storefront congregations led by some charismatic figure. Many of these "missions" offered what is commonly called "compassionate ministry." They commonly served the poor, women, alcoholics and drug addicts, prostitutes and others marginalized by society. These missions often offered not only spiritual help, but also material aid. Early Pentecostals such as Charles F. Parham and Florence L. Crawford expanded the meaning of this term beyond the local level by using it as part of their denominational names: the Apostolic Faith Mission (Baxter Springs, KS) and the Apostolic Faith Mission (Portland, OR).

2. "Weird Babel of Tongues," *Los Angeles Daily Times*, (April 18, 1906), II.1.

3. Joe Creech, "Visions of Glory: The Place of the Azusa Street Revival in Pentecostal History," *Church History* 65:3 (September 1996): 405–434.

4. Joseph Karl Menn, *The Large Slaveholders of Louisiana—1860* (New Orleans, La.: Pelican Publishing Company, 1964), 382–383. By today's standards, Carlin's worth would be about five million dollars.

5. Emma Lou Thornbrough, *The Negro in Indiana before 1900: A Study of a Minority* (Indianapolis, Ind.: Indiana Historical Bureau/Bloomington, Ind.: Indiana University Press, 1985, 1993), 53, 68, 206.

6. Albert J. Raboteau, *Slave Religion: The "Invisible Institution" in the Antebellum South* (New York: Oxford University Press, 1978), 87–88.

7. Cf. *From the Beginning of Bishop C.H. Mason and the Early Pioneers of the Church of God in Christ* (Memphis, Tenn.: Church of God in Christ,

1991), 6; J.O. Patterson, German R. Ross, and Julia Mason Atkins, eds. *History and Formative Years of the Church of God in Christ with Excerpts from the Life and Works of its Founder—Bishop C.H. Mason* (Memphis, Tenn.: Church of God in Christ Publishing House, 1969), vii, x, xii.

8. Mary Mason, Ed. *The History and Life Work of Elder C. H. Mason Chief Apostle and His Co-Laborers* (1924, Memphis, Tenn: Church of God in Christ, rpt. 1987), 92.

9. See, Ithiel C. Clemmons, *Bishop C. H. Mason and the Roots of the Church of God in Christ* (Bakersfield, Calif.: Pneuma Life Publishing, 1996), 21, 22, and 25.

10. Willie Millsaps, "Willie Millsaps Remembers C. H. Mason at Hot Springs," *Assemblies of God Heritage* (Summer 1984), 8.

11. The term "Mother" is common within holiness, Pentecostal, and African American churches. It usually denotes a woman of mature years, whose reputation is flawless, who engages in frequent prayer, and whose wisdom and counsel are highly respected and sought after by other members of the congregation. Church "mothers" often provide advice to pastors and bishops (whether solicited or not), and in many churches they wear special clothing and are given special seating at the front of the congregation.

12. Thomas R. Nickel, *Azusa Street Outpouring* (Hanford, Calif.: Great Commission International, 1979), 5.

13. A. C. Valdez, Sr. with James F. Scheer, *Fire on Azusa Street* (Costa Mesa, Calif.: Gift Publications, 1980), 19.

14. These are the words that Belshazzar and his guests saw being written on the wall by a hand, recorded in Daniel 5. Translated they read "Thou art weighed in the balances, and art found wanting." This may have been hung on the wall of the Azusa Street Mission as a reminder of the need for God to provide interpretation to the tongues that were being spoken in that place, or of the possibility that unknown tongues could be written. In either case, the supernatural character of the warning would not have been lost on Azusa Street's congregation.

15. Camp meetings had been very common events along the American frontier throughout much of the nineteenth century. Many people lived in rural settings where local congregations were often made up of a few family members and a few close friends or neighbors. Camp meetings were regional affairs that brought together many such groups. They typically took place in a field or pasture where tents could be set up. They needed to have access to adequate shade and a decent water sup-

ply nearby that could be used by the worshippers for everything from drinking to washing to baptisms. Often a tent or other temporary structure was constructed. Fire-spitting evangelists using the latest evangelistic methods pioneered by John Wesley or Charles Finney, and preachers intent upon converting their hearers, were the main fare. People were encouraged to sing, shout, dance, cry, moan, and fall. What might have been ruled as disorderly conduct in a local congregation often found a place among campers that a person might never see again. Large segments of the holiness movement emerged from the various camp meeting associations developed by the Methodists. It should come as no surprise that the Apostolic Faith people, who were originally part of the holiness movement, would embrace the camp meeting from the beginning as part of their own spiritual heritage.

16. Scriptural support for this practice is drawn from Acts 19:11–12. Similar practices can be found in popular Catholicism.

17. Free loveism was originally intended as a liberation movement for women. It gave them the freedom to choose their sexual partners as well as the freedom to submit to or decline their husbands' requests for marital sex. Unfortunately, in some places, "free loveism" became an excuse for sexual immorality. It was a common feature among spiritualists at the time. While not all spiritualists were free lovers, nearly all free lovers were spiritualists. The presence of known "spiritualists" at the Azusa Street Mission from time to time, may have led to the accusation being lodged against the Mission.

18. Claims that Seymour broke up marriages sometimes came from men in the city whose wives were converted under his ministry at the Azusa Street Mission. If these women worshipped regularly at the Mission despite the consternation of their husbands, or if they gave money to the Mission, their husbands sometimes made this charge. The local press, of course, looked for and published several such claims.

19. Bart Millard, "I Can Only Imagine," Simpleville Music 2001 (ASCAP)

20. Samuel Terrien, *The Elusive Presence: Toward a New Biblical Theology* (1978; repr. Eugene, Ore.: Wipf and Stock, 2000).

21. See especially, Psalm 150, though one can find similar references in Psalm 30:4 (singing); 47 (clapping and shouting); 81:1–5 (tambourines, harps, lyres, and rams' horns); 92:1–9; 95–96; 98–100; 117; 134 (raised hands); 136 (responses).

22. Eileen Southern, *The Music of Black Americans: A History* 2nd. ed. (New York, NY: W.W. Norton & Company, 1983), 260.

23. "So if the whole church comes together and everyone speaks in tongues, and some who do not understand or some unbelievers come in, will they not say that you are out of your mind?" NIV

24. Lawrence F. Catley, taped interview conducted at the annual meeting of the Society for Pentecostal Studies, May 1974, by Gospel Communicators, P.O. Box 6102, Orange, Calif. 92667, side 2.

25. The term "Patti" is derived from the name of the Italian, Adelina Patti (1843–1919), an internationally known star of opera, who was considered to be the foremost *bel canto* and coloratura soprano of her day. Her name came to be applied to other prima donnas who rivaled her abilities, and by the 1890s it was frequently applied to outstanding African American female singers such as the famous Sissieretta Jones.

26. Arthur G. Osterberg, "I Was There," Full Gospel Business Men's Fellowship International *Voice* (May 1966), 20.

27. Osterberg, "I Was There," 20.

28. Nat Goodwin was an internationally famous stage actor at the time, known especially for his ability to mimic others. He played the major theaters of Boston, London, and especially New York. He moved to Ocean Park in Southern California in 1898.

29. The terms "Pentecost" and "Pentecostal" were commonly used as self-descriptions among those holiness believers who equated the baptism in the Holy Spirit with purification and fire, and thus with sanctification. They dropped this nomenclature when members of the Apostolic Faith movement declared baptism in the Spirit to be a baptism of empowerment that came upon a person who had already been sanctified.

30. Springfield was to become the home base of the Assemblies of God, a prominent Pentecostal denomination.

31. David Douglas Daniels, "The Cultural Renewal of Slave Religion: Charles Price Jones and the Emergence of the Holiness movement in Mississippi," PhD dissertation, Union Theological Seminary, 1992, 275.

32. The preachers to which Ivey Campbell made reference in this quotation were those who attacked the revival in Akron. The account of Ananias and his wife, Sapphira, is found in Acts 5:1–11. Ananias and his wife conspired together to claim that they had given the entire proceeds they had received from the sale of a piece of property, but they had actually withheld part of it. When they were confronted about what they had done, they lied, and they were immediately struck dead. Clearly, Ivey Campbell viewed her attackers as bearing false witness and from her perspective they were in danger of a similar fate.

33. The value of $1,200 in 1906 is equivalent to $25,315 in 2006 according to the website at www.austintxgensoc.org/calculatecpi.php

34. Gary B. McGee, "The Calcutta Revival of 1907 and the Reformulation of Charles F. Parham's 'Bible Evidence' Doctrine," *Asian Journal of Pentecostal Studies* 6:1 (January 2003): 123–143.

35. *Relevant Pentecostal Witness* (Chatsglen, Durban, South Africa: n.p., 1988), 9.

36. *Relevant Pentecostal Witness*, 3–4.

37. John Pollock, *The Cambridge Seven* (London, England: InterVarsity Press, 1955).

38. "So shall they fear the name of the Lord from the west, and his glory from the rising of the sun. When the enemy shall come in like a flood, the Spirit of the Lord shall lift up a standard against him."

39. The dollar-pound rate of exchange in 1907 stood at 4.878 dollars to the pound at year's end. Thus, Polhill's gift of £1,500 amounted to $7,317. The total mortgage at the time of purchase was $15,000. The equivalent value of the property in 2006 dollars would be in excess of $300,000, making Cecil Polhill's gift equivalent to more than $150,000 if he were to give it today.

40. Richard Crayne, *The Mailing List Controversy* (Morristown, Tenn.: Richard Crayne, 2004), 14–15.

41. Owen "Irish" Lee, an immigrant from Ireland and a former Catholic, was a colorful convert who had been an alcoholic. His claim to fame before he came to the Azusa Street Mission was that once in Santa Monica, while in a drunken stupor, he had beaten up a policeman. After he was baptized in the Spirit at the Azusa Street Mission in 1906, he became an evangelist who traveled the world.

INDEX